D0906202

OXFORD
UNIVERSITY PRESS

Great Clarendon Street, Oxford, OX2 6DP,
United Kingdom

Oxford University Press is a department of the University of Oxford.
It furthers the University's objective of excellence in research, scholarship,
and education by publishing worldwide. Oxford is a registered trade mark of
Oxford University Press in the UK and in certain other countries

© Arménio Rego, Miguel Pina e Cunha, and Stewart Clegg 2012

The moral rights of the authors have been asserted

First Edition published in 2012
Impression: 1

All rights reserved. No part of this publication may be reproduced, stored in
a retrieval system, or transmitted, in any form or by any means, without the
prior permission in writing of Oxford University Press, or as expressly permitted
by law, by licence or under terms agreed with the appropriate reprographics
rights organization. Enquiries concerning reproduction outside the scope of the
above should be sent to the Rights Department, Oxford University Press, at the
address above

You must not circulate this work in any other form
and you must impose this same condition on any acquirer

British Library Cataloguing in Publication Data

Data available

Library of Congress Cataloging in Publication Data

Data available

ISBN 978–0–19–965386–7

Printed in Great Britain by
MPG Books Group, Bodmin and King's Lynn

To Tomás and Janinha, Cláudio and Carla, Nélida e José
In memory of my virtuous parents

To Dr Rocha Neves, who helped me to develop the virtues of
persistence and prudence

AR

To my family, friends and teachers, with whom I first learned
what 'virtuosity' means

MPC

To Jonathan, William and their descendants—may they live in a
more virtuous world

SC

Foreword

Kim Cameron

This book by Rego, Cunha, and Clegg—*The Virtues of Leadership*—is a refreshing, much needed, and informative book about a topic that receives too little attention in the world of business leadership. The concept of virtue has, until recently, been out of favour in the scientific community as well as in the world of work. Virtues have been traditionally viewed as relativistic, culture-specific, and associated with social conservatism, religious or moral dogmatism, scientific irrelevance, or steeped in narrow-minded values. Until very recently, scholarly research has paid scant attention to virtues and virtuousness, and these terms have remained largely undiscussable among practising managers faced with economic pressures and stakeholder demands.

As evidence, a survey was done by my colleague, Jim Walsh, in the *Wall Street Journal* from 1984 to 2000. The appearance of terms such as 'win', 'advantage', and 'beat' had risen more than four-fold over that seventeen-year period, whereas terms such as 'virtue', 'caring', and 'compassion' seldom appeared at all. As Rego, Cunha, and Clegg point out in this excellent treatment of virtuousness in leadership, both organizations and individuals may state a desire to be virtuous (e.g. honest, caring, courageous). But in the social sciences as well as in serious conversations about business success, such concepts are often replaced by more morally neutral terms such as corporate social responsibility, prosocial behaviour, employee well-being, citizenship, civility, ethics, and even character. One result of this neutralizing of the language in leadership and organizational studies is that there has been little systematic investigation of the expression and effects of virtues and virtuousness on organizational and leadership success.

However, one of the key attributes of virtuousness is that it is not a means to obtain another end, but it is considered to be an end in itself. It possesses inherent value. Virtuousness is most closely associated with what Aristotle labelled 'goods of first intent'—in other words, 'that which is good in itself and is to be chosen for its own sake'. In fact, virtuousness in pursuit of another more attractive outcome ceases, by definition, to be virtuousness. Forgiveness, compassion, and courage in search of recompense are not virtuous. If kindness toward employees is demonstrated in an organization solely to obtain compliance or an economic advantage, for example, it ceases to be kindness and is, instead, manipulation. Virtuousness is associated with social betterment, but this betterment extends beyond self-interested benefit. Virtuousness creates social value that transcends the instrumental desires of the actor. So, virtuous actions produce advantage to others in addition to, or even exclusive of, recognition, benefit, or advantage to the person displaying virtuousness.

The irony, therefore, is that whereas virtuousness does not require a visible, instrumental pay-off to be of value, if observable, bottom-line impacts are not recognized in organizations, attention to virtuousness usually becomes subservient to the demands of enhancing financial return and organizational performance. Few leaders have consciously invested in practices or processes that do not produce higher returns to shareholders, profitability, productivity, and customer satisfaction. In other words, without tangible benefit, those with stewardship of organizational resources tend to ignore virtuousness. If virtuousness is to be pursued, if leaders are to demonstrate virtues, evidence of pragmatic utility must usually be provided.

One of the best aspects of Rego, Cunha, and Clegg's book on virtuousness among leaders is that they address head-on the dilemmas and criticisms associated with this concept, but they provide interesting and informative examples of leaders who display and exemplify virtuousness in their own lives. They document cases and examples of how virtues and virtuousness have paid off in practical ways. They also illustrate the importance of virtuousness in a complex global environment, and they show how virtuousness is, as it claims, a universal standard for what it means to be human, or to achieve the best of what human beings are capable of being.

As a Nobel Laureate asserted:

> The world is hungry for goodness and it recognizes it when it sees it—and has incredible responses to the good. There is something in all of us that hungers after the good and true, and when we glimpse it in people, we applaud them for it. We long to be just like them. Their inspiration reminds us of the tenderness for life that we all can feel.

This book not only provides evidence that virtuousness pays and has a function in a global business environment, but it also inspires and uplifts us with its examples and illustrations.

Preface

No one will be buried with the epitaph 'He maximized shareholder value'.

(Kay 2011: 79)

We need a more sophisticated form of capitalism, one imbued with a social purpose.

(Porter and Kramer 2011: 77)

The 2000s have been for leadership what Confucian scholars would call 'interesting times'. On the one hand, these have been the days of the politics of commitment, as leaders such as Tony Blair and George W. Bush projected their personally held commitments globally. Not only political leaders seemed to believe that their commitment should shape policy. CEOs have become celebrities because of their commitments to publicity and self-promotion: the names of Jack Welch or Richard Branson spring to mind. Such professionals have reached the status of media or political celebrities, with a name-recognition comparable to political leaders or media stars, even becoming themselves media stars—such as Donald Trump. On the other hand, these have been the years of the global financial crisis. Some of the former star CEOs and other members of their top management teams have suddenly found themselves no longer lauded as the good but loathed as the bad, if not feared, for the ugly effects of their policies on mortgages, savings, jobs, and lives.

Public fascination with charismatic, celebrity CEOs may be causally connected to the crisis of confidence in corporations. Once upon a time, corporations were anonymous and bland, staffed by blue-shirted men in grey flannel suits, in the era of the 'organization man' (Whyte 1956). Business managers were not expected to project an image of success and charisma: rather, they should simply do an honest job. The same might be said of leaders generally: at least until the Kennedy/Nixon television debate, charisma was not required to be a political leader any more than anyone expected their boss to be charismatic. At best, these figures were remote and severe; at worst they were severe and in your face.

Today CEOs and politicians are not expected to be severe and remote: they have to make themselves available—to analysts, to the media, to stakeholders. At worst, the result is that managers and political leaders often resemble stars of the popular media, famed for their image and representation rather than any substance. We do not think that this is fundamentally positive. Politicians and leaders may not be expected to be saints—and some very evidently are not; the name Berlusconi, both tycoon and politician, comes to mind. But they need to be virtuous enough, we contend, if they are to be entrusted with the responsibility of commanding social forces as powerful as states or modern corporations.

We believe that such virtue is especially required of those who run multinational companies with a global reach, in large part because of the extensive privatization of politics and politicization of the private sphere that has occurred in modern times. Where once in history it was only the large oil or trading companies that ran a political remit, today every multinational is a projection, explicitly, of power, because they shape and frame life-chances globally. Whereas virtue might once only have been hoped for in political and public service leaders and decried when its failings were all too evident, today we should expect and we definitely need virtuous leadership across a much broader canvass. The leaders of multinational companies are not often any more anonymous men in the ubiquitous grey flannel suits but media-savvy identities. Showing leadership has become a part of the branding process of large organizations.

Leadership in multinational organizations is a political, ethical, and prudential responsibility, not just a matter of economic performance, although it is rarely explicitly addressed as such. At its best, we argue, leadership can display virtue across the gamut of politics, ethics, and practical wisdom—*phronesis*. We decided to write this book to unite, under a single cover, the research that has been produced in the field of what we will refer to as virtuous leadership. As we will explain, businesses ('the most powerful institution on the planet', Hart 2005: 235) should be forces for good. For this to be true, their leaders need to accept that virtue should not be a notion strange to them. Since Weber, virtues have been considered as critical for the sustainability of organizations. In the 'field', however, managers still view 'realism' as the ingredient for success. We are not against realism. We know that the world in general and the business world in particular may be grounds where virtues may have difficulty flourishing. It is precisely because of this difficulty that we have written this book. We see global leader virtuousness as a social relational process that can position organizations in positive spirals, rather than as an inherent leader trait not amenable to cultivation.

We attempt to share evidence, theoretical, anecdotal, and empirical, on the convergence between good virtues and good results. Businesses can always profit at the cost of relevant stakeholders: this is called exploitation, and it can occur not only in relation to workers but also customers, investors, clients, and communities. Exploitation of good ideas may be virtuous, but not if it comes accompanied by a lack of investment in social and resource relations. Depleting natural resources in non-sustainable ways is no more virtuous than depleting the energies of employees (Pfeffer 2010a), the loyalty of customers, or the trust of those communities in which service and operations are located. Our aim is to help disseminate the idea that managers can be competent and competitive while doing the good things right, thus creating 'shared value' through fostering a fruitful dialogue between economic and societal progress (Porter and Kramer 2011).

When the good are found bad, things can turn ugly. Many celebrity CEOs have recently made media appearances handcuffed, in court or on the way to jail. They may still be celebrities but not the kind that their companies and societies wish to acknowledge. Notoriety is close to celebrity but not quite the same thing, as any number of reality-TV 'celebrities' can testify. Invariably, it is behaviour made public as lax that signals the downfall of celebrity.

We are not against celebrity: in the modern age, we believe that this would be impossible. While not everyone gets the fifteen minutes of fame that Andy Warhol predicted, many strive for it, and many others are prepared to exploit this striving. We hope this book will show that there is another way to become celebrated, maybe a harder one, with less glamour and more sacrifice, but one that will be more aligned with the values that make us more humane. We all are responsible for making the world a better place, and in the contemporary world we increasingly expect organizations to be able to do this through example and actions, examples and actions that, inevitably, become personified. In this sense, we are all equal, but as Orwell said, some are more equal than others. We view this book as a small catalyst for the creation of a theory, not just of organizations but of *better* and *more sustainable* organizations (Hart 2005). It is up to you, dear reader, to make a difference.

Contents

List of Figures

List of Tables

Notes on Authors

Arménio Rego is Assistant Professor at the Universidade de Aveiro, Portugal. He has a PhD from ISCTE – Instituto Universitário de Lisboa, Portugal, and has been published in journals such as *Applied Psychology: An International Review, Journal of Business Ethics, Journal of Business Research*, and *Journal of Occupational Health Psychology*. His research deals with positive organizational scholarship.

Miguel Pina e Cunha is Professor at NOVA – School of Business and Economics in Lisbon, Portugal. His research deals with positive and negative organizing, virtuous and genocidal leaders, transparent and toxic organizational processes. Recently he has been especially interested in the case of the Khmer Rouge, an extreme example of destructive organizing. As this book shows, he also has an interest in what is good and positive.

Stewart Clegg is Research Professor at the University of Technology, Sydney, and Director of the Key Research Centre for Management and Organization Studies, and a Visiting Professor at EM-Lyon, NOVA – School of Business and Economics, and Copenhagen Business School. His research is driven by a fascination with power and theorizing.

Idealism kills deals.

Gordon Gekko

Deals may kill ideals.

Anonymous

I don't believe anger is an effective way of managing.

Matt Winkler, editor-in-chief, Bloomberg (Edgecliffe-Johnson 2010: 16)

1

The Virtues of Leadership: Contemporary Challenges for Global Managers

Business that does not contribute to human growth and well-being is not worth doing, no matter how much profit it generates in the short run.

(Csikszentmihalyi 2003: 35)

To maintain public confidence in our capitalist system it must be managed by men and women of honor and decency.

(Keough 2008: 79)

Virtue and virtuosity

We take the notion of virtuosity from the great German sociologist, Max Weber. He introduces the idea of 'virtuosity' in the context of a discussion of the progenitors of contemporary capitalism, as he sees them—the bearers of the 'Protestant ethic'. In Weber's analysis of *The Protestant Ethic and the Spirit of Capitalism*, written at the dawn of the twentieth century but reflecting back on capitalism's origins, already shrouded in the past, he stresses that the rational foundations of modern capitalism were borne by 'religious virtuosi', strict Protestants with Calvinist convictions (Weber 2001). In Weber's accounts these people were virtuosi, not only because they were highly accomplished in their dedication to the religious life and to the spirit of God that they yearned to move deep within them as virtuous beings, but they were also technically skilled in making minute calculations of the virtue of their actions in every sphere. Roth (1975: 150) says that they were not only 'men of virtue' but also 'highly accomplished technicians in matters moral'. We might say that their virtuosity lies in the sense of virtue in all that they seek to accomplish. For Weber it was this special spirit that constructed a grammar of motives for the ascetic

Protestant, a grammar that saw them dedicate themselves to organizational and civic good works that gave their lives meaning as vessels of God's will. Should they prosper in these affairs then they had little alternative for the virtuosity of their souls other than to reinvest any accumulation of capital back into that which gave life meaning: their work and works.

It was in this way that Weber suggests a solution to the puzzle of primitive accumulation: where the prime capital came from that started the process of capitalism's capital investment. His answer is that it came from the results of the creation of a uniquely socially constructed religious character. Of course, as he pointed out in the final pages of *The Protestant Ethic and the Spirit of Capitalism*, an ethic that proves foundational will not necessarily endure the course. Later capitalism could, and in many cases, did, dispense with these ethical foundations.

In our book we want to build on the notions of virtuosity and virtue, albeit not quite as Weber did. Our gaze is fixed resolutely on the contemporary world, a world of global financial crisis, shyster capitalism, corrupt media organizations, and rapacious bankers. In this world we do not expect to find too many Weberian religious virtuosi; however, we will argue that in the complex world of contemporary globalization we need to develop and cultivate leaders who can show a degree of ethical virtuosity that has been all too lacking in the recent past. Of course, contemporary times require a different type of virtuosity. Weber's virtuosity was strongly inner-directed—in modern parlance it was all about 'me', albeit in relation to transcendent themes rather than immediate pleasures. The need for contemporary virtuosi is to be other-directed, to be reflective, not just on what their actions do for their soul, but what they can do for those others over whose lives they exercise power.

Business virtuousness revival

Today, the unequivocal elites of whom virtuosity is demanded are global leaders. It is to these global leaders that we turn in order to develop our thesis that what the world needs now are more ethical leaders skilled in virtue. In terms of our initial discussion, such leaders would need to be both more reflexive about the powers they yield and the relations they are in, and have a deep appreciation of what it means to be leading globally. Such leaders would represent a marked change from recent examples of leadership in the Global Financial Crisis (GFC). Commenting on the corporate scandals that devastated the corporate landscape in the last couple of decades, Andy Grove admitted he found himself embarrassed and ashamed to be a businessman (George 2003: 2).

Many people will find it difficult to consider the corporate world as a landscape of virtue (Kanter 2008: 280), and the word 'moral' may be the last that the public will use to describe contemporary business leaders (Damon 2004). The virtuosity of many notable leaders—in the global financial sphere especially but also more recently in global media organizations, the British Parliament, and the London Metropolitan Police Service—has been charted less in the ethical realm of virtues and more in their flair for ingenious but ultimately foolish financial innovations and a capacity for rewarding themselves for their ingenuity in doing so that to many seems truly astounding. The very idea that organizational performance may be linked to virtuousness has been ignored until very recently (Cameron, Bright, and Caza 2004), with virtues being out of favour in the management ecology (Manz, Cameron, Manz, and Marx 2008a: 2).

The situation in the political realm is not much different: for instance, Sonia Gandhi described a 'shrinking moral universe' as India grew economically. Nonetheless, virtues and the ethic of virtues have recently been an area of renewed interest (Flynn 2008: 361). The theme of the 2007 *Academy of Management* annual conference was *Doing well by doing good*. Ironically, the conference was held just before the GFC revealed the rottenness beneath the glitter of the corporate veneer. The conference organizers sought to acknowledge that organizational performance should consider, on top of bottom line criteria, the degree to which organizations are willing and able to improve the lives of their members, stakeholders, and those whom they serve. As the delegates returned home to the first news of the unfolding GFC there was much for them to reflect on in the months ahead. Globalization in all its forms, not only just financial crisis, requires attention to the practice of virtues for businesses to operate and prosper in the long run (Fort and Schipani 2004).

Several scholars have stressed that virtue needs to be included in the agendas of business and academia (Gavin and Mason 2004; Gowri 2007; Lilius et al. 2008; Moore 2005; Moore and Beadle 2006; Park and Peterson 2003; Schudt 2000; Wright and Goodstein 2007). Wright and Goodstein argued that character is not 'dead' and that, after the moral and financial collapse of organizations such as Andersen, Dynergy, Enron, Lehman Brothers, MCI, Merck, Tyco, and Worldcom, the business community should be in the process of rediscovering virtues and character strengths as personal and organizational forces for good (Wright and Goodstein 2007: 929). As Melé put it, 'virtues provide interior strength for good behaviour' (2009: 235). The topic is also under intense empirical scrutiny (Bright et al. 2006; Cameron 2003; Cameron et al. 2004; Chun 2005).

The business field echoes this virtuousness paradigm (see, in Table 1.1, how virtues are represented in the codes of conduct of several

Table 1.1. Virtues and character strengths proclaimed in several (global) codes of conduct

Company	Examples of virtues and strengths considered in the codes
BP	Integrity; fairness (e.g. fair treatment and equal employment opportunity); citizenship (e.g. no damage to the environment; safety of the communities)
Casio	Citizenship (e.g. contributing to the development of a sustainable society; striving to be of service to society); creativity; integrity; fairness
Ernst & Young	Integrity; fairness (e.g. respect; inclusiveness); vitality (e.g. energy; enthusiasm); courage; citizenship (e.g. supporting a successful and sustainable society)
General Electric	Integrity; fairness; leadership
Georgia-Pacific	Integrity; perspective/wisdom; humility; fairness and humanity (e.g. treating others with dignity, respect, honesty, and sensitivity); excellence
Google	Integrity; justice and kindness (e.g. respecting each other)
Heinz	Integrity; excellence; fairness (e.g. respect); prudence; citizenship (e.g. acting as a responsible corporate citizen)
KPMG	Integrity; fairness (e.g. treating people with dignity and respect); citizenship (e.g. acting as a responsible corporate citizen); leadership (e.g. leaders as positive models)
Merck & Co.	Citizenship (e.g. being a good corporate citizen); integrity; creativity (imagination); excellence; fairness; integrity; courage; prudence; leadership
Microsoft	Integrity/honesty; excellence; fairness and citizenship (e.g. open and respectful with others and dedicated to making them better; supporting charitable, civic, educational, and cultural causes)
Mitsubishi Chemical Holdings Corporation	Integrity; fairness; prudence; citizenship (e.g. contributing to the affluence and comfort of society by offering socially beneficial goods and services); open-mindedness
Motorola	Integrity; justice (e.g. treating each other with respect and fairness); citizenship (e.g. supporting community, charity and political organizations and causes; protecting the environment and operating businesses in ways that foster sustainable use of the world's natural resources)
Nokia	Citizenship (e.g. aspiring to be among the best in the world in corporate responsibility, actively promoting human rights and environmental protection through our products and solutions); fairness
Novartis	Excellence (e.g. professionalism); citizenship (e.g. being an ethically, socially and ecologically responsible organization); fairness and kindness (e.g. fair, courteous and respectful treatment of employees); integrity; prudence and wisdom (e.g. good judgment and common sense)
Pricewaterhouse Coopers	Excellence; citizenship (e.g. acting in a socially responsible manner); leadership; integrity; courage; fairness and kindness (e.g. respect, dignity, fairness and courtesy)

Samsung Electronics	Fairness (e.g. respecting individuals' dignity); citizenship (e.g. acting as a corporate citizen); excellence; creativity; love of learning (e.g. supporting continuous learning and employee development)
Shell	Integrity/honesty; justice (e.g. respecting people); citizenship (e.g. promoting sustainable development); love of learning (e.g. promoting the development and best use of the talents of employees)
Tata Group	Citizenship (e.g. being committed to good corporate citizenship); fairness; integrity/honesty.

Built from companies' websites

multinational companies) although it is not necessarily expressed in *real* business practices, as a careful attention to Table 1.1 suggests. Bill George, former CEO of Medtronic, expressed his gratitude to the unlikely inspiration coming from Enron and Arthur Andersen, considering that the depth of these companies' misconduct offered an opportunity for the business community at large to question and to reflect on the recent tracks (George 2003: 1). As Chris Brady, Dean of London's BPP Business School, put it, the people who claim not to have admired Jeff Skilling during the halcyon days of Enron, are possibly in a state of denial (Brady 2010). As a result, corporations and society need authentic leaders, 'people of the highest integrity, committed to building enduring organizations. We need leaders who have a deep sense of purpose and are true to their core values. We need leaders with the courage to build their companies to meet the needs of all their stakeholders, and who recognize the importance of their service to society' (George 2003: 5). In other words, what we require are virtuosi versed in virtue.

Virtues are the moral muscle that promotes stamina in the face of challenges and from which originate exemplary cases of positive leadership (Manz et al. 2008a). The virtues of leaders are crucial to build organizations that, in addition to being profitable, also contribute to human and social betterment (Csikszentmihalyi 2003). Making financial capital grow is relatively easy compared to seeding and growing beneficial social capital. Our focus is specifically on global leaders, our aim being to explore how their virtues may make them more effective *and* better able to develop flourishing organizations for the people within and around them, in the various contexts in which they operate. In a globalized world, where multinational companies have extensive power over a huge number of other organizations and millions of people, building positive organizational performance requires global leaders with such positive qualities (Tavis 2000). Leaders with such qualities can have a global positive impact.

We suggest that virtues and character strengths, which we define and characterize in the next section, nourish virtuous global leadership, and that virtuous global leadership fosters positive organizational performance. Pearce, Waldman and Csikszentmihalyi defined virtuous leadership 'as distinguishing right from wrong in one's leadership role, taking steps to ensure justice and honesty, influencing and enabling others to pursue righteous and moral goods for themselves and their organizations and helping others to connect to higher purpose' (Pearce et al. 2008: 214). In a similar vein, we define virtuous global leadership as distinguishing right from wrong in one's global leadership role, taking steps to ensure justice and honesty in operations carried out worldwide, influencing and enabling others to pursue righteous and moral goods for themselves and their organizations, helping others to connect to higher purpose, and fostering society's betterment. The activities that support virtuous global leadership may be identified as the following (see Table 6.1 for details):

- Learning and understanding the complexities of the cultural, economic, and political mosaic;
- Having an accurate emotional and social sense of what happens in the local and global arenas;
- Respecting and adjusting to different people and cultures;
- Interacting positively with stakeholders worldwide;
- Leading respectfully, fostering trust and cooperation, and caring about and developing others;
- Learning with mistakes and adopting a level-5 leadership approach;
- Taking challenging and wise decisions, and facing global and local problems honestly and energetically;
- Pursuing a cosmopolitan ethos, and promoting human dignity and development;
- Appreciating, learning with, and feeling grateful for the splendid diversity of the world;
- Pursuing excellence, sustainable management practices and policies, and meaningful visions and missions.

Positive organizational performance involves enhancing the welfare of the organization and those it serves, such as customers or clients, or the public at large, as well as balancing the needs of its various stakeholders (Pearce et al. 2008). Positive organizational performance includes not only attaining long-term organizational financial performance, for without that the organization will not survive, but also fostering positive and sustainable relationships with stakeholders, contributing to the betterment of society. Figure 1.1 depicts the model. The virtuousness context (e.g. codes of ethics; organizational culture; values prevailing in society) appears as antecedents of virtuous global leadership because global leader's behaviours are influenced by the context in which they operate (Glynn and Jamerson 2006; Pearce et al. 2008). We also posit that global leaders' virtues and character strengths influence the context

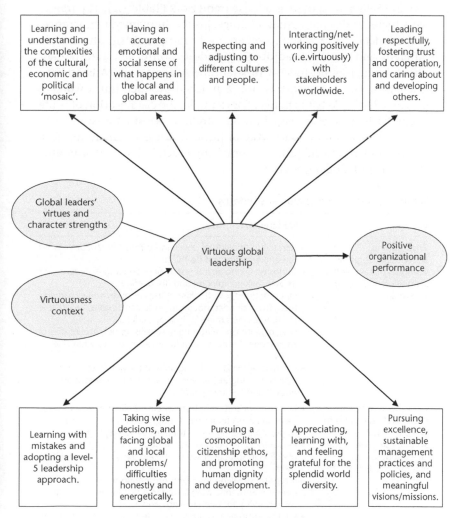

Figure 1.1 A model of virtuous global leadership and outcomes

because global leaders are in a good position to influence organizational culture, practices, and policies. The model summarizes the main arguments of the book.

The golden mean

The character strengths and virtues' classification proposed by Peterson and Seligman is used as a loose framework (Table 1.2). The framework includes six core virtues (courage, justice, humanity, temperance, transcendence, and wisdom) emerging from several (simultaneously different and similar) traditions, including Confucian, Taoist, Buddhist, Hindu, Islamic, Judeo-Christian, and Athenian (e.g. Aristotelian) discourses. The framework is not 'a finished product' but a work in progress that is likely to change. For example, the classification of some strengths is debatable (e.g. humour strength within transcendence virtue, or leadership under virtue of justice). However, the framework is well known and helpful in identifying crucial character strengths and virtues of global leaders.

Table 1.2. Virtues and character strengths

Virtues	Character strengths
Wisdom and knowledge: cognitive strengths that entail the acquisition and use of knowledge	• Creativity: thinking of novel and productive/adaptive ways to conceptualize and do things. • Curiosity: taking an interest in all of ongoing experience for its own stake; exploring and discovering. • Open-mindedness: thinking things through and examining them from all sides; not jumping to conclusions; being able to change one's mind in light of evidence. • Love of learning: mastering new skills, topics, and bodies of knowledge; tendency to add *systematically* to what one knows. • Perspective/wisdom: being able to provide wise counsel to others; looking at the world in a way that makes sense to oneself and to other people.
Courage: emotional strengths that involve the exercise of will to accomplish goals in the face of opposition, external or internal	• Bravery: not shrinking from threat, challenge, difficulty, or pain; speaking up for what is right even when facing opposition; acting on convictions even if unpopular. • Persistence: finishing what one starts; persisting in a course of action in spite of obstacles; taking pleasure in completing tasks. • Integrity: speaking the truth; presenting oneself in a genuine/authentic way; acting in a sincere way; taking responsibility for one's feelings and actions. • Vitality: approaching life with excitement and energy; living life as an adventure; feeling alive and activated.

Justice: civic strengths that underlie healthy community life	• Citizenship: working well as member of a group or team; being loyal to the group. • Fairness: treating all people the same according to notions of fairness and justice; not letting personal feelings bias decisions about others. • Leadership: organizing group activities and seeing that they happen, while promoting good relationships within the group.
Humanity: interpersonal strengths that involve 'tending and befriending' others	• Love: valuing close relations with others; being close to people. • Kindness: doing favours and good deeds for others; helping people and taking care of them. • Social intelligence: being aware of the motives and feelings of self and others; knowing what to do to fit into different social situations.
Temperance: strengths that protect against excess	• Forgiveness and mercy: forgiving those who have done wrong; giving people a second chance; not being vengeful. • Humility/modesty: letting one's accomplishments speak for themselves; not seeking the spotlight. • Prudence: being careful about one's choices; not saying or doing things that might later be regretted. • Self-regulation: regulating what one feels and does; being disciplined; controlling one's appetites and emotions.
Transcendence: strengths that forge connections to the larger universe and provide meaning	• Appreciation of beauty and excellence: noticing and appreciating beauty, excellence, or skilled performance in all domains of life. • Gratitude: being aware of and thankful for the good things that happen. • Hope: expecting the best and working to achieve it. • Humour: liking to laugh and tease; bringing smiles to other people; seeing the light side. • Spirituality: having coherent beliefs about the higher purpose and meaning of life; having beliefs about the meaning of life that shape conduct and provide comfort.

Built by Rego et al. (2012), from Peterson and Seligman (2004)

Peterson and Seligman defined virtues as 'the core characteristics valued by moral philosophers and religious thinkers: wisdom, courage, humanity, justice, temperance, and transcendence' (Peterson and Seligman 2004: 13). Character strengths are the psychological ingredients (processes or mechanisms) that define virtues, or the distinguishable routes through which virtues are expressed. For example, courage is displayed via four main human strengths: bravery, persistence (involving perseverance and industriousness), integrity (authenticity and honesty), and vitality (zest, enthusiasm, vigour, and energy). These four strengths animate a life lived with excitement and energy. They involve emotional strengths that imply the exercise of will to accomplish goals in the face of opposition, whether external or internal (Wright and

Table 1.3. How virtues support global leaders' activities

Wisdom and knowledge	Helps global leaders to understand the complexity of a world where there is no uniformity in customer preferences, competitive circumstances, economic conditions, employee relations, or governmental regulations across the various countries and cultures (Bingham et al. 2000).
Courage	Helps global leaders to show decisiveness and integrity in countries where human rights are violated, and impels them 'to walk the talk', thus creating the trust necessary for stimulating fluid and collaborative work relationships with individuals, teams, and organizations from many different economic, legal, political, social, and cultural systems (Beechler and Javidan 2007).
Justice	Allows global leaders to better articulate and integrate individuals and organizations that are geographically dispersed and promote enhanced cooperation among the members of a global network.
Humanity	Helps global leaders to develop networks around the world, to care for customers, employees, communities, and other stakeholders, to behave for the benefit of society, thus making the world a better place.
Temperance	Is crucial to avoid being dazzled by the media spotlight, to practise self-restraint rather than make megalomaniac decisions (just because one can), to respect partners with fragile power positions in developing countries, to avoid excesses when working in remote cultures where human rights are disregarded, and to avoid consumption habits that may appear extravagant, ostentatious, and disrespectful when interacting with people from deprived economic contexts.
Transcendence	Helps global leaders to act in favour of higher and virtuous purposes, to feel grateful for having the opportunity to experience the splendid diversity of the world, and to pursue excellence in the company and the global network of which it is part.

Goodstein 2007). Virtues and character strengths are crucial for helping global leaders to reach positive organizational performance. Table 1.3 depicts several examples of how they may have an impact upon leader behaviour.

It is important to note that virtues are not absolute endeavours. They are tendencies, acquired through habit, allowing balance between extremes in conduct, emotion, desire, and attitude (Aristotle 1999; Martin and Schinzinger 1996). Aristotle's 'doctrine of the mean' (Aristotle 1999) suggests that virtues work best in the range of the 'golden mean' between the extremes of excess and deficiency. For example, courage is the middle ground between foolhardiness (the excess of hardiness) and cowardice (the deficiency of self-control and clear thought in the face of danger). Excessive demonstrations of virtues are, in essence, not virtue but vices, as we discuss in the following chapters, after considering the relevance of each virtue for the global leaders' positive performance. An individual gives proofs of virtuosity when, in the presence of a specific event, reason and experience are used to interpret the idiosyncrasies of the event's context, charting a course of action located between the extremes of deficiency and excess—the mean between both being *virtue,* Aristotle argued.

To illustrate our arguments, examples will be presented across the book. That we mention a particular leader does not mean that the leader in question is necessarily virtuous. For example, the fact that a leader has shown courage at a certain time or in making certain decisions does not imply that (s)he may be considered a courageous or virtuous leader in general. A leader can show courage in certain moments *and* cowardice in others, which does not destroy the courage demonstrated in the former action and its positive consequences. Likewise, the examples of leaders who failed to behave virtuously do not mean that such leaders are devoid of virtue. In short, several examples presented in the next chapters retail virtuous episodes, not necessarily reflecting consistently virtuous leaders. Being humans we are not always virtuous. But some of us are more virtuous than others. If in the past, research has turned to toxic organizations and leaders and their effects on organizations (Frost 2003), it is now timely, as the Positive Organization Scholarship (Cameron and Spreitzer 2012) scholars suggest, to look not just at the bad and the ugly but also to try to find the good as an exemplar for practice.

Before proceeding, it is also important to note that character strengths and virtues are relevant both for global and local leaders. The increased complexity, uncertainty, and diversity (Beechler and Javidan 2007; Bird and Osland 2004; Gregersen et al. 1998) that global leaders have to face make their character strengths and virtues particularly relevant, however. In a global risk society, where the dysfunctional effects of business can flow globally far from the places where investments were made or costs incurred, global leaders have far-reaching responsibilities (Beck 1999). They have to be able to make virtuous performances before many different audiences and stakeholders simultaneously. They have to be able to soothe the anxieties of investors, nurture innovation, nourish the communities in which they operate, and invest in the growth and development of those they employ, globally. Indeed, they have to be virtuosi. As in any form of endeavour, virtuosity in virtue requires endless training, practice, and discipline. Our use of 'discipline' in this context is two-fold: first we mean it in the same way that one might ask what discipline one is studying or has mastered. We offer the curriculum for a discipline of virtuous leadership. But we also mean discipline in the terms of drill and practice: the book offers appropriate tools for the acquisition of virtuosity in the realm of virtue.

Global leaders have to display character strengths and virtues in a different way from local leaders. Local leaders play to the local crowd; they play on their home ground. There are no away games when the organization takes place in one domain. Global leaders play away all the time. All leaders must be able to manage uncertainty, but 'the degree of uncertainty that global managers face is exponentially higher' (Gregersen et al. 1998: 25). For example, although the understanding of consumer needs is important in any business and place around the world, 'its importance is magnified exponentially in the global context because of the many variables involved in effectively selling a product outside one's home country' (John Pepper in Bingham et al. 2000: 288). Although strong character is important for every leader, it is put to the test especially when leaders face ethical dilemmas involving social norms and beliefs that collide with those prevailing in their culture. As an extreme example, consider the case of an American manager working in China who, because of company policy, notified the police that he had fired an employee for theft and who later discovered, to his horror, that the ex-employee had been executed (Stone 2002; Wright et al. 2003).

Virtuosity in virtuousness is not the result of summing and subtracting virtues

As will be discussed, virtuousness does not necessarily proceed from the sum and subtraction of virtuous acts. It is not an additive or conjunctive process (Irwin 1997). For example, a courageous, prudent, creative, curious, and open-minded leader cannot be called virtuous if (s)he is poor in integrity and uses these virtues in a dishonest way or for dishonest purposes. In such cases, it is more appropriate to consider virtuousness as a multiplicative process, in such a way that dishonesty neutralizes the potential virtuousness of the other virtuous acts. Virtuosity in virtue is not a zero-sum game: the deficits in integrity cannot be made by a credit in courage, if that courage is plied in the name of evil enterprise.

There are many examples of leaders who express some virtues in the absence of others. You will find references in chapter 5 to the legendary modesty and frugality of Ingvar Kamprad, founder of Ikea, the Swedish flat-pack furniture retailer. A recent book, however, portrays Ikea as a sort of secretive dictatorship managed by Kamprad and his family with an iron fist (Stenebo 2010). An internal network of 'spies' reports on any signs of disloyalty by senior managers. Another well-known example of how some forces may coexist with the lack of other forces is provided by Al Dunlap, nicknamed 'Chainsaw Al' and also known as 'Rambo in pinstripes' and as 'serial killer' (Kellerman 2004). Dunlap showed bravery in terms of the company's stock value when selling pieces of Scott Paper and eliminating thousands of jobs, with positive consequences for shareholders in the short run, if not for those whose jobs were lost. These strengths convinced some that he was the right man to solve Sunbeam's problems. Sunbeam's shareholders initially viewed him as the company's saviour (Kellerman 2004). However, his callousness, hubris, dishonesty, inhumanity, and rashness turned him into one of the most hated CEOs in the world. The saviour would eventually become Sunbeam's gravedigger (Kellerman 2004; Nirenberg 2001). Dunlap defended his style thus: 'If you want a friend, get a dog. I'm not taking any chances; I've got two dogs' (Dunlap and Andleman 1996: xii). People are not in business to be liked, or to please stakeholders, he argued:

> The most ridiculous term heard in boardrooms these days is 'stakeholders.' (. . .) Stakeholders [including employees and home communities] don't pay a penny for their stake. There is only one constituency I am concerned about and that's the shareholders. (Dunlap 1996: 196–197)

Thus, bravery and persistence, if not accompanied with justice, humanity, wisdom, temperance, and transcendence, can give rise to abrasive forms of leadership (Kellerman 2004), with perverse consequences for followers, the community, and the leaders themselves, as demonstrated by the criminal consequences for the leaders of Enron, Worldcom, Lehman Brothers, and other companies caught in recent scandals (Hamilton 2006). In Europe, Parmalat's founder, Calisto Tanzi, was sentenced to eighteen years in jail for fraudulent bankruptcy of the dairy products giant (Moloney and Pizzo 2010). In Asia, microfinance, once seen as the ideal weapon to combat poverty is now compared to 'bloodsucking' the poor. Among others, the accusations hit Muhammad Yunus, the Nobel Prize winner, whose work attracted global admiration (Kazmin 2010). Barbara Kellerman presented several examples of bad and evil leaders who expressed bravery, persistence, and even appreciation of beauty and excellence (Kellerman 2004). And, as is well known, the flower of Germany's 1940s' intellectual elite, over-represented in the SS, listened to the artistic creations of Brahms and Beethoven in the camps while the gas did its work and the ovens burnt.

Some virtues have more multiplicative effects than others. For example, in performing challenging, complex, and ethically difficult leadership roles, the absence of humour, curiosity, and creativity has not the same relevance as the lack of courage and integrity. A global leader rich in humour, curiosity, creativity, and even kindness, but not in the courage required for taking difficult and necessary decisions and in the integrity to use the right means, cannot be considered virtuous. In contrast, one can imagine a virtuous global leader (even an imperfect one, (Irwin 1997)) with a limited sense of humour, minor creativity, and occasional kindness—but whose courage, integrity, love of learning, prudence, humility, appreciation of beauty and excellence, and self-regulation are 'bullet-proof'. We are not arguing that humour, creativity, and kindness are not important to a global leader. Rather, we are suggesting that, for some global leaders' activities and positive performance, some virtues are more critical than others.

Virtuousness is not necessarily where it is supposed to be

Global leaders may benefit from moral good luck (Michaelson 2008). Sometimes, when observed retrospectively, their behaviours are apparently virtuous in the sense that they were the result of conscious and deliberate actions. However, such positive consequences of past behaviours may have been more the result of positive circumstances than of the agent's will and intentions. The apparent morality, or virtuousness, of an act or strategy may be not the consequence of the agent's intentional control; rather, it may result from a convergence of factors and circumstances beyond the person's control. The examples presented in this book are not free from such a risk, which is the reason why we ask our readers to interpret the examples advanced throughout the book with a number of virtues, including caution and prudence.

It can also be naïve to attribute virtuous traits to someone on the basis of the person's discourse. Words and deeds, or what is said and what is done, can often differ markedly. Kenneth Lay, former CEO of Enron, defended the relevance of highly moral and ethical environments in which individuals may express their 'God-given potential' (Glynn and Jamerson 2006). He repeatedly expressed his role as guardian of the company's central values, including respect, integrity, and sincerity (Glynn and Jamerson 2006). Prior to allegations of Enron's misconduct, the company's 2000 Annual Report stated that (Enron 2000: 53):

> We treat others as we would like to be treated ourselves. We do not tolerate abusive or disrespectful treatment. (...) We work with customers and prospects openly, honestly and sincerely. When we say we will do

something, we will do it; when we say we cannot or will not do something, then we won't do it.

During the 1990s, under the leadership of Lay, the company became a generous financial donor, especially to the Republican Party, and encouraged its employees to be involved with charities (Glynn and Jamerson 2006). Considering what it is now known about the company and its leaders' misconduct at that time, it is not possible to assert peremptorily whether Kenneth Lay was merely a shameless man or one who started *virtuous* and ended up badly embroiled in *vicious* cycles of unethical behaviour. Both explanations are plausible. One may even argue that bad barrels corrupt good apples, and that Lay's decisions were shaped within a larger political, regulatory and economic context conducive, or, at least, not vigilant enough, to misconduct (Glynn and Jamerson 2006). What we cannot disregard is that true virtuousness is more than virtuous discourse and intention: deeds must match words; thus, the examples presented across this book should be approached with prudence.

Organization of the book

The book is organized around five chapters. Chapter 2 clarifies the tasks and activities that characterize the global leaders' role, and discusses the Herculean challenges borne out of the complex and heterogeneous context where these professionals necessarily operate. We argue that traditional competencies are not enough because global leaders make a real difference in a world where several constituencies, both local and global, expect that they reduce poverty and contribute towards making the world a more peaceful and prosperous place (Fort and Schipani 2004; Kaku 1997; Maak 2009; Tashman and Marano 2010).

Chapters 3 to 5 discuss how virtues and character strengths help global leaders to carry out their activities and responsibilities. Chapter 3 focuses on cognitive and energizing virtues (wisdom/knowledge and courage), chapter 4 on the amiability and citizenship virtues (justice and humanity), and chapter 5 on transcendent virtues (temperance and transcendence). The taxonomic criteria from which this clustering has been derived is the following:

- Wisdom/knowledge and courage enable global leaders to interpret the complexity of the world and to energetically face its challenges, difficulties, and opportunities.

- Justice and humanity allow global leaders to develop positive human relationships with a wide range of constituencies (e.g. employees, customers, communities, governments, NGOs), and to act as responsible citizens of the world.

- Temperance and transcendence enable global leaders to control impulses and emotions, and to act in favour of a high purpose—in short, to release inner energies in favour of outer virtuous aims.

In each of these three chapters, we use the same structure. We start by explaining the meaning of the virtue and its corresponding character strengths. References to the opposites and the excess of the strength are also made. Then we explain how the strength contributes to the global leaders' positive performance. Examples are provided to support the arguments—although, as remarked previously, such examples must be interpreted with caution. We also suggest that 'excessive' levels of virtues may be dysfunctional. As Gunther and Neal argued, 'any organization's strength, taken to an extreme, can become a weakness' (Gunther and Neal 2008: 277). The discussion reflects the golden mean paradigm, showing that virtues are in the middle between two opposite sides (e.g. courage representing a middle way between cowardice and foolhardiness). Virtuosity in virtue requires balance: just as a tenor in opera or trumpeter in jazz who hits too many high Cs unnecessarily shows off a wonderful attribute just a little too often, so too does a leader whose excessive display of a single virtue hides a lack of facility in others.

Chapter 6 integrates the above arguments. Different groups of strengths (i.e. core virtues) tend to support different roles, activities, and competencies. Therefore, global leaders must combine different virtues for being effective and a source of positive impact. Thus, we suggest the relevance of strengths is contingent upon the global leaders' roles and missions. For example, integrity, bravery, perseverance, prudence, and self-regulation may be more relevant for working and interacting with partners from contexts where corruption is extensive, and for working in countries where human rights and dignity are disrespected. Reciprocal influences between strengths are also discussed.

The chapter also suggests that human strengths and virtues may serve as facilitators and enablers of global leader development. We argue that individuals with character strengths and virtues will be better motivated to accept or look for, and to take advantage of development experiences. For example, individuals with high levels of curiosity, love of learning, and bravery are more likely to accept and look for international assignments, responsibilities in international teams, and for participating in international meetings and forums. Finally, the chapter points up some research directions and implications. Some issues discussed in this chapter may appear excessively academic for practitioners. However, considering the adolescence of the topic in the (global) leadership literature, such perspective may help scholars to identify useful avenues for future research and practitioners to focus their practice more virtuously. Chapter 7 discusses practical implications.

From good theories to good organizations and businesses: in search of heliotropic effects

There is a tendency in the management literature to romanticize corporate leaders as heroes, who often subsequently show feet of clay. The fact is that they are neither as extraordinary as is sometimes assumed nor will they end up displaying fewer character and ethical flaws than the rest of us. Nonetheless, it would be wrong to say that such leaders do not make a difference—they often do—but they do so more by setting parameters, tone, examples that are adopted by those reporting to them, and admired or denigrated in consequence.

In a globalized world, where multinational companies and military and political leaders have extensive power over a huge number of other organizations and millions of people, global leaders may make a real difference. Cameron pointed out that a focus on the positive produces so-called heliotropic effects (the tendency of all living systems toward positive energy and away from negative energy). Therefore, in his view, 'leaders who capitalize on the positive similarly tend to produce life-giving, successful outcomes in organizations' (Cameron 2010: 46). By emphasizing the positive influence of global leaders' virtues on positive organizational performance, we hope to boost heliotropic effects.

Human motives, for most of us, most of the time, are part altruistic and part self-serving. Global leaders are no different from the rest of us. However, to do good work, our self-oriented needs need not be discounted; rather our moral sense needs to be kept active, particularly in face of pressures (Damon 2004). The advantage of focusing on virtues results from the convergence between self-interest and the interest of others (Solomon 1999). Kanter replied to sceptics who claimed that the philanthropic and citizenship activities of organizations such as IBM, Cisco, or Timberland are self-interested (Kanter 2008: 282):

> Of course, they are [self-interested]. And they should be. Enlightened self-interest makes efforts sustainable because employees, customers, and shareholders reward good conduct with their loyalty.

We have lived through a vicious cycle whose effects are still unwinding, a cycle whose viciousness sprang from many causes but which condensed in the practices of many of the less regulated global financial institutions. As the GFC ebbs slowly away, leaving a tsunami of damage in its wake, we want to turn the thoughts and minds of businesses, business school academics and students, and organizations more generally, to how they might construct virtuous cycles. As William Damon observed, 'a pervasive belief in the inevitability of moral degeneracy can become self-fulfilling' (Damon 2004: 43): such inevitability he suggests, can be contested by showing examples of business leaders who treated customers and employees in a respectful manner and prospered (Damon 2004: 14). We consider that a pervasive belief in the benefits of global leaders' and organizational virtuousness can also become self-fulfilling—but positive.

Right and good management theories

The book is inspired by the idea that 'management theories must be both right and good' (Ghoshal and Moran 2005: 17). Being right results from being well grounded in coherent theory and empirical research, while being good comes from promoting ethically sound outcomes. By disseminating theory about *good* and about the human *goodness* potential, we may contribute to building and spreading the expectations that organizations are able to be virtuous spaces where human beings achieve higher purpose, including happiness. In turn, happiness may nurture individual and organizational excellence (Danna and Griffin 1999; Grant et al. 2007; Huppert 2009; Lyubomirsky et al. 2005; Wright and Cropanzano 2004). As argued by Csikszentmihalyi, (2003: 25) 'any manager who wants his or her organization to prosper should understand what makes people happy, and implement that knowledge as effectively as possible'.

Reciprocal relationships may also occur: higher performance frees resources for improving employees' benefits and well-being, thus leading to self-reinforcing virtuous spirals. Spreading ideas of virtuous relationships is not irrelevant for the type of management practices adopted in organizations. As argued by Ghoshal et al., (1999: 19) ideas matter and, 'in a practical discipline like management, the normative influence of ideas can be powerful, as they can manifest themselves as uniquely beneficial or uniquely dangerous'. Ghoshal (2005: 77) offered a helpful metaphor to illustrate the argument:

A theory of subatomic particles or of the universe—right or wrong—does not change the behaviors of those particles or of the universe. If a theory assumes that the sun goes round the earth, it does not change what the sun actually does. So, if the theory is wrong, the truth is preserved for discovery by someone else. In contrast, a management theory—if it gains sufficient currency—changes the behaviors of managers who start acting in accordance with the theory. A theory that assumes that people can behave opportunistically and draws its conclusions for managing people based on that assumption can induce managerial actions that are likely to enhance opportunistic behavior among people. (Ghoshal and Moran 1996)

Solomon agreed that if our representation of business is that of a game of cut-throat, dog-eat-dog competitions, then that is the world that would be created as people play such games (Solomon 1999: xxii). However, if business were constituted on the basis of trust and collective gain, a process directed and executed by virtuous people, a different understanding would emerge. Therefore, considering that theories are self-fulfilling and that expectancies influence behaviours and social relationships, through painting a more positive picture of human beings and organizations the chances are higher of making the world a better place in which to live and organizations better places in which to work (Ferraro et al. 2005, 2009; Ghoshal 2005; Ghoshal and Moran 2005; Ghoshal et al. 1999; Pfeffer 2010a). If we keep on disseminating pessimistic assumptions about the nature of individuals and organizations, we will contribute to the perpetuation of bad management and leadership practices. As Ghoshal et al. (1999: 10) observed,

People are right in their intuition that something is wrong. But this is not because large corporations or management are inherently harmful or evil. It is because of the deeply unrealistic, pessimistic assumptions about the nature of individuals and corporations that underlie current management doctrine and that, in practice, cause managers to undermine their own worth.

We do not want to appear as naïve and idealist scholars who believe that good intent is enough to change the world and that human beings are *necessarily* good. Human beings are not, in our view, necessarily anything other than bipedal mammals with a set of capacities for growth and development. All human beings, including business and organization leaders, have the potential for good and evil deeds. However, if we represent organizations as characterized *only* by cut-throat competition, greed, and selfishness, we end up fertilizing the soil on which venality flourishes. There is an argument that says that much of what has traditionally been taught in business schools has in fact done this (Khurana 2007; Clegg 2008). On the contrary, by focusing on the bright side of organizations, we aim to increase the possibilities that organizational virtuousness will be self-fulfilling.

More specifically, if theoretical and empirical evidence suggests that organizational performance comes mainly from global leaders' behaviours characterized by greed, brashness, and a Spencerian survival of the fittest, it is not wise to expect that most global leaders will behave virtuously. However, if evidence suggests that organizational performance *may* be built over global leaders' character and virtuousness, and that doing the right things represents a moral advantage (Damon 2004), then it is more likely that virtuous behaviours will emerge and contribute to building good businesses (Csikszentmihalyi 2003) and virtuous organizations (Gavin and Mason 2004; Manz et al. 2008b).

Writing about virtuousness is not the same as being virtuous

To borrow from a Spanish proverb, we acknowledge that it is not the same thing to talk of bulls as to be in the arena. That is to say that 'it is not the same thing to talk of leadership as to be in a leadership situation; to *talk of* leadership, as we do here, is not the same thing *as* leadership' (Thayer 1988: 254; italics in original). It is easier to talk about leadership than to lead virtuously. It is not difficult to preach the virtues of virtuous virtuosity in leadership. However, for those who compete in the global market, the discourse of virtuousness may sound naïve, unrealistic, or plain foolish (Brenkert 2009). Scholars must avoid behaving as 'Monday's experts': those who after the game have plenty of advice for a football player.

> Monday's Experts
> Always know what's best
> Always tell you what you should've done
> Monday's Experts
> Always know what's cooking
> How the game was lost and how it could've been won (Weddings, Parties, Anything 1993)

The book is intended to be neither a sermon nor a collection of pious guidelines aimed to preach virtuous virtuosity to global leaders. Our aim is to discuss how global leaders' virtues may contribute to positive organizational performance, meaning better and more effective organizations producing greater human and social good. We consider that the primary concern of leaders will be to build and develop businesses that create 'shared value' for all stakeholders (Porter and Kramer 2006). We do not expect that shared value will mean the end of struggles over who gets what shares: in our view, power relations and struggles are a constitutive feature of social life. However, where shared value can be represented in increasingly positive terms, and less in terms of zero-sum politics, then there is a capacity for positive power being built. As Maak and Pless (2009: 539) suggested,

> given the power, potential, and abilities of business leaders to make this world a better place the least we can expect from business leaders is that they recognize their co-responsibility for addressing some of the world's most pressing problems; not as one-dimensional agents of shareholder interests, but as active and reflective citizens of the world who happen to be managers and leaders in a corporation.

We are not denying the positive value of competition and competitiveness. In fact, both are important for economic and social development. However, as Solomon warned, an overemphasis on competition can destroy the much-needed sense of community and collaboration, ingredients of cooperation that are critical for business sustainability (Solomon 1999: xxi). Whether it is competition or collaboration that leads to the survival of a species depends on the context in which the species finds itself: nothing else. As the ecologist Tim Flannery notes, in the arid wastelands of Australia it was collaboration rather than competition that more often determined species survival (Flannery 1994).

Solomon argued that the combination of an amoral conception of the corporation and the quasi-exclusive emphasis on competition is 'doubly disastrous' and may result in an impoverished sense of meaning, distrust, loss of productivity, and poor employee morale. In his view, promoting virtuousness would be necessary for building good businesses. For this author, who sought inspiration from ancient Greek philosophers, having a good life requires working for a great corporation—'great not just in the sense glossily celebrated in the Annual Report, but great in the sense of great to work for, great to be a part of, great in a sense that speaks to our pride and our spirituality, and not just to our pocketbooks' (Solomon 1999: xxii). Such an endeavour requires changing orientations and facing the current moral crisis with compassion, as Jeffrey Sachs suggests, otherwise economic productivity may be obtained at the cost of our humanity (Sachs 2010).

In short, the book follows Kanter's value-based capitalism paradigm, according to which the best companies fulfil three conditions (Kanter 2008): (1) they obey the laws and regulations; (2) they are guided by an enlightened self-interest, and (3) they are guided by values that stimulate them to make a positive difference. Building such organizations is a difficult task, but, as Muhammad Yunus, the Nobel Prize Laureate, noted (Yunus 2006: 246):

> We get what we want, or what we don't refuse. (...) We wanted to go to the moon, so we went there. We achieve what we want to achieve. If we are not achieving something, it is because we have not put our minds to it. We create what we want. What we want and how we get it depends on our mindsets. It is extremely difficult to change mindsets once they are formed. We create the world in accordance with our mindset. We need to invent ways to change our perspective continually and reconfigure our mindset quickly as new knowledge emerges. We can reconfigure our world if we can reconfigure our mindset.

Anticipating some criticism

Virtues and character may not be dead (Wright and Goodstein 2007), but talking and writing about virtues and virtuousness may not be the most direct route to success and popularity in most business and academic settings (Cameron et al. 2004). Scepticism abounds in both fields. Therefore, presenting compelling arguments about how virtues and virtuousness are worthy endeavours in the business arena may help guarding against accusations of naïvety. In addition to the arguments presented across the book about the possible positive impact of global leaders' virtues and character strengths, we discuss here some possible specific arguments against the discourse of virtuousness that we are advocating.

The sceptics may argue that virtuous and virtuousness neutralizes, decreases, or makes it difficult to develop power relations, a crucial resource to be a successful leader. Power, at its simplest, refers to the ability to shape behaviour by getting people to do things that otherwise they would not do (Pfeffer 1992b: 30). It is the touchstone of management and leadership and a constitutive process of organizing (Krishnan 2003; Pfeffer 1992a, 1992b, 2010b; Schriesheim and Neider 2006; van Knippenberg and Hogg 2006). Power can be used to benefit organizations and society rather than individuals alone (Pfeffer 2010b). Being virtuous and addressing the real needs of followers may actually be a way to build power relations that generate positive power, in the sense that contemporary theory addresses this phenomena: as the power to achieve things rather than to stop them happening (Clegg and Haugaard 2009; Krishnan 2003; Pfeffer 2010b), and several character strengths (e.g. humility, wisdom, persistence: Pfeffer 2010b) may help leaders to develop and sustain positive power relations. There are many ways to build power relations and one may do so either by being or not being virtuous (Machiavelli 1992; Mintzberg 1983). In essence, power is conceptually agnostic, neither good nor bad (Fairholm 1993; Simpson 1994). Power relations can be used in virtuous or corrupt ways, in the service of positive or negative goals, as inner-directed or in the service of others.

A degree of reflexivity about power that is still unusual is required to move from inner-directed to other-directed actions: leaders of all kinds, especially political and business leaders, are fixed in the midst of complex relations of power that they can shape and frame as well as be shaped and framed by. Power, however, is something that contemporary elites are rarely explicitly educated about. Implicitly, they learn a great deal: they learn complex disciplines of accounting, inventory, training, and management, all of which are oriented to the control of subjects and objects—often subjects treated as if they were objects, such as head count that has to be let go. The disciplines of management function as devices of instruction, drill, and performativity with which managers are able to practise the essence of their being managers: they do the maths, they check the figures, they run the programmes and can feel in control in consequence. Explicitly, the control that they experience leaves little room for reflexivity about the power relations that constitute their capacities for action. Executive control assumes predictability, routine, and repetition. It is often only when events disrupt, interrupt, and disorder the normalcy of control that reflexivity becomes evident, when the relationships between causes and effects need to be pondered because action no longer produces predictability. Contemporary executives are, above all, engaged in power steering of those organizations they seek to command. To the extent that this steering has been indifferent to the fate of those commanded and affected, then the crisis induced by unanticipated external contingencies, or events, is less likely to be resolved by reflexivity that engages all the talents available. Management that has run monadically, in power terms, seeking to inscribe its writ unilaterally, will have far fewer resources of imagination and insight to draw on than that which sought to make power more positive.

How is positive, ethical power built? When using power to manage others, always remember that those you are seeking to manage probably also will be trying to manage you with power. Thus the old adage 'do unto others as you would have others do unto you' is worth recalling. Although you may think of their response as resistance, to do so presumes a value legitimacy that may not be justified on your part. They are trying to manage your management of power through their management of the power that they can enact in the situations in which they find themselves or that they can create. Power is nothing if not creative. Crucially, managing with power means achieving common definition, a genuine accord, on which to base strategies, tactics, and actions. Positive uses of power make things happen that would not otherwise have happened—not by stopping some things from occurring, but by bringing new things into creation, involving less force and more listening, working with, rather than against, others.

Managing with power does not always mean seeking to impose a specific meaning on an uncertain context because it entails arbitrary structuring of others' realities. In contrast, power frequently means giving way in the organization conversation, not claiming a special privilege because of title or experience, and not being selectively inattentive to others, but listening and attending to them. Coercive power should be the refuge of last resort for the diplomatically challenged and structurally secure, not the hallmark of management's right to manage. Organizations may listen or may not, may work with the creativity and diversity of people's identities or work against them, based on active listening rather than assertive denial through the instrumentality and ritual of established power. To build such organizations—ones that seek to extend the organization conversation rather than to exploit its lapses— would seem to be one of the more pressing aspects of the agenda for future virtue. In a truly liberal society power relations would moderate both the patriarchal autocracy ensconced in family-dominated firms such as News Corp as well as the casual autocracy spurred by market analysis.

There are plenty of well-documented models and research available in the pages of journals such as *Economic and Industrial Democracy* that posit alternative models that are routinely neglected in the syllabi of management curriculum around the world, something that is remarkable when one thinks of the success of firms such as the UK retailer John Lewis. Indeed, cooperatively owned and managed firms are once again appearing as positive models for future organization. For instance, Maurice Glasman's *Unnecessary Suffering: Managing Market Utopia* (1996), makes a case for the kind of social market developed in West Germany after the Second World War, one in which democratic organizations and institutions—many of them devoted to developing and maintaining vocational skills—prevented domination by either state or market. The book suggests a 'third way' politics, rather different from that of Blair and New Labour, by contrasting a virtue economy with a virtual economy. The virtue economy represents a truly skilled and productive society governed by democratic and participatory norms, which he contrasts with a virtual economy dominated by the banks and driven by market demands. In the former we would expect the virtues, more generally, to flourish with greater vigour than in organizations dominated by markets and hierarchy.

Virtues and character strengths may support global leaders' power relations and help them to use power more effectively (Finkelstein 1992; French and Raven 1959; Raven 2001; Yukl 2009). We suggest that global leaders' virtuousness and power are not incompatible. Without several virtues (e.g. courage, humanity, and temperance), Anne Mulcahy would not have had enough power to 'save' Xerox by leading 'one of the most extraordinary turnarounds in business history' (Gunn and Gullickson 2006: 10). Mandela's virtues and character strengths (e.g. wisdom, bravery, persistence, integrity, vitality, citizenship, love, prudence, humility, self-regulation, forgiveness, and mercy) were the foundations for the power relations he was able to build and join together, albeit that they were made possible through a vicious campaign and civil war waged by the African National Congress against the apartheid regime's state-sanctioned brutality. However, power is not just concerned with extraordinary individuals: its virtues are expressed relationally through how leaders do what they do.

Why have virtues been neglected?

If virtues are so positive and relevant for the good functioning of individuals, organizations, and society, why have they been neglected? Why have so many corporate scandals occurred over the last years? Several explanations are plausible. First, the belief in unidirectional linear progress so typical of the modern (mainly Western) societies may have led people to neglect the relevance of some old virtues, and the pursuit of new values such as enhanced marketization of almost everything, with a concomitant stress on interpersonal competition, personal achievement, and material wealth. Second, in the past, virtues were frequently associated with religiosity. Secularization (Alvey 2005; Bruce 2002; Ecklund et al. 2008; Fuller 1997; Gorski and Altinordu 2008; Smith 2003) may have led people to ignore virtues seen as founded on religious beliefs and practices.

A third possible explanation is that globalization and rampant neoeconomic liberalism may have destroyed what Lisa Newton called 'the village', the spontaneous form of human community that created limits via the mechanisms of transparency and moral consistency. According to this line of reasoning, the destruction of this communitarian ethos contributed to corporate scandals (Newton 2006). In the old village, virtuous practices were a condition for staying in business, and honesty was the best policy, because the village was panoptical: it saw everything and everyone in its limited purview. In these tight-knit communities, sometimes built around a company and its values (for example, the nineteenth-century employees of Cadbury in Bournville, Birmingham, or the employees of Titus Salt's Saltaire Mill in Bradford), individual virtues were structured within an explicitly defined moral community with architectural lines of sight and efficient surveillance of the subject population to ensure either conformance or that deviance was made public (Cadbury 2010). Vicious behaviours and frauds were socially reproved and business people who breached trust had their affairs (as well as personal and family life) destroyed. The business community promoted moderation, compassion, restraint, and decency. In such contexts, greed was a matter of personal and community self-control (Newton 2006). In contrast, the anonymity of the industrialized and urbanized world frees individuals from the village's social and moral precepts, leading them to pursue a life with no limits:

> From an aristocracy of gentility, that took seriously its obligations to maintain the culture they have inherited, we have moved instead to an aristocracy of extravagant entitlement. (Newton 2006: 61)

A new old village?

Several disciplines, from evolutionary biology to moral philosophy and theology indicate that human nature contains both the capacity for evil and for good, for harming and helping, offending and forgiving, retaliating or reconciling (McCullough et al. 2009). Human beings are *hard-wired* with opposite tendencies to violence and greed, as well as to cooperation and kindness. These tendencies are built into our genetic heritage, and codified in our genes over tens of thousands of years of selection.

Humans are social animals who need cooperation, social approval, and group loyalty for satisfying needs to belong and gain protection from enemies, implying respect for social norms and imperatives of virtuousness and morality but they are also capable of greed and violence and taking advantage of others. In the absence of the eyes of the village, conditions for anonymity and self-focus grow. In a greedy context, adopting virtues may appear as naïve. By observing how greedy individuals succeed and prosper, people may feel ashamed to affirm and reinforce moral ideals and virtues.

The consequence is perverse for businesses and the market, at least in the long run, as demonstrated once again by the succession of corporate scandals and the crisis of confidence in corporations. As argued by Adam Smith (who also wrote *The Theory of Moral Sentiments* [1759] as well as the much more cited *An Inquiry into the Nature and Causes of the Wealth of Nations* [1776]) and Hayek (1988), businesses do not succeed unless the participants have qualities such as honesty, integrity, industry, and con-scientious respect towards all affected by the market (Fort and Schipani 2004; Newton 2006). To increase cooperation and self-restraint, we may need an equivalent of those 'witnesses' that regulated life in the village:

> In the public light of day, completely visible, with everyone watching, we will not do what we know to be wrong. In the village, where everyone is watching all the time, and where we are expected to be able to give an account of ourselves and our actions to neighbors, we will not do what we and the villagers hold to be wrong. (Newton 2006: 75)

The emergence of digital technologies is increasing the level and depth of panoptical scrutiny via a globally distributed network of neighbours:

> A decade ago, secrets often remained buried until a professional journalist could be persuaded to reveal them. Today anyone with a cell phone and access to a computer has the power to bring down a billion-dollar corpora-tion or even a government. (Goleman et al. 2008: 3)

The role that social media have played in recent social movements is well documented (Castells 2009). Most recently we have seen the role it played in Tunisia and Egypt, and elsewhere in the Middle East, in bringing down corrupt and venal dictators. WikiLeaks has projected social media to new heights. As a consequence, one may expect modern information and communication technologies (e.g. blogosphere) to replace, at least in part, the panoptical role of the old village in such a way that greed and dishonest practices are punished by the market, and being virtuous is rewarded. This explains why transparency, a reflex but also a facilitator of virtuousness, may be a crucial policy in order to compete and prosper:

> Organizations need candor the way the heart needs oxygen. Ironically, the more corporate and political leaders fight transparency, the less successful they are. The reason for this is not, unfortunately, the inevitable triumph of good over evil but the reality-shifting power of the new technology. Whether leaders like it or not, thanks to You Tube, there is no place to hide. (Bennis, in Goleman et al. 2008: ix)

Virtuousness beyond naïvety

Virtues like gratitude (McCullough et al. 2008; Polak and McCullough 2006) and forgiveness (Hruschka and Henrich 2006; McCullough et al. 2009; Nowak and Sigmund 1993) have evolutionary bases, arise by natural selection, and are intrinsic to human nature. Moreover, Darwinism is incomplete as an explanation of human behaviour (O'Hear 1997). Therefore, adopting virtues is not necessarily a naïve way to conduct personal and business life (Damon 2004; Goleman et al. 2008; Solomon 1999). If virtues were not really important, why would Jeff Immelt, the CEO of GE, have argued that he wanted GE to be known as a virtuous company, in order to attract and motivate the most talented people (Gunther and Neal 2008)? Why did the level of character strengths seem to increase in America in the aftermath of the 9–11 events (Peterson and Seligman 2003; Rhee et al. 2008)? Why do we admire virtuous leaders like Mandela or Gandhi? How can one ignore virtuousness in a business landscape damaged by the perverse consequences of the leadership practices that caused consecutive waves of corporate scandals? How can one shut one's eyes to the benefits of virtues and virtuousness when observing exemplary companies that have succeeded both financially and in terms of service to their communities and to society (Kanter 2008)? How could we ignore that organizational members interpret leaders' behaviours using virtue frames, and such interpretations have implications for the degree to which they develop organizational identification and affective commitment toward the organization, rather than cynicism and distanciation (Rhee et al. 2008)? How can we neglect theoretical and empirical evidence suggesting that there are significant advantages associated with more collaborative and communal forms of organization (i.e. more humane and virtuous)? How to explain the proliferation of initiatives, organizations, and institutions rewarding virtuous practices? Why do even greedy leaders adopt a façade of virtuosity when communicating with stakeholders?

Conclusion

Virtues and virtuousness are not dead and should be put at the centre of the stage, not in order to depreciate competition and competitiveness but to hitch them to other virtues that foster individual, organizational, and societal betterment. Global leaders' virtues and character strengths may be strong drivers of such an endeavour. One cannot demand of them that they be morally pure (Brenkert 2009) or that they assume responsibility for solving the most pressing public problems in the world (Maak and Pless 2009) but, we argue, that they may be part of the solution, contributing both towards making the world a better place and to the realistic desiderata (Rawls 1999: 127) of a values-based capitalism (Kanter 2008).

2

The New Virtuosi: Global Managers

Far from being villainous or exploitative, management as a profession can be seen for what it is—the primary engine of social and economic progress.

(Ghoshal et al. 1999: 13)

The age of globalization demands we recognize international interdependencies of resources and stakeholders. This interconnectedness requires mutual respect for societal impacts and mindfulness of the collective ramifications. Effectively balancing all these considerations with a social conscience to create value for corporate sustainability is at the heart of value-centric leadership.

(Henry 2009: 46)

One heterogeneous world?

In some accounts, global leaders straddle a largely unified, borderless, flat, and homogenous world. There is, we find, a remarkable degree of idealism in much contemporary discussion of the globalizing world. In his book *One World*, Peter Singer argued that 'as the nations of the world move close together to tackle global issues such as trade, climate change, justice, and poverty, our national leaders need to take a larger perspective than that of national self-interest' (Singer 2002: ix). The author used expressions such as 'one atmosphere', 'one economy', 'one law', and 'one community' to characterize our changing planet, arguing that *global* problems and challenges need to be faced with ethically *global* approaches and solutions.

The sentiments are well directed, but the reality is that we do not live in a borderless or a flat world but one highly stratified in terms of inequalities, opportunities, and freedoms. To see the world as flat (Friedman 2005a, 2005b) is to see very little at all. While it is clearly not a mistake to consider the planet visible from outer space as 'one world' that is homogenous in terms of phenomena such as climate change, where effects of national policies and practices respect no boundaries, it would be a mistake to think that just because risks are shared globally that countries agree on what to do. Nor is such global agreement to be found in the private sector. There is no uniformity of customer, competitive frames, economic conditions, governmental regulations, and labour relations between countries (Bingham et al. 2000). As Pankaj Ghemawat argues: (a) the vast majority of companies continue to be deeply rooted in their home countries, (b) distances really matter for firms in search of growth, (c) 'even the icons of globalization are less global than the rhetoric suggests', (d) 90 per cent of the world's people will never leave the countries where they were born, (e) only 2 per cent of all telephone calling minutes are international, and (f) 95 per cent of the news people get is from domestic sources (Ghemawat 2011). Moreover, Black (2006) states, the experience of international travel indicates that myriads of borders still exist and the prognosis is that they are not likely to disappear soon. A terrain that may look flat from cruise altitude may in fact be full of details and irregularities when considered at the ground level. Similarly, strategies formulated at the top for a globally flat world rarely run smoothly on the ground, no matter how much care is put into their formulation (Black 2006).

If the world were borderless, the challenges to global leadership would correspond to those of domestic leadership. Likewise, if all places were completely different, global strategies would be useless. Everything should be considered local (Black 2006). Companies need effective *global* leaders precisely because they face both pressures and opportunities for *global* integration and pressures and requirements for *local* responsiveness. The globalized environment is full of local idiosyncrasies that can change the ways in which leaders conduct business and the competencies they need to be successful. Global leaders must be curious and inquisitive about the specificities of what is local. In consequence, Hitt et al. (2007: 2) argued that a global company, with a complex web of global interdependencies,

> needs managers who can understand and are able to deal with excessive levels of ambiguity and diversity, managers who have the appropriate knowledge about diverse sociocultural and institutional systems and have the intellectual capacity to absorb but not be paralyzed by high levels of complexity, managers who have the personal attributes that enable them to work closely and effectively with those from other cultural regions of the world, managers who can build sustainable trusting relationships with individuals,

groups, and organizations in different countries to ensure that they help [the company] achieve its global ambitions.

More and more, corporations need global leaders who can (a) expand overseas businesses, (b) conceive strategies on a global basis, (c) deal effectively with a complex set of constituencies, (d) identify potential business opportunities, (e) motivate geographically dispersed and diverse individuals and teams, and (f) facilitate the development of a network of internal and external connections with individuals, teams, and organizations from many different economic, legal, political, social, and cultural systems (Bartlett and Ghoshal 1992; Beechler and Javidan 2007; Caligiuri 2006; Caligiuri and Tarique 2009).

In such global business contexts, where the global meets the local in a process of *glocalization* (Gould and Grein 2009; Robertson 1995), traditional hierarchical approaches in which the centre commands the periphery are now even less appropriate (Kanter 2010). The contemporary need is (a) to foster fluid and collaborative work relationships, (b) to promote self-organized communities able to deal with local and glocal problems (Kanter 2010), and (c) to promote trust and speed of decision-making and action throughout a global network of interconnected internal and external activities designed to accommodate diverse customer needs in several parts of the world (Beechler and Javidan 2007; Cunha and Rego 2010).

The tight coupling of organizational systems in a digitally connected globality makes coordination by remote control increasingly less viable. Therefore, earlier models of organization, supported by logics of efficiency, hierarchy, control, and centralization, are giving way to models based on decentralization, partnership, and minimal structuring (Kedia and Mukherji 2000). Kanter (2010) argues that the complexity of globalization favours distributed rather than the concentrated forms of leadership typical of traditional bureaucracies. An early description captures the complexity and capabilities required:

> [The ideal global manager should have] the stamina of an Olympic runner, the mental agility of an Einstein, the conversational skill of a professor of languages, the detachment of a judge, the tact of a diplomat, and the perseverance of an Egyptian pyramid builder. [And] that's not all. If they are going to measure up to the demands of living and working in a foreign country they should also have a feeling for the culture; their moral judgment should not be too rigid; they should be able to merge with the local environment with chameleon-like ease; and they should show no signs of prejudice. (Aitken 1973, in Townsend and Cairns 2003: 317)

Global leaders operating in a complex mosaic

Global firms require effective global leaders. Global leaders are the high-level professionals whose jobs include some leadership activities with global reach (Caligiuri and Tarique 2009). According to research, they perform ten global leadership tasks (Table 2.1) that were found to be common and unique to those in global leadership positions (Caligiuri 2006; Caligiuri and Tarique 2009). In a context characterized by diversity, complexity, uncertainty, and strong international competition, they are resources that, in a formula, are valuable, rare, inimitable, and non-substitutable (Ng et al. 2009).

One hypothetical example of a global leader's day is provided by Nardon and Steers (2007): (s)he is located in Bangalore, and interacts with her/his business partner in California, a client in Hong Kong, Australian clients, and a partner in Mexico, before preparing for a trip to Germany. This profile may characterize many agendas, for instance, the company's CEO, one of its executive directors, one of the heads of vertical business units, the chief global delivery officer or chief marketing officer, or of a European expatriate who is leading a cross-cultural team working on the development of a new product.

Rosabeth Moss Kanter provided the example of an IBM leader, working in Russia as research lab director. Such a leader performs several tasks with global impact:

> She reports locally to the country general manager and worldwide to a vice president of development in the systems and technology group in the United States. She has dotted-line relationships to the other product lines on which the lab is working. She is a member of the IBM Academy of Technology (. . .) for which she led a team studying globalization issues related to technology. She also interacts with U.S. headquarters as a member of informal teams with

Table 2.1. Tasks that are common among (and unique to) those in global leadership positions

Global leaders . . .
. . . work with colleagues from other countries.
. . . interact with external clients from other countries.
. . . interact with internal clients from other countries.
. . . may need to speak a language at work other than their mother tongue.
. . . supervise employees from different nationalities.
. . . develop a strategic business plan on a worldwide basis for their unit.
. . . manage a budget on a worldwide basis for their unit.
. . . negotiate in other countries or with people from other countries.
. . . manage foreign suppliers or vendors.
. . . manage risk on a worldwide basis for their unit.

Caligiuri (2006)

people in strategy, sales, services, and research. She works with labs in Mainz, Germany; Poughkeepsie, New York; and Beijing, China, and participates in bimonthly lab directors' meetings to set priorities and assign projects among labs. And, to top it all off, she maintains numerous informal relationships. She fields near-daily instant messages from a colleague in California that he sends before he goes to the gym in the morning to learn from her, ten time zones away, if there are any issues he should address during the day. (Kanter 2010: 594)

Different leaders face different challenges, but they all operate within a complex and diverse context. They all need to have a 'global mindset' (Beechler and Javidan 2007; Javidan et al. 2007; Levy et al. 2007). A global mindset can be defined as the set of attributes, psychological and cognitive, that allows a leader to exert influence over individuals, groups, and organizations over the world (Beechler and Javidan 2007). The three critical components of global mindset are intellectual capital, psychological capital, and social capital (Table 2.2). Leaders with global mindset are able to perceive, analyse, and decode the global operating environment, possessing the cognitive and behavioural flexibility necessary for identifying effective managerial actions on diverse environments (Beechler and Javidan 2007; Javidan et al. 2007).

Expatriate assignments are major developmental experiences for those pursuing global leadership careers (Jokinen 2005). However, leadership and expatriate assignments represent different roles and concepts. Although there is some overlap between both, and many competencies necessary for the success of expatriates conceptually overlap with many global leadership competencies (Mendenhall 2006), a global leader is not necessarily an expatriate, and vice versa (Caligiuri 2006; Jokinen 2005; Suutari 2002).

In fact, expatriation missions may not require global competencies. For example, a German computer engineer working in Angola may confine her activities to the local context, without having any integrative role. Likewise, many global leadership activities require cross-cultural and international business savvy without the need to live abroad. In spite of being performed domestically, such activities require international business knowledge, cross-national skills, and a global mindset (Caligiuri 2006; Levy et al. 2007; Otazo 1999). For example, a global leader with limited cross-cultural savvy, located in the US or Europe, may be unable to understand the idiosyncrasies of the work carried out by an expatriate in Asia or the Middle East—namely the lengthy time necessary to create personal ties for further developing and closing business deals. Such global leader's cross-cultural inability may

Table 2.2. Three dimensions of global mindset

Dimension	Definition	Components
Intellectual capital	Capacity to understand culture, history, geography, and political economic systems in different parts of the world.	• Knowledge of the global industry (e.g. knowledge of global business, competitors and industry) • Knowledge of the global value network (e.g. knowledge of global supply chains) • Knowledge of the global organization (e.g. understanding the tension between global efficiency and local responsiveness) • Cognitive complexity (e.g. ability to empathize with those who hold conflicting views) • Cultural acumen (e.g. cultural awareness; understanding cultural similarities and differences; knowledge of other languages)
Psychological capital	Having a passion for diversity, the quest for adventure, and self-assurance that make the individuals able to thrive in unfamiliar environments.	• Positive psychological profile (self-efficacy, optimism, hope, and resilience) • Cosmopolitanism (e.g. positive attitude towards other cultures) • Passion for cross-cultural and cross-national encounters (e.g. curiosity about and interest in other cultures and peoples)
Social capital	Having intercultural empathy, interpersonal impact, and diplomacy that make the individual able to develop global connections with people from diverse backgrounds.	• Structural social capital (resources resulting from the position the individual occupies in a network and the contacts that provide him/her with access to information and other benefits) • Relational social capital (resources derived from interactions with other people in the network) • Cognitive social capital ('resources providing shared representations, interpretations, and systems of meaning among parties' (Beechler and Javidan 2007: 159)

Built from Beechler and Javidan (2007)

impel him/her to evaluate hastily and erroneously the performance of the expatriate, leading to premature repatriation and misspending of the relational capital (s)he had developed meanwhile.

Global leadership: a Herculean task

Leading globally is a complex job, a Herculean task full of disorienting challenges (Osland et al. 2006) that result from the interaction between four main aspects of the complex global context (Lane et al. 2004): multiplicity, interdependence, ambiguity, and flux.

Multiplicity. The first dimension of complexity is the multiplicity of competitors, customers, governments, NGOs, and other stake-holders from vastly different backgrounds (Den Hartog 2004). These interlocutors represent many and different voices, viewpoints, and constraints—which are also distinct from the voices and perspectives of the organization's executives. For example, customers in different places have different priorities and preferences; customers in developing markets differ significantly in their needs and desires from those in developed markets.

Interdependence. The second dimension is interdependence among a great variety of stakeholders and socio-cultural, economic, political, and environmental systems. Globalization creates a world of interdependence that leads companies to engage in interdependent relationships via mechanisms such as outsourcing and alliances (Lane et al. 2004). The 2008 financial meltdown was the epitome of such interdependence: in a few days, the crisis spread around the globe, affecting many economies and companies.

Ambiguity. The third contextual dimension is ambiguity, constituted in part by the inability of top managers to understand and interpret effectively the huge amounts of data that they can be exposed to in such a way that it can unambiguously guide companies' action. Ambiguity results from three main sources. The first is the unreliability of what is taken to be informational clarity (e.g. even audited financial statements can be ambiguous and unreliable, as demonstrated by the surprising debacles of Enron and Worldcom). The second source refers to ambiguous cause–effect relationships (e.g. does critical mass created via international acquisitions really matter for profitability?). The third source is equivocality, meaning that multiple plausible interpretations of the same fact are possible. For example, Shell faced equivocality when it decided to destroy and sink its Brent Spar oil platform in the North Sea when it was no longer functioning; unexpectedly, the expected approval by Greenpeace was equivocal, forcing the company to cancel its plan (Sluyterman 2010). Another source of ambiguity is culturally bound: verbal and non-verbal messages, intentions, and behaviours have meanings and are interpreted differently in different cultural contexts.

Monsanto offers one illustration of these three aspects. After entering the market for genetically engineered crops, Monsanto faced different reactions to genetic engineering from different entities around the world, ranging from unquestioning support to open hostility (Hart 2005) (multiplicity). The application of this new technology would influence many social, cultural, environmental, and economic factors (interdependence). And the long-term impact of genetically modified organisms, both on humans and the environment, was (and still is) unclear and subject to different interpretations (ambiguity). Moreover, the three aspects interact continuously, creating a dynamic complexity that makes Monsanto's leadership a very demanding task, especially when, as a result of its earlier work on genetic modification, it came up with what was labelled as the 'Terminator' gene—making users of its patented seeds ever more dependent on Monsanto because the plants would not reproduce but were genetically engineered to terminate instead.

Flux. The continuous interaction between multiplicity, interdependence, and ambiguity influences the fourth dimension of flux, meaning that the whole system is always changing at a fast rate. For example, climate changes may not only influence the way people think about (and support or oppose) genetic modification but also influence the effectiveness of the modifications themselves. Governments, public opinion, and the media may also change, while companies act and decide according to preceding circumstances. New scientific findings and discoveries may also change the whole system, and have implications in terms of the multiplicity of entities and variables at stake, interdependence among them, and ambiguity of cause–effect relationships.

Institutional, integrative and identity work. Kanter analysed three main aspects of globalization (Kanter 2010). The first is an increased uncertainty (more surprises and frequent, rapid, and unexpected changes). The second is an increased complexity (more moving parts, more variables at play simultaneously). The third is the increased diversity (a wider variety of people and organizations, and more facets of difference among those in contact). Such aspects require that global leaders perform three kinds of work:

- Institutional work, to deal with uncertainty. It includes tasks such as establishing and transmitting values, giving people working in different places the opportunity to carry out meaningful work, performing corporate diplomacy with a wide range of stakeholders (both at the national and transnational levels), and contributing to the improvement of life conditions in underprivileged contexts.

- Integrative work, to deal with complexity. It includes, for example, connecting people from different and distant places, what Kanter calls the building of social capital through 'management by flying around'. Although one might be doubtful about this activity as an adequate interpretation of how to build social capital as a collective community-based phenomenon, its symbolic and representational significance, in conjunction with local policies that lower the centre of gravity and encourage self-organizing in dispersed places around the world, can assist in developing leadership competencies at lower levels.

- Identity work that addresses diversity, including tasks such as respecting differences and effectively managing people with different identities, seeking to build a sense of community among individuals from different cultures.

Virtuousness and global leadership: the traditional competencies

Several researchers (Beechler and Javidan 2007; Gregersen et al. 1998; Kets de Vries et al. 1992; Moran and Riesenberger 1994) suggest that global leadership roles pose challenges that require specific competencies and characteristics. Not surprisingly, there are many recommendations as to what these should be. For instance, Kets de Vries and Mead propose that global leaders must have: (a) a capacity for envisioning and being able to give meaning to the vision; (b) an ability to instil values and inspire others; (c) an ability to build and maintain organizational networks at the global level; (d) a capacity to understand increasingly complex environments and recognize complex patterns in the environment; and (e) a sensitivity to cultural diversity and cultural adaptability (Kets de Vries and Mead 1992).

Pepper (in Bingham et al. 2000) emphasized four key global leadership competencies: (1) dealing with uncertainty; (2) knowing customers; (3) balancing tensions; and (d) appreciating diversity. More expansively, Moran and Riesenberger (1994) suggest twelve globalization competencies: (1) global mindset; (2) ability to work as an equal with persons from diverse backgrounds; (3) long-term orientation; (4) capacity for facilitating organizational change; (5) capacity for creating learning systems; (6) motivating employees to excellence; (7) negotiating conflicts; (8) managing skilfully the foreign deployment cycle; (9) leading and participating effectively in multicultural teams; (10) understanding one's own values and assumptions; (11) accurately profiling the culture of others; and (12) demonstrating knowledge and respect for other countries. These competencies and capabilities seem remarkably generic: it is hard to imagine that most of them would not be required of top managers in most situations, barring those that are explicitly globally oriented.

Better businesses for a better world

Transnational companies have an impact on hundreds of thousands of organizations and millions of people worldwide. The decisions of these organizations can exacerbate economic crisis or expansion of a country, and can create or destroy thousands of jobs (Maak 2009). However, in the decisions that they make, these considerations are not as likely to be as uppermost as effects on the bottom line and shareholder value for most CEOs, especially those whose remuneration is closely linked to these performance outcomes. If global companies were to seek to respect not only the interests of the shareholders but also a broader set of stakeholders outside the company, they would need to become more virtuous. As a start, they would need to demand success in the promotion of individual, organizational, and societal well-being (Cameron 2010; Cameron and Caza 2004; Fort and Schipani 2004). Such leaders would be expected to develop good businesses (Csikszentmihalyi 2003) *and* perform good work (i.e. successful and responsible, masterful and moral work, Damon 2004), as well as promoting human rights and social and environmental justice (Maak 2009), and contribute to the creation of a better planet (George 2003, 2009; Singer 2002). As argued by Maak (2009: 361),

> instead of being part of the problem by failing to protect human rights, by aggravating poverty or by polluting the environment, corporations should ask themselves what they can (pro-)actively contribute to positive social and environmental change as 'agents of world benefit'.

Not all leaders will be able to make the transition. Table 2.3 alerts us to the demands that will be made on these transitional leaders in their capacity to lead, their commitment to leading transitionally, and the character required of them in doing so.

Organizations' decisions, investments, and activities can make a difference for the better by reducing poverty, contributing to peace through commerce that develops a multiplicity of weak ties, and by developing more sustainable new practices (Fort and Schipani 2004, 2007; Singer 2002; Tashman and Marano 2010). Multinational corporations, and their leaders in particular, 'have the means and thus the power to act as agents of world benefit' in tackling pressing public problems such as poverty, access to clean drinking water, HIV/AIDS, and global warming (Maak and Pless 2009: 538). Donaldson, using a social contract-based approach, suggests that global firms have three obligations in any society in which they operate (Donaldson 1989): (1) to enhance the long-term welfare of employees and consumers; (2) to

Table 2.3. Virtues and character strengths assisting positive leadership

Core constructs	Factors (Dimensions)
The capacity to lead	1. Capacity to reason and make good decisions (Critical thinking and decision-making; numerical and financial acumen) 2. Capacity to see and realize the future (Seeing the future; strategic and execution excellence; global acumen) 3. Capacity to communicate and influence (Inspiration and influence; conflict management; leadership presence) 4. Capacity for technical knowing (Job and industry knowledge; business knowledge) 5. Capacity to persevere and adapt (Energy, adaptability, and humour)
The commitment to lead	6. Commitment to excellence (Pursuing success; passion for results) 7. Commitment to people and relationships (Building talent; diversity and culture; interpersonal effectiveness) 8. Commitment to personal growth (Insatiable curiosity; self-awareness and development) 9. Commitment to stakeholders (Customers; team members; organization; shareholders; community)
The character to lead	10. Personal integrity and ethics (Personal integrity; ethics; openness) 11. Organizational integrity and courage (Organizational integrity; courage; power) 12. Humility, gratitude, and forgiveness (Humility; gratitude; forgiveness)

Sources: Peterson and Seligman (2004); Thompson et al. (2008)

minimize the drawbacks, including the environmental ones, of large productive organizations; and (3) to refrain from violating minimal standards of justice and human rights. These obligations are defined in terms of ten fundamental rights (Table 2.4). Global firms should avoid deprivation of any of these rights, and in some circumstances they will have an obligation to protect potential victims against deprivation of these rights by others.

Global leaders enjoy a position in circuits of power relations that enable them to influence the global market for the benefit of the many, including the distant poor and needy (Maak and Pless 2009). They have the *privilege* of living well in developed countries, a privilege that generates special responsibilities, including contributing to improving people's livelihoods in poor regions of the world, and acting

Table 2.4. Ten fundamental rights that companies must respect and, in some circumstances, protect

- Freedom of physical movement
- Property ownership
- Freedom from torture
- Fair trial
- Non-discriminatory treatment
- Physical security
- Freedom of speech and association
- Minimal education
- Political participation
- Subsistence

Donaldson (1989)

as beneficial rather than hostile agents in terms of people's social relations, resources, and rights. Considering their position in wide networks of stakeholders, they have the *potential* to mobilize people and institutions around the world and foster social betterment to assist those in need.

Those characteristics do not imply that global leaders and their companies are responsible for, or should be held accountable for, solving all the problems of the world—but that they should recognize their '*co-responsibility* for addressing *some* of the world's most pressing problems' and work as active and reflective citizens of the world in addressing such problems (Maak and Pless 2009: 539; italics in the original). More precisely, global leaders and their corporations may choose to assume (or not) their responsibilities in new moral forms of the division of labour (Nagel 1991). Choosing to stay on course with default settings oriented only to shareholder value is, of course, an option. But it is one that is an ethical choice just as much as opting for transitional strategies. Some companies seem to realize this: Ryuzaburo Kaku, former president and chairman of Canon (the Japanese word for the Buddhist Goddess of Mercy, Shelton and Darling (2003), went further and considered that contributing to social betterment is a necessary condition for companies' survival:

> Many companies around the world believe that they have a moral duty to respond to global problems such as Third World poverty, the deterioration of the natural environment, and endless trade battles. But few have realized that their survival actually depends on their response. Global corporations rely on educated workers, consumers with money to spend, a healthy natural environment, and peaceful coexistence between nations and ethnic groups. This reality is to me a great source of hope: at this watershed period in history, it is in the interests of the world's most powerful corporations to work for the advancement of global peace and prosperity. To put it simply, global companies have no future if the earth has no future. (Kaku 1997: 55)

Global organizations fostering peaceful societies

Nancy Adler suggests that global corporations, considering their more extensive and integrated global experience, compared with the more discrete and geographically bound experience of most countries and governments, are in a good position to promote society's betterment by fostering peace and security (Adler 2008). In her perspective, respecting democracy and human rights, adopting sustainable development practices and policies, and promoting health, poverty reduction, and more equitable income distribution, can accomplish these goals. By facilitating peace and security, companies not only contribute to societal betterment, they also build better conditions for operating and developing their businesses (Fort and Schipani 2004), especially where environmental problems leading to resource shortage and disease, extreme poverty and excessive income inequalities are a paramount cause of social tension (Adler 2008; Fort and Schipani 2004). Prosperity and peace support each other in a virtuous circle (Adler 2008).

According to Adler, business leaders rather than political, military, or humanitarian leaders may be better at tackling questions of societal well-being (Adler 2008). She goes as far as to suggest that the contributions of some companies in creating societal well-being are so extraordinary that the Nobel committee may need to consider private-sector initiatives as candidates for future Nobel Peace Prizes!

Tashman and Marano (2010) argue that as globalization proceeds, some functions previously assigned to nation states are increasingly being transferred to for-profit businesses. Private companies are increasingly expected to protect citizens in particularly troubled regions where crime and civil discontent flourishes, such as South Africa and Iraq; they do so on a commercial and fee basis but, when done well through intelligent design, community building, and social capital enhancing initiatives, by doing so they can intervene in power relations to promote more peaceful behaviours (Tashman and Marano 2010). Power can be exerted via at least four routes (Fort and Schipani 2004, 2007; Tashman and Marano 2010): participating in economic development, exercising track two diplomacy (i.e. unofficial forms of diplomacy), adopting external evaluation principles, and developing a sense of community both within and outside the company. Table 2.5 summarizes these four routes.

Economic development. Companies can contribute to the kind of economic development that breaks the spiral of violence and poverty. In environments where resources are scarce, competition for the

Table 2.5. How corporations may contribute to fostering peaceful societies

The four routes	Examples of global leaders' activities
Fostering economic development	• Providing jobs to the local residents. • Investing in the communities' long-term development. • Transferring know-how and managerial capabilities to the local people. • Paying taxes.
Exercising track two diplomacy	• Global leaders have the capability to deal directly with government officials and impact society. • They are in a good position to persuade politicians and governments of the advantages of peaceful conflicts resolution. • Global leaders are frequently perceived as unofficial ambassadors for their countries. • By employing diverse employees, global companies may promote positive relationships between people in conflict, thus allowing them to see that 'the enemy has a face'.
Adopting external evaluation principles	• Adopting transparency practices and policies. • Adopting efforts to limit or eliminate corruption. • Complying with legal requirements. • Educating people about laws and how they can be useful.
Nourishing a sense of community both within and outside the company	• Creating connections among employees and providing them with senses of security and identity. • Encouraging employees to use voice within the organization and in the communities where they live.

Built from Fort and Schipani (2004)

necessities of life may give rise to conflicts and violence, a context that is perverse for initiatives to operate and develop businesses. Companies may contribute to peace and stability in several ways. The first consists in providing jobs to residents of the countries where the company operates. In this way, a number of possibilities are created: the local economy can develop, and where a conscious attempt is made to ensure that child labour is not exploited, children may go to school instead of being made to work, health care facilities improve, and people can become more active politically as they assert their voice for the extension of those rights secured. The second way is investing in the communities' long-term development, through training and development policies, and by providing cultural and educational benefits to the community. The third way is transferring resources, including technological know-how and managerial capabilities to the local people. The fourth way consists in paying taxes, thus providing the country with resources for public policies. These benefits, of course, depend on how local government makes use of the collected taxes.

Track two diplomacy. Companies may also be vehicles for 'track two diplomacy' (i.e. unofficial diplomacy). For example, the 2002 nuclear showdown between India and Pakistan, it has been suggested, was mitigated by business leaders who convinced the Indian government of the benefits of a peaceful resolution of the conflict. In this regard, Friedman (2002) noted: 'in the crunch, it was the influence of General Electric not General Powell that did the trick'.

Companies may exercise track two diplomacy in several ways. First, global leaders command significant resources and thus are generally respected: this means that, in their positions of influence in elite social relations and the circles in which they can freely move, they can deal directly with government officials; thus, they are in a good position to persuade politicians and governments of the perverse economic and social consequences that might arise from open conflicts. Second, global leaders are frequently perceived as unofficial ambassadors for their countries; effectively, throughout history, in many imperial and colonial situations, companies such as the East India Company and British Petroleum were de facto agencies of government. Third, employing diverse employees, global companies may promote positive relationships between peoples in conflict (e.g. Protestants versus Catholics in Ireland). Working together, people may realize that 'the enemy has a face' and, thus, be more open to peaceful forms of conflict resolution.

Adopting external evaluation principles and transparency. Companies may also contribute to a peaceful environment by adopting transparency practices, which require willingness to have actions evaluated by external entities. Two main transparency routes are worthy of mention: transparency with respect to corruption and support of the rule of law. Companies may reduce violence by adopting transparency practices and making efforts to contain or eliminate corruption. Companies may also support the rule of law by, for example, complying with legal requirements and educating people about laws and the legal system. In today's information society, where information and communication technologies are at the disposal of millions of anonymous citizens, activists, and the media, transparency is crucial for organizational health (Goleman et al. 2008). Bad practices can become subject to everyday comment rapidly by spreading across the global competitive landscape, damaging a company's reputation in nano-seconds of Internet time. As argued by Bennis, Goleman and Biederman,

> The leaders who will thrive and whose organizations will flourish in this era of ubiquitous electronic tattle-tales are the ones who strive to make their organizations as transparent as possible. (In Goleman et al. 2008: 17)

Developing a sense of community. Companies may promote peace in the communities where they operate by developing a sense of community both within and outside the company. Such an endeavour may be carried out in several ways, including: (1) creating connections among employees and providing them with senses of security and identity; (2) tolerating dissent and encouraging employees to participate and use voice, thus developing voice in the communities where the company operates. By promoting the virtues of citizenship inside the company, employees are potentially better citizens at the community level.

In search of global leaders' character strengths and virtues

Some authors have explicitly referred to character strengths and virtues (e.g. integrity, character, and courage) as crucial for global leaders' performance (Brownell 2006; Conner 2000; Gregersen, et al. 1998; Kanter 2010). For example, Gregersen, et al. argue that global leaders should have, on top of other competencies, an *unbridled inquisitiveness* (e.g. being driven by a strong sense of curiosity and a desire to see and experience new things) and *personal character* (e.g. expressing a sincere interest in and concern for others; making efforts to really listen to people and understanding different viewpoints; showing high levels of trust and integrity, even when challenged by questionable ethical actions and behaviours common in other cultures). Conner (2000: 149) also argues that global leaders must have a strong character:

> They can be counted on to do what is right. Should they be pushed to do something they oppose, they aren't reluctant to resist. They understand that there are changing employee expectations. They inspire trust in others, and they value and respect the differences each person brings to the workplace. Global leaders with strong character meet commitments, act consistent with their words, and are interested in the well being of others. They use their power and influence to benefit the organization rather than for personal gain.

Bird and Osland (2004) propose a pyramid of leadership global competency development. At the first level there are four dispositions ('threshold traits'): integrity, humility, inquisitiveness, and hardiness. These dispositions are prerequisites to the effective development of attitudes and orientations (e.g. global mindset), interpersonal skills (e.g. intercultural communication), and system skills (e.g. making ethical decisions). McCall and Hollenbeck (2002) considered that global executives must have, in addition to other competencies, open-mindedness, honesty, and integrity, if they are to excel in their jobs.

Brownell (2006) argued that global leaders must possess several distinctive competencies (e.g. cultural sensitivity; cultural intelligence; empathy; self-control; self-efficacy; passion; sound judgement), including character ('an innate sense of fairness, honesty, respect for others, and humility'). According to the author, character is becoming the most resonant quality of global leaders. In his view, while the relative importance of other distinctive competencies is influenced by situational variables, such as organizational culture, strategy, and environment, character is essential to all global leadership contexts: character is relevant across situations without being situation-specific. Character works as the lens used by leaders to interpret events and choose courses of action (Brownell 2006), and is also crucial for developing the other distinctive competencies.

In other taxonomies, character strengths and virtues are not explicitly mentioned but are clearly necessary for developing global leadership competencies. For example: (a) the strengths of wisdom, open-mindedness, and social intelligence are crucial for understanding and respecting cultural differences; (b) vitality is necessary for travelling through different time zones, dealing with massive exposure to information, and working long days in adverse conditions; (c) prudence is crucial for avoiding inconsiderate decisions when dealing with unknown customs; (d) integrity and bravery are necessary for dealing with unethical behaviours and disrespect for human rights in some contexts.

We explore the character strengths and virtues that make global leaders more effective *and* better able to develop vibrant and positive organizations and communities in the contexts in which they operate. The character strengths and virtues framework proposed by Peterson and Seligman is used as a guide (Table 1.2). In the following chapters, we discuss how the virtues, and the correspondent character strengths, may help global leaders to perform their roles successfully in both 'technical' as well as social and humanitarian terms. We aim to show how global leaders' virtuousness may help them to be more effective builders of positive organizational performance.

Character strengths and virtues are important for leadership of the self (Crossan et al. 2008). Today's leaders must not just lead the self, the organization (leadership *of* the organization), and others (leadership *in* organization), but also must act responsibly toward all stakeholders in business, society, and the environment. We consider that the interconnection between the four levels is especially relevant for turning global leaders into sources of positive change in global organizations as well as for the planet: their personal strengths and virtues make them more able, in a virtuous way, to lead people and organizations operating worldwide, fostering virtuous and responsible relationships with a broad network of partners, thus contributing to societal betterment.

Virtues may contribute a positive difference

The book is inspired by the idea that global leaders' virtues should increasingly be reckoned as crucial ingredients for successful global leaders and businesses (Damon 2004; Fort and Schipani 2001). We consider that the success of global leaders should be interpreted and assessed in light of four criteria (Damon 2004). First, that these leaders achieve their goals. Second, that they build satisfying and enduring careers for those whom they employ as well as for themselves. Third, that they live honourably, behaving in a fair, honest, and responsible way. Fourth, that they feel proud to make a positive difference in the world. Czikszentmihalyi (2003: 34) argues that, under the guidance of virtuous leaders, many businesses can be both successful and humane, making a reasonable profit but also contributing to the happiness and well-being of their employees:

> Contrarily to common perception, there are many successful executives who understand that 'good business' involves more than making money, and who take the responsibility for making their firms an engine for enhancing the quality of life.

Virtuous leaders articulate three major principles of 'good business'. The first principle is vision beyond the self, rooted in a sense of that ethos that Weber referred to as a calling, a dedicated commitment to being a professional who models integrity and honour in their dealings with others (Weber 1978). Demonstrating this kind of vision and modelling it in everyday behaviours attracts and fosters the physical and psychological energies of other people and makes them willing to work beyond the call of duty. The second principle refers to practices characterized by trust, respect, organic solidarity, personal growth of organizational members, and opportunities for experiencing flow. Such practices make it possible to translate the vision into virtuous, flourishing, and effective organizational practices. In the absence of virtuous organizational practices, workers are less willing to genuinely commit to the vision. The third principle refers to creating products and services that help humankind,

Table 2.6. The principles of good business

Major principles	Main components of the major principles (i.e. ways through which the principles are realized)
1. **A vision beyond the self** (leaders believe in a goal that benefits not only themselves but also others, and act moved by a sense of calling)	1.1. Doing one's best, in search for excellence.
	1.2. Helping people (employees, customers, suppliers, the community).
	1.3. Contributing to building a better world.
2. **Positive business operating practices** (leaders lead organizational members to make the vision a reality)	2.1. Trusting and respecting people.
	2.2. Concern for the personal growth of organizational members.
	2.3. Creating/developing organizational/work opportunities so that organizational members experience flow (a mental state of optimal functioning, in which the individual fully immerses in carrying out the task, with focus, involvement and success).
3. **Products/services that help humanity**	3.1. Generating products and services that improve human health and well-being.
	3.2. Being selective in investments (e.g. abandoning cotton produced by industrial means and moving towards the adoption of organic cotton).
	3.3. Respecting and preserving the natural environment.
	3.4. Devoting earnings to philanthropic causes (addressing, for example, health, education, arts, and culture issues).

Source: Czikszentmihalyi (2003)

that make a difference rather than just a buck. As Porter and Kramer (2011: 75) put it, 'not all profit is equal'. By participating in the making of such products and services, organizational members can feel more energized and derive greater meaning from work.

It is not difficult to see how leaders' virtues may support such principles, as we suggest in Table 2.6. Flynn (2008) noted that the challenge of constructing a great and sustainable company critically depends on the action of virtuous managers who combine high principles, inspired standards, a passion for people, and the search for profits. Without profits all else is impossible; the point is that all else should not be sacrificed to create them. We consider that global leaders' virtues make them able to develop organizations according to the three principles of good business referred to above.

What is the business of business?

There is a reasonable consensus about the inadequacy of the 'the business of business is business' aphorism, associated with Friedman's (1970) proposition that the social responsibility of business is to increase its profits (Adler 2008). Solomon argued that business is as much about integrity as it is about profits. He also considered that profits mean little when they imply the sacrifice of integrity. As he put it, 'in other walks of life, this is called "prostitution"' (Solomon 1999: xiii). In the Zermatt Summit, a new annual event whose motto is humanizing globalization, that was held in Switzerland in 2010, Philippe de Woot, Emeritus Professor at the Catholic University of Louvain, observed that Friedman's belief in shareholder primacy is today 'an absurdity, an obscenity' (Fraser 2010). Mary Bush, a former US representative on the International Monetary Fund's board, agreed that Friedman has had a corrosive influence: 'I think his views are politically and morally unacceptable and we should call them by their proper name: obscene.'

The rival World Economic Forum at Davos also acknowledged the need to rethink the ways businesses should be run. The affiliated Forum of Young Global Leaders (YGL) acknowledged that the global financial crisis of 2008 and the ensuing economic recession 'brought under question the character and trustworthiness of business managers around the world' (http://www.globalbusinessoath.org/). As a consequence, the YGL proclaimed the Global Business Oath (Table 2.7), along the following lines:

> The YGL Global Business Oath aims to transform the value system dominant today among business leaders around the world by (a) explicitly recognizing that the ultimate purpose of management is to serve society by bringing together people and resources to create sustainable and inclusive prosperity that no single individual can create alone, (b) recognizing that the effects (good and bad) of managerial decisions in the welfare of society are amplified by the accumulation of resources under legal corporations, and (c) proposing a code of conduct—a modern day 'Hippocratic Oath of Business'—that spells out a commitment to 'doing no harm' throughout the practice of management.

Table 2.7. YGL Global Business Oath

'As a business leader I recognize that
- The enterprise I lead must serve the greater good by bringing together people and resources to create value that no single individual can create alone.
- My decisions can have far-reaching consequences that affect the wellbeing of individuals inside and outside my enterprise, today and tomorrow.
- As I reconcile the interests of different constituencies, I will face choices that are not easy for me and others.

So I promise that
1. I will manage my enterprise diligently and in good faith and will not let personal considerations and compensation supersede the long-term interest of my enterprise and society at large.
2. I will understand and uphold, both in letter and spirit, the laws and contracts governing my own conduct and that of my enterprise.
3. I will respect and protect the human rights and dignity of all people who are affected by my enterprise and will oppose all forms of discrimination and exploitation.
4. I will respect and protect the right of future generations to enjoy a clean and resourceful planet.
5. I will not engage in nor tolerate bribery or any other form of corruption.
6. I will represent the performance and risks of my enterprise accurately and honestly to each of the constituencies that are affected by it.
7. I will actively engage in efforts to finding solutions to critical social and environmental issues that are central to my enterprise, and
8. I will invest in my own professional development as well as the development of other managers under my supervision.

In exercising my professional duties according to these principles I recognize that my behavior must set an example of integrity and responsible conduct.'

Source: http://www.globalbusinessoath.org/businessoath.php (retrieved December 28, 2011)

The degree to which these statements are more than pious intentions, to be neglected or forgotten as soon as the crisis dissipates and a new wave of economic optimism washes pessimism away, is impossible to predict. But the intention has been stated and, once committed to, a standard set. Elias (1969) advises that the cultivation of a sense of shame is an essential step in the civilizing process; hence, such oaths, when malfeasance occurs in spite of them, set up the preconditions for the civilizing of global leaders to occur as a sense of collective shame can be institutionalized.

Conclusion

In the recent past, intellectual movements such as positive organizational scholarship (Cameron and Spreitzer 2012) devoted their energy to the transformation of organizations via research on the theory and practice of positive and virtuous leadership and organizing. Scholars such as Ed Diener and Martin Seligman, prominent members and leaders of the positive psychology movement (Seligman and Csikszentmihalyi 2000), have recommended going 'beyond money' to building an economy of well-being. Others have promoted the economics of happiness (Diener and Seligman 2004; Donal et al. 2008; Graham 2005, 2006).

This book positions itself alongside these positive streams, generated mainly in the positive organizational scholarship movement. In a globalized world, where multinational companies implicate a huge number of other organizations and millions of people in extensive power relations, global leaders may make a positive difference where they are persuaded that they need to be endowed with virtues and character strengths. In the next chapters, we analyse the nature of these virtues and character strengths.

3

Cognitive and Energizing Virtues

> The lessons from this crisis are evident: if we select people principally for their charisma and their ability to drive up stock prices in the short term instead of their character, and we shower them with inordinate rewards, why should we be surprised when they turn out to lack integrity?
>
> (George 2003: 5)

> If a CEO of an organization was said to be wise, it means that she/he was astute or showed good judgment in his/her transactions. If the 'getting of wisdom' is considered a necessary attribute of today's managers, why is it that few management programs offer courses in managerial wisdom? (...) Why is there no debate or discussion in contemporary management thinking about the relevance of managerial wisdom?
>
> (Small 2004: 753)

The strengths of wisdom and knowledge

The virtues of wisdom and knowledge comprise five character strengths: creativity, curiosity, open-mindedness, love of learning, and perspective/wisdom (Table 3.1). Creativity refers to the ability to produce original and useful ideas. Curiosity may be defined as an 'active recognition, pursuit, and regulation of one's experience in response to challenging opportunities' (Peterson and Seligman 2004: 125). Open-mindedness is the willingness to engage in a search for evidence to which one will give fair consideration even though it might invalidate one's beliefs (Peterson and Seligman 2004). In the management literature, the evidence-based management perspective epitomizes a commitment to open-mindedness—as long as the boundaries of what will be considered as evidence are not drawn so securely as to exclude all but the most arrant positivism and arid

Table 3.1. Strengths through which the virtues of wisdom and knowledge are displayed

Strength	How individuals with this strength behave (examples)	Opposites	Excess
Creativity (originality; ingenuity)	• They develop novel and useful ideas for dealing with problems and opportunities. • They present original, adaptive and practical ideas and approaches. • They suggest new ways to achieve goals and objectives. • They suggest new and practical ideas and plans to increase quality, to originate innovation, and to improve performance.	Dullness; unimaginativeness; insipidity.	Excessive fantasy; lack of realism.
Curiosity (interest; novelty-seeking; openness to experience)	• They reveal active interest in understanding novel events, situations, and people. • They pursue experiential novelty, variety, and challenge. • They seek novel and exciting experiences to elevate stimulation to an optimal level.	Disinterest; boredom; ennui; world-weariness.	Inconvenience; bedazzlement with novelty; adventurism.
Open-mindedness (judgement; critical thinking)	• They take into consideration evidence that goes against their beliefs. • They revise beliefs in response to new evidence. • They see several possible angles when confronted with complex issues in which evidence for and against a belief must be examined and pondered.	Inflexibility; rigidity; ethnocentrism; dogmatism; stereotyping.	Naivety; chameleon behaviour, switching views without regard to the quality of the evidence as different interpretations emerge.
Love of learning	• They experience positive feelings when they are acquiring skills and knowledge, satisfying their curiosity, and/or learning something completely new. • They like to develop capacities for carrying out tasks in which they are not proficient.	Intellectual resistance; ignorance.	Obsessive passion; not knowing when to stop learning and start practising.
Perspective/ wisdom	• They integrate accumulated information and knowledge and use it deliberately to improve well-being in others and themselves. • They have a strong need to contribute to others and society.	Thoughtlessness; foolishness; idiocy.	Self-righteousness; fundamentalism, excessive extreme idealism; arrogance.

(continued)

Table 3.1. Continued

Strength	How individuals with this strength behave (examples)	Opposites	Excess
	• They listen to others, evaluate what they say, and offer good advice. • They are able to see to the heart of important problems and opportunities.		

empiricism (Pfeffer and Sutton 2006). Love of learning involves the positive motivation to acquire new skills and knowledge or building on existing skills and knowledge. Perspective/wisdom refers to the ability to approach life in 'large terms'. It results from knowledge and experience, and is much more than merely accumulating information (Peterson and Seligman 2004).

These strengths, frequently operating in a blended way, are crucial for global leaders' effectiveness. For example, curiosity, open-mindedness, love of learning, and perspective/wisdom help to avoid cultural imperialism and allow the adoption of a prudent perspective (Beer 2003). Many global organizations display impatience and pursue business strategies that reflect an individualistic, short-term orientation. They are pressed by a sense of urgency and the will to get results quickly. Such strategies, however, may clash with cultures where the values of collectivism, long-time orientation, interpersonal harmony, patience, and respect for tradition prevail. Wise leaders will be more prepared to arrive at a synthesis between both orientations when necessary.

The virtue of wisdom helps global leaders to develop four kinds of knowledge (Jokinen 2005): knowledge of tasks, organization, business, and people. They are all important for dealing with the levels of complexity, ambiguity, and uncertainty that characterize the global leadership role:

- The knowledge of *tasks* refers to the technical knowledge (e.g. language skills, technical expertise, understanding and utilizing financial concepts and principles) needed to get the job done.
- The knowledge of *organization* includes: (a) knowledge of the firm worldwide, (b) organizational astuteness, (c) a capacity to recognize the key constituencies and decision makers and to manage with power; (d) an ability to understand the key organizational processes, systems, procedures, and methods, (e) the capacity to understand the strategic roles and competitive advantages of different business units, and (f) an awareness of human resources and training needs available worldwide.

- The knowledge of *business* includes: (a) the knowledge of the company's worldwide business structure, (b) the knowledge of international business issues, (c) the capacity to cope with the interdependence of business activity around the world, (d) the ability to recognize business opportunities around the world, (e) the understanding of international marketing and finance, and (f) the ability to analyse market trends and conditions.

- The knowledge of *people* includes (a) understanding the impact of culture on behavioural communication, (b) getting insight into the needs, goals, demands, and problems of different organizational constituents, (c) being able to appreciate cultural differences, (d) managing cross-cultural ethics and diversity, and (d) building, hiring, developing, assessing, and rewarding systems that respect the norms and values of other cultures.

Although the five strengths have similarities (they all refer to positive cognitive traits related to the acquisition and use of information in the service of good life), and reveal reciprocal influences (e.g. curiosity may feed the love of learning, and love of learning may trigger curiosity), each may make a unique contribution to the global leaders' positive performance, as discussed next (see the synthesis in Table 3.3).

Creativity: facing the world's diversity with creative moral imagination

Global leaders' creativity may help them develop innovative strategies in countries where the home company's strategy does not work. Creativity may help global leaders to find new and useful ideas for dealing with unexpected situations in different markets and societies, and for developing creative products and services in markets where the more traditional ones do not meet local needs. Daimler-Benz's leaders gave proofs of creativity, in 1992, when facing pressures both from the German Green Party (pressing the company to be more ecologically responsible) and from the Brazilian government (pushing foreign companies to expand the local content of their products). Daimler-Benz developed a new high-tech factory making headrests and seats out of coconut fibres from locally grown trees (Fort and Schipani 2004; Lodge 2002). Thousands of people from the surrounding communities were employed in the project, higher retention rates for school children were achieved, and health care facilities improved.

Global leaders with high levels of creativity may be more effective in negotiating globally, by discovering new and useful cooperative solutions that may satisfy idiosyncratic needs of partners from different cultures and by overcoming apparently insoluble disagreements (Brett 2001; Imai and Gelfand 2010; Kurtzberg 1998; Rosenbloom 2002). Brett (2001) argued that negotiators have to be creative while facing cultural differences. Namely, they must accept that diverse cultural strategies may coexist.

Brett also suggested that creativity is required for finding agreements in negotiations where parties come from different ideological spaces. A widely cited example of a creative negotiation that overcame ideological differences about repatriation of profits is the agreement between Pepsi-Cola Company and the government of the USSR, in the 1970s and 1980s. In return for selling soft drinks in the USSR, Pepsi-Cola agreed to buy and export vodka in lieu of repatriating profits (Brett 2001; Okoroafo 1992). South Korean companies also accepted Libyan debt in payment of Czechoslovakian obligations (Lewis and Turley 1991).

When negotiating international mergers and acquisitions, strategic alliances, and licensing and distribution agreements, or when working within management teams of joint ventures, creativity may also help global leaders to deal with differences in values, ambitions, and strategies—thus overcoming the 'same bed, different dreams' syndrome (Jackson 2002). The creativity of global leaders may also be crucial for facing scarcity in some contexts and developing products and solutions that meet the needs of the 'base of the pyramid' (London 2009; Prahalad 2005). The base of the pyramid represents 4 billion customers with low income that, combined, spend more than $2 trillion each year, being the target of initiatives of companies such as Hewlett-Packard, Unilever, Ericsson, Cemex, Motorola, Monsanto, DuPont, Citigroup, Monsanto, Johnson & Johnson, Novartis, Philips, and Danone (Elaydi and Harrison 2010; Gabel 2004; Hart and Christensen 2002; London 2009; London and Hart 2004; Tashman and Marano 2010; Yunus et al. 2010).

In countries suffering from deep poverty, new products and services need to be imagined and developed with a sophisticated understanding of how poverty constrains needs and shapes consumption patterns (Elaydi and Harrison 2010; Simanis and Hart 2009; Yunus et al. 2010). Facing such scarcity through creativity and innovative products designed for the base of the pyramid enables firms to (a) make money and develop dynamic capabilities (Tashman and Marano 2010), (b) contribute to alleviating poverty if local entrepreneurialism is channelled, (c) as well as improve the well-being of billions of people (Yunus et al. 2010), (d) reduce the imbalance between wealthy and poor nations and,

thus, (e) make a small contribution to reducing the human tide of economic refugees and illegal immigration (Adler 2008; Collier and Dollar
2002; Kaku 1997; Tashman and Marano 2010; Yunus et al. 2010). In this
way, they can contribute to creating a more inclusive capitalism (London
and Hart 2004) and to fostering peace, a crucial condition for operating
and developing businesses (Fort and Schipani 2004).

Creativity and moral imagination (Damon 2004; Solomon 1999) led
the Nobel Peace Prize winner Muhammad Yunus to build and develop
micro-credit and the Grameen Bank (Adler 2008; Yunus et al. 2010). This
innovation has contributed to taking millions of people around the
world out of poverty, and has been a source of inspiration for other
creative solutions (e.g. Grameen Phone, Grameen Veolia, Grameen Danone) for improving the life of millions of people in underprivileged
nations. Recent criticisms of micro-credit (*The Economist* 2010b), however, show that unscrupulous individuals and a failure to imagine the
consequences of well-intentioned social interventions creatively can
corrupt even good ideas. On the latter point, for instance, one micro-
entrepreneur in a small community who is armed with a mobile phone
which is hired out for calls can make a profit; once there is multiplicity
of such entrepreneurs in the small locale doing the same, all are con-
demned to poverty and another race to the bottom. The success of
individual cases of micro-finance can easily lead to an uncreative reple-
tion of its success that will breed failure.

Daniel Vasella, from Novartis, expressed creativity and moral imagination when the company introduced Gleevec (George 2003). The drug,
aiming to target a cancer called chronic myeloid leukaemia (CML), was
put in limbo because of the small number of patients. However, Vasella
recognized the drug's potential and accelerated clinical trials. The FDA
eventually approved the drug in record time. Next, Vasella introduced
Gleevec in a creative way (George 2003: 135). Recognizing the great
difficulties of low-income patients in purchasing the drug, he decided
to provide it for free for anyone with an income below $40,000, and at a
reduced price for patients with incomes up to $100,000. The drug has
had a strong positive impact on Novartis' reputation in the USA, far
exceeding its initial sales.

Curiosity fuelling the global mind

Curiosity and enthusiasm are crucial leadership forces (Greger and
Peterson 2000). Several authors have considered inquisitiveness as an
important competency of global leaders, referring to it in terms such as

learning – multiple disciplines [handwritten]

curiosity and concern with context (Jokinen 2005). For example, Black and associates (Black 2006; Black et al. 1999; Gregersen et al. 1998; Black 2006) referred to inquisitiveness as the fuel of a global mind. Morrison (2000: 126) also noted that:

learning from mistakes [handwritten]

> true inquisitiveness produces the action associated with learning, and learning is essential for keeping savvy, character, and perspective fresh. Without inquisitiveness, an individual will never develop a solid understanding of global markets nor will s/he establish the type of vibrant internal relationships necessary to effectively access the resources of the global organization.

curiosity → learning → people, relationships [handwritten]

Curiosity helps global leaders to develop motivation and willingness to enter and confront unfamiliar situations (e.g. accepting international assignments in culturally distant countries), to seek opportunities for learning continuously, to avoid limiting and biased assumptions, to be open to criticism, and to engage in continuous improvement and personal transformation (Jokinen 2005). Curiosity may nourish creativity, in such a way that curious global leaders are more likely to be inquisitive about how to solve problems creatively and take advantage of opportunities.

John Pepper, former CEO of Procter & Gamble, used to visit several families' homes in each country, before going to his hotel or office, thus seeing first hand how local people used the firm's products (Gregersen et al. 1998). Doing this, he learnt that the French preferred front-load washers instead of top-load washers. This, in turn, helped him better to manage the introduction of a new cold-water detergent brand globally and led to the invention of an innovative plastic ball into which customers put the detergent, with the ball evenly distributing the detergent through small holes.

Curiosity is crucial for seeking knowledge and expertise outside established boundaries, and drawing information from many sources in several ways (Jokinen 2005). It fuels the passion for cultural difference (Beechler and Javidan 2007), and helps to acquire knowledge of how culture influences those leadership behaviours that are accepted or rejected in different contexts, as well as consumers' tastes and preferences, the most appropriate ways to communicate, negotiate, and behave within cross-cultural teams, and the best ways to deal with authorities. In summary, curiosity is a powerful driver of a global mindset (Beechler and Javidan 2007).

Curiosity was one of the pillars of Anita Roddick's capacity to build and develop The Body Shop, inspired by the lessons learned with women from poor countries. According to Damon (2004: 77–78), what began as youthful curiosity and enthusiasm for the practices of native cultures matured into a systematic method of examining these practices and adapting them for universal uses. (. . .) Roddick's creative gift was the capacity to look at what indigenous people were doing with fresh eyes and learn from their wisdom (. . .) It was an approach founded on a deep respect for the native people whom she journeyed across the world to meet (. . .).

The Body Shop has not been without its critics (Purkayastha and Fernando 2007), some of whom have accused it of overstating its green commitments and general corporate social responsibility agenda, as well as singling out the 2006 decision to sell the company to L'Oreal for particular invective, given that Anita Roddick had frequently criticized their practices. Jon Entine, a particularly virulent critic, coined the now-familiar term 'greenwashing' in the context of an invective aimed at the organization in *Business Ethics* magazine. Moreover, claims that Body Shop was a major supporter of charities were not borne out by the records of the Charity Commission. Clearly, in this case, curiosity there may have been, but it was also combined with what at best was 'clever' marketing; at worst, with a degree of duplicity in claims that were being made (Entine 2004). Curiosity in itself is insufficient: it is how the virtues hang together that is important.

Open-mindedness

To accept and to face the world's complexity, challenges, and contradictions with creativity and a cosmopolitan ethos requires open-mindedness (Maak and Pless 2009). Leaders of Norske Skog (a world-leading producer of newsprint and magazine paper, with fourteen paper mills around the world as per October 2010) gave proofs of this strength when the company transformed itself from a domestic to a global company (Adler 2002). In creating an organizational culture that would be globally integrated, locally responsive, and skilled at worldwide learning, the company did not confine itself to replicate what other global companies had done but adopted an heterodox approach. Norske Skog invited the children of its employees, worldwide, to help understand what global cooperation means, and could mean, for society, companies, and individuals. According to Adler, this open-mindedness approach helped the company to reach impressive performance and growth from being a modest player to becoming one of the largest world suppliers of newsprint paper (Adler 2002).

Open-minded global leaders are less vulnerable to stereotypic conceptions of leaders and partners in other countries (Burns et al. 1995). They are also able to appreciate cultural differences (Jokinen 2005) and to develop cultural intelligence (Earley and Mosakowski 2004; Earley et al. 2007). Cultural intelligence is the personal capability to adapt to new cultural contexts successfully and involves four components (Table 3.2): metacognitive, cognitive, motivational, and behavioural. Open-mindedness and cultural intelligence facilitate the reception and

avoid (handwritten)
insensitivity (handwritten)

Table 3.2. The four dimensions of cultural intelligence

Dimension	Definition	Examples of cultural intelligence
Metacognitive	Control of cognition: the processes individuals use to acquire and understand cultural knowledge, including knowledge of and control over individual thought processes.	• The individual is conscious of the cultural knowledge (s)he uses when interacting with people with different cultural backgrounds. • The individual is able to adjust the cultural knowledge as (s)he interacts with people from a unfamiliar culture. • The individual checks the accuracy of his/her cultural knowledge as (s)he interacts with people from different cultures.
Cognitive	Knowledge of the norms, practices and conventions in different cultures, acquired from education and personal experiences.	• The individual knows the legal, economic, and social systems of other cultures. • The individual knows the cultural values and religious beliefs of other cultures, and is able to understand similarities and differences across cultural situations. • The individual knows the rules for expressing nonverbal behaviours in other cultures.
Motivational	Capacity to direct attention and mobilize energies toward learning about and functioning in situations characterized by cultural differences.	• The individual enjoys and feels intrinsically motivated to interact with people from different cultures. • The individual is confident that (s)he can deal with the stress of adjusting to a new culture. • The individual enjoys living in unfamiliar cultures.
Behavioural	Capacity to exhibit appropriate verbal and nonverbal behaviours when interacting with people from different cultures.	• The individual changes his/her verbal behaviour (e.g. accent, tone) when a cross-cultural interaction demands it. • The individual adjusts his/her nonverbal behaviour to the cultural situation (s)he is experiencing. • The individual alters his/her facial expressions when a cross-cultural interaction requires it.

Built from Ang et al. (2007); Ng et al. (2009)

processing of unbiased information from other cultural contexts (De-Frank et al. 2000). Such strengths are crucial for global leaders to switch national contexts, learn new patterns of social interaction, and devise the right behavioural responses to these patterns (Alon and Higgins 2005). Both open-mindedness and cultural intelligence help global leaders to adopt cooperative approaches when making cross-cultural negotiations (Imai and Gelfand 2010).

When they are impoverished in open-mindedness and cultural intelligence, global leaders are likely to develop stereotyped and ethnocentric views of other cultures and people, thus experiencing cultural shock and failures when performing international assignments. Stereotypes and ethnocentric views also create difficulties in negotiating effectively and in developing positive relationships with employees, customers, authorities, partners, and other stakeholders in other countries. To an American or European global leader, the following anecdotal excerpt from Roger E. Axtell (author of *Gestures: The do's and taboos of body language around the world*) illustrates how open-mindedness is crucial for dealing with partners of apparently exotic cultures (Axtell 1998: 39):

> On my first trip to the Middle East, my Arab business contact and I toured the city, walking along the street visiting customers. He wore his long robe, the air was hot and dusty, a muezzin chanted the call to prayers from a nearby minaret, and I felt as far away from my American home as one could possibly be. At that moment, my business friend reached over, took my hand in his, and we continued walking along, his hand holding mine. It didn't take me long to realize that something untoward was happening here, that some form of communication was being issued... but I didn't have the faintest idea what the message was. Also, I suddenly felt even farther from home. Probably because I was so stunned, the one thing I didn't do was pull my hand away. I later learned that had I jerked my hand out of his, I could have committed a Sahara-size *faux pas*. In his country, this act of taking my hand in his was a sign of great friendship and respect.

Axtell was deprived of *cognitive* cultural intelligence regarding this Arab country, although having it would not guarantee that he would feel comfortable to reciprocate appropriately with the Arab partner. Open-mindedness may also support flexibility and innovative and successful strategies that take advantage of the current stage of globalization and the inherent properties of international exchanges (Ozer 2002). Open-mindedness guided Leung Qingde, co-founder of the Chinese company Galanz, a textile and garment manufacturer (Ge and Ding 2008; Hart and Christensen 2002). In 1992, after Mr Qingde visited Japan for business in 1991, Galanz decided to enter the market for microwave ovens, although the global market for microwaves was mature and shrinking, being hard to differentiate products because most of them were good enough to satisfy customers' needs in developed countries. At this time, due to low labour costs, China was mainly a manufacturer, rather than consumer—only 2 per cent of all Chinese households owned a microwave oven. Furthermore, most Chinese families did not have kitchens large enough to accommodate the available models (designed to fit Western homes).

Rather than profiting from inexpensive Chinese labour to make low-cost ovens for export, Qingde chose to compete against non-consumption in the Chinese market, launching a simple, energy-efficient and cheap model, one also small enough to fit in Chinese kitchens. As the market expanded, economies of scale allowed the costs and price to diminish, with Galanz's domestic market share rising from 2 per cent in 1993 to 50 per cent in 1996, and to 76 per cent of a much larger market in 2000. Armed with a successful business model, the company moved upmarket, disrupting the microwave-oven markets in developed economies (the global market share in 2002 was of 35 per cent). In 2000, Galanz launched an effort to replicate its disruptive success in the home air-conditioning industry. In 2004, the annual export volume reached 1.56 million units, the highest among all Chinese air-conditioner exporting companies (Ge and Ding 2008).

Love of learning to understand the richness of the world

Love of learning shares several features with the other cognitive strengths, mainly with curiosity and open-mindedness. However, an individual may be extremely curious and open-minded, although less motivated to learn new skills or knowledge, or to build on existing skills and knowledge. One could even argue that the positive effects of global leaders' curiosity and open-mindedness require, or are facilitated by, a strong love of learning.

Global leaders' love of learning is most likely to be deployed in dealing, communicating, and negotiating with employees, customers, authorities, communities, partners, and other stakeholders of different cultural contexts, rather than in scholarly pursuits; also these are invaluable. Oriet Gadiesh, chairman of Bain & Company, revealed a strong love of learning when he pointed out the following (Csikszentmihalyi 2003: 163):

> I read history, I read biographies, I read military history. (...) I read books about math and science—I read philosophy. Whenever I travel to a country, especially if I am on vacation, I will buy books that are written by authors in

that country—it gives you a lot of insight into the way people really feel. I love theater, I love to travel. And I am curious about anything up to a point. (...) One of the things that is fun for me is to keep learning all the time.

Love of learning helps global leaders to develop cultural intelligence and a global mindset. They are often able to learn from cultural mistakes, adopting more effective behaviours, attitudes, and strategies. Anita Roddick claimed that success means consistently learning how to do things better (Csikszentmihalyi 2003). Joaquin, a Colombian working in Malaysia as president of a Japanese high-tech firm, gave proof of love of learning when faced with the idiosyncratic habits and attitudes of the Malaysian employees (Otazo 1999). The prototype of a Malaysian leader is a kind of father of the village—loving, benevolent, and able to resolve conflict together with other elders in the village—but someone who is also decisive. Joaquin faced a company whose morale was exhausted by bad management practices of two previous managers, one from Japan (who was aggressive and communicated via an interpreter) and another from Taiwan (who treated employees as if they were beneath contempt).

Before taking the job, Joaquin submitted himself to coaching that helped him to understand cultural issues that would affect his business effectiveness. Once in Malaysia, he spent the first two months listening and benevolently doing favours. Every day, he sat down with people and reflected with them. He learned Malay, becoming fluent enough to participate in meetings with government officials. Joaquin also creatively implemented several measures that helped him to build respect and charisma among employees and the community. He helped to open a kindergarten without support from the Japanese head office, and to create a system that allowed ten employees per year to go to Mecca without having to take vacation days.

On the other hand, Leroy Jackson (Otazo 1999), CEO of an Indonesian subsidiary of an American oil company, revealed a weak inclination to learn the local culture. He adopted leadership behaviours that collided with the prototype of an Indonesian leader, a type similar to the Malaysian one. He either did not use coaching, or gave it only lip service. Eager to show who was the boss, he adopted a policy that stated that no American needed to learn Indonesian *Bahasa*. Moreover, he adopted cost-cutting policies that reduced the time employees could spend with their families, a disastrous decision in such a strongly family-oriented culture. A severe slowdown in productivity dictated Leroy's fate. Having lost sight of the needs of employees and the Indonesian culture, Leroy survived only six months in Jakarta before being repatriated.

Wisdom: using knowledge to adopt sensible global perspectives

Den Hartog (2004) considered wisdom a crucial aspect for effective strategic global leadership, arguing that such strength involves the ability to take the right action at the critical moment, and discernment. Wisdom is more than being simply analytically smart by virtue of having brainpower (Den Hartog 2004; Sternberg 1997). It can be seen as 'the product of knowledge and experience' (Peterson and Seligman 2004: 106), combined with an accurate view of one's own strengths and weaknesses as well as of the situation's challenges. This is particularly relevant because global leaders operate in conditions of liminality, betwixt and between spaces (Cunha et al. 2010).

Using this definition, it is possible to identify some CEOs who seem to have the appropriate combinations of reflexivity, knowledge, and experience. Born in Brazil, French by nationality, raised in Lebanon, and having worked in France, Brazil, US, and from 1999 in Japan, Carlos Ghosn is often portrayed as the 'saviour' of Nissan (Millikin and Fu 2005). He embraced the cultural differences between himself and Japanese interlocutors and used differences in cultural perspective as opportunities for personal growth and for becoming a better leader. He approached the Nissan–Renault alliance as an opportunity for mutual learning, considering that both could learn from the strengths and perspectives of the other. Regarding Japanese culture, he said: 'I did not try to learn too much about Japan before coming, because I didn't want to have too many preconceived ideas. I wanted to discover Japan by being in Japan with Japanese people' (Millikin and Fu 2005: 121). Immersion is an essential trait for global leaders. It denotes a grain of anthropological curiosity, essential to managing the complexities of a subtle and culturally different quotidian life.

Wisdom, in contrast, was not present when leaders at IBM did not understand, or refused to understand, that marketing PCs was different from selling and servicing the big mainframes that had given the company global dominance (Keough 2008). With a mainframe mindset, IBM missed the opportunity to take advantage of the emerging market in PCs. This and other mistakes (e.g. neglecting data about business trends) took the company to the brink of disaster (Collins 2009; Keough 2008). According to Donald Keough, former CEO of The Coca-Cola Company, it was as if IBM management 'was standing on the bank of a river' neglecting the fact that one never bathes in the same river twice:

The reality was that the executives at IBM were too busy looking downstream happily watching those beautiful, profitable mainframes floating down the river and around the world. The final curtain on this little business history episode is that the ThinkPad, IBM's PC, ended up in the laptop factories in China under the brand of Lenovo. It's sad because IBM had such a head start. They're recovered, of course, but it wasn't easy. (Keough 2008: 33–34).

Wisdom was also absent when the Medical Systems division of General Electric acquired *La Compagnie Generale de Radiologie*, in France (Mendenhall et al. 2003). It was a time when, under the influence of the new CEO, Jack Welch, General Electric adopted the vision of being #1 or #2 (or be sold). During one of the initial integration meetings, US managers put up English posters in the meeting room that declared 'GE is #1'. They also asked French managers to wear T-shirts with similar slogans. The French managers felt insulted by these and other moves, the consequence being severely perverse for the new unit's profits. HR experience and wisdom would have helped US managers to be more sensitive to the French managers' idiosyncrasies and sense of 'pride'. What works in Peoria might not play in Paris.

Wise global leaders make better expatriate selection decisions, weighing the technical, social, emotional, and motivational features of candidates, thus reducing the risks of premature repatriation and contributing to the expatriates' success (consider, for example, the informal approach used by Jon Huntsman, from Huntsman Corporation: Black and Gregersen (1999)). They are better able to identify leadership behaviours that are more appropriate in different contexts (Javidan et al. 2006; Morrison 2000).

Wise leaders develop business and organize expertise (Mendenhall 2006; Osland et al. 2006) in a global perspective, integrating diverse knowledge bases (Gupta and Govindarajan 2002), and developing strategies that take local and global issues into account. Wisdom also helps in making good international acquisitions and mergers (Hutzschenreuter et al. 2009), and in adopting appropriate policies and practices. Such strengths helped Danone successfully to lead a transformation process in a company acquired in Moscow. By recognizing specificities of the local company (greatly influenced by the Soviet legacy), the CEO established a reassuring sense of community and adopted a paternalistic, autocratic leadership, a style 'still seen by Russians as a guarantee against anarchy' (Kets de Vries and Florent-Treacy 2002: 301; Fey and Shekshnia 2011).

Wisdom helps global leaders to get more pervasive insights from the cultural, economic, and political environment, and thus decide what is more appropriate (i.e. leaving versus keeping investing) when operating in a country where human rights and dignity are violated (Beaver 1995; Cavanagh and Bandsuch 2002; Mitchell 1994). This discernment also makes them able to identify appropriate strategies to adopt in difficult countries, and to discover ways to contribute to the reduction of poverty within the communities in which their companies operate. Wise global leaders can understand that Western-style patterns of economic development may not apply to initiatives targeting low-income markets (London and Hart 2004), and thus become more likely to develop creative ways for meeting the needs of these markets.

Global leaders with perspective/wisdom are also more prepared to provide counselling and mentoring to impatriates (Harvey and Novicevic 2004) and to individuals who are preparing for international assignments (Jassawalla et al. 2006), thus helping their cross-cultural and psychological adjustment and helping them to be more effective. When working abroad, global leaders with perspective/wisdom develop better cross-cultural adjustment, and are better able to build social and working relationships, thus becoming more effective and reducing the risks of expatriation failure and premature return (Lee 2007; Lee and Liu 2006). Perspective/wisdom also helps them to develop cultural intelligence and global mindset (mainly its intellectual component; Table 3.2). They are also more willing to coach local employees and facilitate localization (Law et al. 2004; Selmer 2003), helping to develop local management teams and reducing the organizational needs to resort to expatriates, who are more expensive than locals, for managing subsidiaries.

When wisdom becomes vicious

As discussed in the first chapter, virtues are a golden mean between extremes. Too little virtue (deficiency) may certainly be detrimental. However, an excess of virtue potentially represents a vice. For example, excessive creativity may give rise to developing fanciful or unrealistic strategies and products or services—or behaviours that, although creative, are foolish in the cultural context where the leader is operating. Excessive curiosity may lead global leaders to ask questions that are inconvenient to stakeholders of idiosyncratic cultural contexts, or to become confused and fascinated with novelty, focusing only on satisfying immediately defined needs and neglecting *action*. Excessively curious leaders may incur unnecessary risks when accepting certain international assignments or confronting unfamiliar situations.

Table 3.3. Wisdom and knowledge assisting several global leaders' activities

Creativity	• Finding new and useful ideas for dealing with unexpected situations in different markets and societies.
	• Developing creative products and services in markets where the more traditional ones do not meet customers' needs.
	• Developing creative/adaptive strategies in countries where the home company strategy does not work.
	• Negotiating globally, discovering new and useful cooperative solutions that may satisfy idiosyncratic needs of partners from different cultures.
	• Dealing with differences in values, ambitions, and strategies when negotiating international mergers and acquisitions.
	• Facing scarcity in some contexts and developing products and solutions that meet the need of the base of the pyramid and reduce the imbalance between wealthy and poor nations.
Curiosity	• Developing motivation and willingness to enter into and confront unfamiliar situations.
	• Fuelling the passion for cultural difference.
	• Acquiring knowledge about how culture influences leadership prototypes, consumers' tastes and preferences, and appropriate ways to communicate, negotiate, and behave in different contexts.
	• Seeking opportunities for learning continuously.
	• Avoiding limiting and biased assumptions about cultural idiosyncrasies.
	• Nourishing creativity.
	• Seeking knowledge and expertise beyond boundaries.
	• Drawing information from many sources in several ways.
Open-mindedness	• Accepting and facing the world's complexity and its challenges and contradictions with creativity and a cosmopolitan ethos.
	• Avoiding stereotypic conceptions about individuals and entities from other countries.
	• Appreciating cultural differences and developing cultural intelligence.
	• Negotiating effectively in cross-cultural contexts.
	• Developing positive relationships with employees, customers, authorities, partners, and other stakeholders in different countries.
	• Nourishing innovative and successful strategies that take advantage of the current stage of globalization and the inherent properties of international exchanges.
Love of learning	• Developing cultural intelligence and a global mindset.
	• Learning to deal, communicate, and negotiate with employees, customers, authorities, communities, partners, and other stakeholders of other cultural contexts.
	• Accepting coaching before and during international assignments.
	• Reducing risks of cultural shock when working abroad.
Perspective/wisdom	• Making wiser expatriate selection decisions (balancing technical, social, emotional, and motivational features of candidates), thus reducing the risks. of premature repatriation and contributing to the expatriates' success.
	• Identifying leadership (as well as negotiation and conflict management) behaviours that are more appropriate in different contexts.
	• Developing global organizing expertise for a global perspective.
	• Integrating diverse knowledge bases.
	• Developing strategies that take into account local and global issues.

(continued)

Table 3.3. Continued

- Getting better insights from the cultural, economic and political environment and deciding what is more appropriate when operating in a country where human rights and dignity are violated.
- Providing wise counsels and mentoring to impatriates and individuals who are preparing for international assignments.
- Developing better cross-cultural adjustment when working abroad, being more able to build social and working relationships, and reducing the risks of expatriation failure and premature return.
- Coaching local employees, thus fostering 'localization' and helping to develop/build strong local management teams.

Excessive open-mindedness may make global leaders naïve interpreters of a culturally distant context, or impel them to adopt a chameleon strategy that makes them inauthentic. For example, Japanese managers operating in the US who adopt Americanized leadership styles were interpreted by the American employees as not genuine (Thomas and Ravlin 1995). The more effective leaders are not those who merely adopt a chameleon style, nor are those who follow the style suitable in their home countries, but rather those who know how to apply cultural knowledge in a sensitive way (Liu et al. 2004). In fact, evidence suggests that excessive mimicry in intercultural interactions may be interpreted as insincere and even devious (Thomas 2006; Thomas and Ravlin 1995). As Thomas (2006: 88) warned:

> For example, when I (a North American) go to Japan it is obvious to Japanese people that I am not Japanese, and they don't expect me to mimic their behavior. While they may be favorably impressed if I am courteous, polite, and somewhat reserved, they do not expect me to have mastered intricate social skills of Japan such as bowing appropriately. In fact, if I try to do so they may view my behavior as at best amusing and at worse offensive. In addition, in contrast to mimicry, there are cases where the desired outcome in the intercultural interaction will be accomplished by not adapting at all.

Excessive love of learning may lead to an unbridled passion or obsession to explore, originating difficulties in knowing when to stop learning and to start taking decisions and *doing*. And an excess of wisdom may make global leaders appear as arrogant, self-righteous, or naïvely idealistic, that is, as more *thinkers* and *talkers* rather than *doers*.

When curiosity, open-mindedness, and love of learning are combined in excess, global leaders may experience such a great level of flow in the specific activities they are performing that they neglect other activities (Csikszentmihalyi 2003). For example, a global leader operating abroad may become so absorbed and fascinated by the idiosyncrasies of the novel culture that (s)he pays it too much attention in comparison with other duties and the goals of his/her mission as defined by the home firm.

The degree to which the 'excesses' are perverse for global leader performance depends on other virtues. For example, giving proof of leadership, prudence, and self-regulation may mitigate the negative effects of an excessive open-mindedness.

Strengths of courage

Courage can be defined as 'the mental or moral strength to venture and persevere to withstand danger and difficulty' (Malloch 2010: 757). It refers to doing the right thing despite costs, dangers, and threats. Without courage, many of the other virtues and strengths are nothing more than good intentions (Solomon 1999). Aristotle considered courage the first virtue, arguing that it makes all the other virtues possible. Churchill echoed this perspective, presenting courage as the first among all human qualities (Longstaffe 2005). Nelson Mandela is one of the highest epitomes of courage, whose courageous actions have contributed to real and positive change (Mandela 2010).

Courage is displayed via four main human strengths (Table 3.4): bravery, persistence, integrity, and vitality. Bravery is the ability to do what needs to be done and what is right without fear and hesitation. Persistence is the voluntary continuation of a goal-directed action in spite of obstacles, difficulties, or discouragement (Peterson and Seligman 2004). Integrity is the character trait of people who are true to themselves (Peterson and Seligman 2004). Vitality is the capacity to feel alive, full of zest, and to display enthusiasm and vigour.

Although the four strengths have similarities (all represent the will to accomplish goals in the face of opposition, either internal or external), and reveal reciprocal influences (e.g. bravery facilitates integrity, and vice versa), they make unique contributions to global leaders' positive performance. This is what we discuss next (synthesis in Table 3.7). Bravery and persistence are discussed together. Often, bravery is consequent only if the individual is perseverant. And perseverance may be threatened if the individual is not brave. To simplify, we use the term 'courage' when referring to both.

Table 3.4. The four strengths through which courage is expressed

Strength	Examples of how individuals with this strength behave	Opposites	Excess
Bravery	• They adopt voluntary actions and are able to judge and take risks in order to do what is necessary and right. • They confront the status quo when necessary to restore justice and other important values. • They are prudently brave (i.e. not inconsiderate or reckless).	Cowardice; spinelessness.	Recklessness; foolishness; self-righteousness.
Persistence (perseverance; industriousness)	• They do not desist from doing what is necessary. • They persevere towards goals, despite obstacles and failures. • They have lots of courage to complete things. • They are diligent and work earnestly towards long-term goals. • They do not procrastinate.	Laziness; sloth; vacillation; cutting corners.	Obstinacy; stubbornness.
Integrity (authenticity; honesty)	• They behave consistently with their espoused values. • They assume their moral convictions, even if they are not popular. • They treat others with care and are sensitive to others' needs. • They are open/authentic and honest about their feelings. • They follow through their commitments and promises.	Deceitfulness; insincerity; falseness; phoniness; dishonesty.	Integrity is never excessive (although honesty is excessive when, for example, the truth is told even if it is uncalled for or is harmful). Some kinds of purity for preserving an important value may be unrealistic and/or jeopardize more important values: to protect some values, one may have to sacrifice others (Brenkert 2009: 463).
Vitality (zest; enthusiasm; vigour; energy)	• They have energy and spirit. • They feel energized. • They are energetic and fully functioning. • They rarely feel worn out. • They are mentally and physically vigorous.	Sluggishness; dullness; lethargy; listlessness; sloth.	Restlessness.

Bravery and persistence

Courage is relevant for any leader (Carey et al. 2009) but the complexity and ambiguity involved in global business make it especially relevant for global leaders (Morrison 2001; Mulcahy 2010a, 2010b; Treasurer 2009). For example, courage helps global leaders to display decisiveness and integrity when making decisions (e.g. closing a plant in a poor region of a developing country; disinvesting in a country where human rights and dignity are violated) involving political, labour, and NGO issues in other countries, thus preventing problems from escalating worldwide (Carey et al. 2009).

When news disseminates swiftly at the global level, and a mistake made in one country may damage the company's reputation worldwide, courage is necessary to be transparent with stakeholders, to assume responsibility for mistakes, and to display uncomfortable data about the company's actions and to recall products (Bennis et al. 2008; George 2009). Courage made James Burke, CEO of Johnson & Johnson, able to deal with the Tylenol criminal contamination with cyanide, in September 1982. Seven people died (Beck 1982; Cavanagh and Bandsuch 2002; Lucero et al. 2009; Maak 2008; Shrivastava et al. 1988) and the incident jeopardized a company whose credo said: 'We believe our first responsibility is to the doctors, nurses, and patients and to mothers and all others who use our products.' Market share dropped from 35 per cent to 8 per cent. Although J&J had no responsibility for the incidents, and the cases of poisoning seemed to be restricted to a limited area (Maak 2008), Burke made himself available to the media, showed honesty with all the stakeholders, and decided to pull 31 million bottles of tablets back from retailers, a recall that cost J&J more than $100 million. In the long run, the company was able to save the brand, sustain brand loyalty, boosting consumer trust and enhancing J&J's reputation as a responsible organization (George 2003). Apparently, Burke acted for the right reasons, doing justice to the company's commitment to its customers: the rationale for the recall was justified not with financial or reputational reasons, but by the company's values regarding the health of customers (Maak 2008). Hamilton (2006) also stressed that successful crisis management was catalysed by Burke's courage and wisdom:

> James Burke (...) has been praised not only for knowing what actions needed to be taken but also for having the strength to make difficult decisions to act on that knowledge (Bierly et al. 2000; Shrivastava et al. 1988). In other words, fostered by the leadership example set by Burke, Johnson & Johnson demonstrated organizational wisdom in management of the

Tylenol crisis and was able to avoid negative consequences that could have arisen and precipitated demise of the organization.

Burke's actions were justified by social astuteness (he realized that the short-term losses originated by the recall were minor compared to likely long-term damage of the company's reputation), but ethics also played a role (Ketchen Adams, and Shook 2008). Social astuteness, in this case, has much to do with prudence and a sense of accountability. Cavanagh and Bandsuch (2002) also noted that for Burke and others, the emphasis on good moral reasoning is a better leadership foundation than business skills and techniques.

After retiring, Burke became president of the Business Enterprise Trust, a non-profit organization that annually identified and rewarded business firms that were especially responsible, providing an example of courage, integrity, and social vision. Unfortunately, long-term funding failed to materialize, and the organization ceased operating in 1998—a practical demonstration, perhaps, of the value ascribed to organizational and leadership virtuousness by businesses and society in the recent past. Nor did his example seem to endure at J&J. In 2010, J&J was forced to make other recalls of several products, including Tylenol, due to quality problems (Rockoff and Kamp 2010), costing the company hundreds of millions of dollars.

It is not possible to estimate the implications of such recalls for the company's reputation and profitability. However, there are reasons to fear that bravery and wisdom have been in short supply these days when cost cutting has gone so far and taken precedence over quality and safety. In fact, 'among the allegations is that J&J waited as long as two years to admit or address some quality problems and sent consultants in the guise of shoppers to buy all packets of Motrin suspected of releasing too little active ingredient rather than issue a recall' (Neff 2010). One may ask if and how Burke's legacy was, at least partially, undermined by the contemporary competitive landscape.

Arrogance also helps to explain a negative surprise experienced by Mercedes-Benz in China (Pu and Que 2004). The company, whose cars are one of the highly prized status symbols in the People's Republic, probably never thought that its image of high quality and prestige could be tarnished. This led Mercedes-Benz to refuse recalls after receiving consumer complaints—having even threatened the customers with legal action. The company only changed its attitude when criticism from almost all major media outlets became deafening. China Central Television (CCTV) featured the event in its primetime talk show, *Telling the Truth*. The media coverage magnified the impact of the incident, the number of announced consumer complaints increased, and a nation-wide association of Benz victims was formed. The company underesti-mated the very strong consumer activism in China and the highly nationalistic attitude of the Chinese press when Western companies are involved (Ip 2007). To build long-term success in the country, West-ern companies must act as positive citizens demonstrating sincere con-cern for local customers, and avoid acting as rigid and arrogant outsiders coming to grab a profit (Pu and Que 2004).

Bravery was what Robert Eckert, the CEO of Mattel Toys, did not demonstrate when, in 2007, the company was compelled to recall millions of toys containing excessive lead (George 2009). Eckert reacted by blaming the Chinese contract manufacturers, neglecting that, since the company's name was on the toys, Mattel was responsible for certify-ing that the products met safety standards. Eckert's reaction and his testimony before the US Congress resulted in a public outcry against Chinese manufacturers. A wave of xenophobia grew. Senator Brown-beck said 'Made in China has now become a warning label' (George 2009: 99). Later, the owner of a supplier committed suicide. Several weeks later, facing a loss in the company's reputation, Mattel's executive vice president was forced to apologize to the Chinese minister for hav-ing shifted criticism to China. The negative effects of the lack of courage are transversal to all companies, and they are magnified when global leaders are imprudent and neglect the political, cultural, and patriotic implications of their companies' actions.

Courage is also crucial for dealing with angry environmental activists (Swartz 2010), or with unions—especially when global or regional cam-paigns are fought against actual or announced unit closings (e.g. the European 'strike' to protest against the restructuring of Electrolux in 2005). Courage is also crucial for dealing with xenophobic attitudes in the countries where a company operates (Kets de Vries 2001).

Courageous and honest leaders do not abandon the principles of their organization's visions when their efforts to realize the vision suffer serious setbacks and failures. Rather, they see difficulties and failures as opportunities for learning, and persevere with determination and, if necessary, personal cost (Mendonca 2001). Darwin Smith, two months after becoming CEO of Kimberly-Clark, was diagnosed with nose and throat cancer, with doctors giving him less than a year of life. When informing the board of his illness, he said 'he had no plans do die anytime soon. Smith held to this demanding work schedule while commuting weekly from Wisconsin to Houston for radiation therapy. He lived 25 more years, 20 of them as CEO' (Collins 2001: 68).

Courage may also sustain high purpose visions. Novartis chairman and CEO Daniel Vasella has a revealing life story. He faced tremendous challenges in his early years but reached the top of the global pharmaceutical industry (George et al. 2007). Born in 1953 to a modest family in Fribourg (Switzerland), his early years were filled with medical problems. He suffered from food poisoning at age 4, asthma at 5. He was sent alone to the mountains of eastern Switzerland for two summers. At age 8, he had tuberculosis, followed by meningitis, having been an in-patient in a sanatorium for a year. These experiences and 'the human gestures of forgiveness, caring, and compassion' (George et al. 2007: 133) he experienced in the health institutions where he was cared for, fed his motivation to become a physician. His resilience and perseverance were put to proof again several times later. At age 10, his 18-year-old sister died after suffering cancer for two years. Three years later, his father died during surgery. Left to his own devices when his mother went to work in a distant town, he 'derailed' for three years, until he met his first girlfriend, whose affection changed his life.

At age 20, Vasella entered medical school, and graduated with honours. He was rejected for the position of chief physician at the University of Zurich because of his young age; he then talked with the head of the pharmaceutical division of Sandoz, who offered him the opportunity to work in the company's US affiliate. A few years later, when Sandoz merged with Ciba-Geigy (giving rise to Novartis), Vasella was named CEO, in spite of his age (still young) and limited experience. What happened next was the following (George et al. 2007: 133):

> Once in the CEO's role, Vasella blossomed as a leader. He envisioned the opportunity to build a great global health care company that could help people through lifesaving new drugs, such as Gleevec, which has proved to be highly effective for patients with chronic myeloid leukemia. Drawing on the physician role models of his youth, he built an entirely new Novartis culture centered on compassion, competence, and competition. These moves established Novartis as a giant in the industry and Vasella as a compassionate leader.

The many corporate scandals that have taken place in recent years, with global consequences, could perhaps have been avoided if these companies' leaders had acted in a brave and honest way (George 2003, 2009). One recognizes such authenticity readily when one sees it. One of the most widely admired statesmen of modern times, Nelson Mandela, is recognized, above all else, for the integrity of his character despite the tribulations he had to endure and the fact that, in some assessments, he would be regarded as a terrorist.

Integrity, bedrock of character

Integrity is crucial for leader effectiveness (Reave 2005). The GLOBE project showed that it is one of the few positive leadership traits that are universally endorsed (Dorfman et al. 2004). This strength is especially relevant to operating and leading in the global arena. When discussing Google leaders' decision to stay in China in spite of the Chinese government's pressures for filtering the Internet, Brenkert (2009) argued that businesses will always confront difficult and challenging ethical situations wherever their operations are but especially in international contexts. These complexities and difficulties have led several authors (Bird and Osland 2004; Gregersen et al. 1998; McCall and Hollenbeck 2002; Mendenhall 2006; Morrison 2001, 2006; Osland et al. 2006; Spreitzer et al. 1997; p. 79–81 this volume) to suggest that integrity is crucial to global leaders' effectiveness. Morrison noted that integrity marks the bedrock of character and is essential for global leaders. In his perspective, all managers confront ethical issues but global leaders confront them more regularly (Morrison 2001).

Kanter (2010: 575) recognized integrity as crucial for the performance of every leader but also considered such a classical strength to be especially relevant for global leaders:

> Integrity work is also classic and enduring, but it does increase in importance in a globalizing world because of the fourth aspect of globalization: increasing information flow and pressures for transparency, from regulatory bodies policing companies and companies assessing governments, and NGOs examining both. Misconduct is more readily exposed and risks to reputation more readily communicated by watchdog groups using Internet tools, so the task of ensuring that the organization meets high standards grows in importance and takes on global dimensions.

Global leaders with strong integrity are more prepared to deal with ethical dilemmas, which are magnified when a company operates across several cultures and has to face different conceptions of ethical leadership in different countries (Martin et al. 2009)—the case of Google operating in China is paradigmatic (Brenkert 2009). As Donaldson and Dunfee stated, global leaders often navigate grey, liminal areas between cultures. In the authors' perspective, 'the Gordian knot of international business ethics is formed around the vexing question, how should a company behave when the standards followed in the host country are lower than those followed in the home country?' (Donaldson and Dunfee 1999: 45–46).

Integrity helps global leaders to refuse to deal with organizations with low ethical standards (Morrison 2006), to avoid unethical deals and bribery, to obey the (spirit of) law, and to respect human rights—thus avoiding reputational harm (Morrison 2006; Sliter 2007; Williams and Barrett 2000). Lee Kun Hee, former chairman of Samsung, caused severe damage to the company's reputation, after being convicted of embezzlement and tax evasion (Kollewe 2010; Sang-Hun 2009). He returned to the firm after receiving a special amnesty from South Korea's President.

Dishonesty may also be the originator of significant losses to communities and society. According to Mokhiber, in a paper published in the anti-corporate publication *Multinational Monitor* on the top 100 'corporate criminals' of the 1990s, there is 'an emerging consensus among corporate criminologists: corporate crime and violence inflicts far more damage on society than all street crime combined' (Mokhiber 1999: 10). He also argued that while 19,000 people are murdered every year in the US, 56,000 people 'die every day on the job or from occupational diseases such as black lung and asbestosis and the tens of thousands of others who fall victim to the silent violence of pollution, contaminated foods, hazardous consumer products and hospital malpractice' (Mokhiber 1999: 10). With this scenario in the US, one can imagine what has happened in countries where the rule of law does not occur as effectively.

Being under constant public scrutiny, honest global leaders promote a positive external company image (Morrison 2006). They also foster a corporate culture where employees operating in different countries are motivated to behave with integrity (see in Table 3.5 how ethics and integrity are fundamental competencies at 3M: Alldredge and Nilan (2000), even if such conduct may imply refusing to make profitable but unethical deals (Damon 2004; George 2003). Honesty, together with bravery, is especially relevant in contexts where corruption is salient and human rights are disrespected (Morrison 2000, 2001). As Bill George pointed out, there are cases where a company must lose business to secure reputation to gain future business (George 2003).

Global leaders with character and integrity are more attractive to other competent global leaders. Youngsuk Chi, Vice Chairperson and Global Managing Director of Academic and Customer Relations of Elsevier, after being a prominent leader in the field of international publishing, when interrogated about what led him to follow other leaders during his career, gave the following answer (Dalton 2007: 194):

[They need] to have a great sense of character and a strong set of ethics. This sort of individual knows how not to compromise what is good for what is

Table 3.5. Ethical business conduct guidelines by 3M

'3M's higher standard

Ethical business conduct sometimes requires more than strictly complying with the law. Moreover, there are no laws governing many business activities. Even when laws apply, sometimes they set a standard of behavior that is unacceptably low for 3M. When you are confronted with such situations, you need to make a good, ethical decision that will reflect well on 3M and you. This section contains advice to help you do that. (. . .) Ethical decision-making requires evaluating and giving due consideration to alternative courses of conduct in light of these corporate standards:

- Show uncompromising honesty and integrity in all of your 3M activities and relationships.
- Avoid all conflicts of interest between work and personal life.
- Respect the dignity and worth of all individuals.
- Encourage individual initiative and innovation in an atmosphere of flexibility, cooperation and trust.
- Promote a culture where promise keeping, fairness, respect and personal accountability are valued, encouraged and recognized.
- Create a safe workplace.
- Protect the environment.

Making ethical decisions

You should be able to answer 'yes' to the following questions before taking any action on behalf of 3M:

- Is this action consistent with 3M's corporate values of uncompromising honesty and integrity?
- Can this action withstand public scrutiny?
- Will this action protect 3M's reputation as an ethical company?

If you can't answer 'yes' to all these questions, but still believe the proposed action is lawful and ethical, you should review the proposed action with your supervisor, management or your assigned 3M legal counsel because it may not be in the best interest of 3M or you to proceed.'

Source: http://solutions.3m.com

easy; by 'good', I don't mean good for meeting goals, but good for the society we serve. The person needs to be an example in action, and that includes everything from work ethics to priorities in life. I can only work for someone who embraces the attitude of 'family first'. However successful a person might be, if they cannot understand that their most important responsibility is to raise a family that is an example to society, I cannot respect them.

Honesty helps global leaders to create conditions for higher levels of service quality, worker safety, equality in hiring, equality of opportunities, comparable compensation, and freedom of expression (Morrison 2001). Tony Wang, Vice President of KFC for Southeast Asia in the late 1980s, refused to follow Chinese partners' pressures to lower the company standards for quality, service, and cleanliness. Local partners argued that Chinese customers were not accustomed and did not value the standards KFC used in other countries (Morrison 2006).

Honest global leaders adopt high personal standards in all their interactions, and 'their personal reputations are based on treating people with the same degree of respect irrespective of where they are in the world' (Morrison 2001: 72). Integrity makes them walk the talk and respect people, thus creating personal positive reputation, credibility, and the trust necessary for stimulating fluid and collaborative work relationships with individuals, teams, and organizations from different economic, legal, political, social, and cultural systems (Beechler and Javidan 2007; Csikszentmihalyi 2003; Reave 2005). They are able to develop trust with their collaborators and to persuade them to accept challenging international assignments. With integrity, global leaders foster ethical organizational climates and are a source of ethical influence over employees and other stakeholders around the world (Reave 2005).

For global leaders, maintaining integrity both at the individual and organizational level is a difficult endeavour, requiring significant amounts of work, commitment, and sacrifice (Emler and Cook 2001; Hanson and Rothlin 2010; Morrison 2001, 2006). Sir Adrian Cadbury argued that his grandfather experienced such difficulties more than a century ago (Cadbury 1989). Queen Victoria issued an order to his company to send a decorative tin with a bar of chocolate inside to all of her soldiers who were serving in South Africa. Aiming to develop the company and benefit his employees from the additional work but fired by Quaker principles, he was publicly opposed to the Anglo-Boer War. He decided to accept the order but declared that he would not take any profit from doing so.

The case illustrates how global leaders may have to face ethical dilemmas and incur personal and organizational costs. Leaving a country in protest against human rights violations (including freedom of expression) is, to a certain degree, a modern version of Cadbury's dilemma. Exiting the country is not necessarily the more ethical way to work in favour of human rights (Beaver 1995; Brenkert 2009)—in the same way that refusing to sell chocolates would not have been the best way to help Cadbury's employees to get higher rewards and British soldiers to fight a war that they certainly would prefer to avoid.

When moral compromises do not subvert integrity

Google leaders experienced ethical dilemmas when they agreed to censor its China search engine (Google.cn) in some ways, in exchange for

Chinese government permission to enter the market in January 2006 (Gwynne 2010; O'Rourke IV et al. 2007). In consequence, while Google was accused of contributing to human rights violations in China, there is reason to believe that the company adopted what can be called a *moral compromise* (Table 3.6) that represents the lesser of several evils.

The company needed to take into account values other than freedom of expression. By leaving China, the company would place itself at a considerable competitive disadvantage in the Chinese market (with spill-over effects in other markets), and it could jeopardize the investment of stockholders. Google had responsibilities to protect and develop jobs and employment possibilities for the Chinese people. If the company refused to filter the Internet, it would put its Chinese employees at risk of fines, harassment, or imprisonment. On the contrary, continuing to operate in the People's Republic, the company was able to provide information that the Chinese could not obtain otherwise, for example about AIDS, environmental problems, avian flu, and so forth. The opponents of Google have legitimate reasons for accusing the company of infringing the right to freedom of speech, but one must see the company's situation in its full context. All things considered, the decision to remain in China at that time seemed morally acceptable, and Google leaders made a prudent decision:

> Google could refuse to enter the Chinese market. But this, I am supposing, would have significant negative implications for its use in China. It would slowly decline to the role of a very minor player. We might further suppose that this would negatively impact Google's future. If it did not filter what the Chinese government wanted filtered, its employees might be subject to fines, harassment, or imprisonment. If it tries to protest this filtering to the Chinese government, it is unlikely that the government will change its course. (Brenkert 2009: 467)

A moral compromise may be a fragile or ephemeral tool for improving conditions in the operating arenas where global companies make business, as reported by the following excerpt from the *Information Management Journal* (2010: 6):

> Google may leave China (. . .), after a December cyber attack on its network that resulted in theft of its intellectual property. (. . .) In recent months, The New York Times said, the government has also blocked Google's YouTube service. Last summer, the government briefly blocked access nationwide to Google's main search engine and other services like Gmail. It also forced the company to disable a function that lets the search engine suggest terms, arguing that it was trying to remove pornography from Google's search

Table 3.6. Criteria for justified moral compromises: the case of Google in China

Criteria	Specific aspects to be taken into account	Did Google have reasons to adopt the moral compromise (i.e. to compromise the respect for freedom of expression)?
Fairness	• If the company's moral compromise results in unfair disadvantage for others who do not violate the rule, value, or principle in question, the moral compromise is less justified.	Yes. All Google competitors violated this human right.
	• If the demands of morality place an unfair or unrealistic burden on the company, in such a way that the violation/infringement of the moral principle, value, or principle seems warranted, the moral compromise is justified.	Yes. By leaving China, Google would place itself at a considerable competitive disadvantage in the Chinese market (with spill-over effects in other markets), and it could jeopardize the investment of its stockholders. Google employees and Chinese people also would be harmed.
Harm	• If the moral compromise threatens the lives of those affected by the violation, it is less justified.	Yes. No one's life was directly threatened by the company's compromise. Moreover, Google adopted measures to reduce such a possibility.
	• If the negative consequences of the moral compromise do not add additional harm, the moral compromise is justified.	Yes. Whether or not Google operated in China, the harm done by Google's own filtering did not increase the harm already experienced by the Chinese. On the contrary, the Chinese would benefit from Google staying in China.
	• If the interests at stake for the company outweigh the harm that would be caused to innocent third parties, the moral compromise is justified.	Yes. Google was not imposing any additional harm on the Chinese people more than they were already experiencing. The company joined others who were also not providing relevant information to the Chinese. If Google left China, the Chinese would not have more information, and they would have less.
Integrity	• If the company adopted the moral compromise for arbitrary or capricious reasons, rather than for 'higher motives', the moral compromise is not justified.	Yes. Google compromised the value of freedom of speech in favour of other important values. All things considered, it can be said that Google maintained its integrity.
Mitigation	• If the company attempts to mitigate the consequences of the moral compromise, the moral compromise is more justified.	Yes. Google adopted several mitigation actions (e.g., placing a notice on one's screen when a webpage was blocked, even against Chinese Government pressures for removing the notification; O'Rourke IV et al. 2007). However, other mitigation actions would be carried out (e.g. working with other Internet companies and stakeholders to develop conjoint actions for promoting freedom of expression in China).

Built from Brenkert (2009)

engine results. The U.S. government has expressed its support for Google and sent a diplomatic note to China formally requesting an explanation for the attacks, according to Reuters.com. (. . .). Google said these attacks, combined with increased curbs on free speech on the Web, had led to the review of its business in China.

Indeed, as a result of hacking of its site housed in Tsinghua Science Park, or so it claimed, Google moved its China operation to Hong Kong, outside of the mainland regulators. Critics suggest, instead, that it was the loss of market share to the domestic search engine, Baidu, that was the main reason for Google's move. On this analysis, Baidu was simply a better fit for the Chinese context than the foreign-owned and inspired search engine.

Moral compromise is not a panacea for dealing with ethical dilemmas. First of all, morally questionable actors may try to use the space thus opened to take advantage of the pioneer's action (Brenkert 2009). Consider, for example, the presumed moral compromise adopted by some transnational companies that make arrangements with dictatorial governments of developing countries, to explore natural resources. When companies such as Shell dealt with governments such as the Nigerian dictatorship, they accepted the right of the governments to sell the country's resources (Singer 2002). Such money, however, may end up being used primarily to enrich dictators and to help them to consolidate their rule. On the other hand, companies may try to use their power to improve the living conditions of the people, providing a corporate benchmark for people to evaluate governmental activity. In the case of Shell's involvement in the Niger delta, it has clearly been compromised. That refusing such deals will jeopardize a country's development is a fragile argument, at least if one considers data showing that the living standards of resource-rich countries are much lower than expected (Singer 2002). Refusing to accept that a dictatorial government is entitled to sell off the resources of the country is not the same as imposing a total boycott on that country. Such boycotts, in fact, can be harmful to citizens. Therefore, in dealing with complex and delicate issues, global leaders must display several strengths, including integrity but also bravery, persistence, and wisdom. Several other strengths are necessary to face accusations of hypocrisy (Brenkert 2009; O'Rourke IV et al. 2007) and to build diplomatic and political competencies that allow for dealing with issues involving the countries' international policies.

Vitality: energizer of resilience

Vitality is crucial for global leaders. Pfizer CEO Jeffrey Kindler resigned from the top job in December 2010, citing fatigue as a main reason for stepping down (Rockoff 2010). The vitality of global leaders acts as a strong energizer of other leaders and employees operating worldwide, and a powerful positive influence over customers, suppliers, communities, and partners. Communicating with enthusiasm and energy is crucial for conveying relevant messages and missions to employees and other stakeholders worldwide (Briggs 2008), thus creating the glue (Den Hartog 2004) that may prevent centrifugal forces of fragmentation (Kanter 2010). For example, following a period of acquisitions by the Vodafone group, Sir Christopher Gent (chief executive at the time) invested time in building relationships with the employees, starting a major internal communication programme that involved 18 countries and more than 30,000 people over a year (Briggs 2008: 13).

Anne Mulcahy radiated vitality when she was charged with the mission of recovering Xerox (Powley and Cameron 2008), a process described as 'one of the most extraordinary turnarounds in business history' (Gunn and Gullickson 2006: 10). Contradicting critics who doubted that she could be the catalyst to remake Xerox into a profitable company, she visited employees all over the world, 'living on planes' and deciding to speak the truth directly to employees, including the bad news about shutting down a business unit or making lay-offs (Caminiti 2005; Collins 2009; George 2009). With vigour, she did not take a weekend off for two years and rebuffed advisors' repeated suggestions that she consider Chapter 11 (a chapter of the US bankruptcy code, which permits reorganization under bankruptcy laws). By 2006, the profits of the company exceeded $1 billion and, in 2008, the *Chief Executive* magazine selected Mulcahy as chief executive of the year.

Vitality may be a facilitator of other global leaders' virtues and strengths. A global leader with vitality is more likely to be persistent and courageous when facing strong ethical dilemmas and human rights violations. S(h)e is able to deal with worldwide crises, or to act vigorously and promptly to avoid the overflow of a local crisis to other contexts. A vigorous and energetic global leader is also more likely to face cultural *faux pas* with humour, which helps to learn from mistakes, sustaining self-efficacy and maintaining better conditions within which to continue flourishing.

Vitality is necessary for global leaders to accept challenging international assignments, to face global challenges and missions abroad with

Table 3.7. Courage assisting several global leaders' activities

Bravery and persistence	• Showing decisiveness and integrity when making decisions that involve political, labour, and NGO issues in other countries, thus preventing problems from escalating worldwide. • Being transparent with stakeholders, assuming responsibility for mistakes and displaying uncomfortable data about the company's actions and, eventually, recalling products—thus avoiding reputational damage. • Dealing with environmental activists' campaigns and unions at the glocal scale. • Dealing with xenophobic attitudes in countries where the company operates. • Pursuing and nourishing high purpose even if demanding visions. • Following the principles implicit in the organizational vision, especially in contexts where human rights and dignity are disrespected. • Behaving with integrity.
Integrity	• Facing complex, difficult, and unavoidable ethical situations/dilemmas in the global arena. • Safeguarding the company's reputation when critical ethical issues need to be dealt with. • Adopting moral compromises. • Refusing to deal with operators with low ethical standards. • Safeguarding the community, society and other stakeholders' higher interests. • Fostering a corporate culture where employees operating in different countries are motivated to behave with integrity. • Fostering conditions for service quality, worker safety, equality in hiring, equality of opportunities, comparable compensation, and freedom of expression and ensuring they are respected in the different countries where the company operates. • Avoiding any forms of cultural imperialism. • Stimulating fluid and collaborative work relationships with stakeholders from many different economic, legal, political, social, and cultural systems.
Vitality	• Being persistent and courageous when facing strong ethical dilemmas and human rights violations. • Accepting challenging international assignments and facing global challenges and missions abroad with excitement and commitment. • Working long days. • Dealing with the emotional stress experienced when living far away from the family during international assignments. • Developing resilience when working in strange cultures or dangerous places. • Travelling regularly across different cultures and time zones. • Dealing with excessive amounts of information. • Conveying, with vigour and enthusiasm, relevant messages and missions to employees and other stakeholders worldwide. • Creating the 'glue' that prevents centrifugal forces of fragmentation to occur. • Developing other virtues and strengths (e.g. curiosity, love of learning, bravery, persistence, integrity, humour, and gratitude).

excitement and commitment, and to develop resilience when working in strange cultures or dangerous places—thus avoiding cultural shocks and the correspondent negative effects upon performance (Russell and Aquino-Russell 2010). With vitality, global leaders are more prepared to deal with huge amounts of information, to work long days, and to deal with the emotional stress experienced when living far from the family during international assignments.

Vitality is also crucial to travel regularly across different cultures and time zones (DeFrank et al. 2000). Lacking vitality, global leaders experience stress, the consequence potentially being emotional upset, physical illness, decreased work performance, and problems in achieving company objectives (DeFrank et al. 2000; Striker et al. 2000). As an example of the roughness of frequent travelling, consider the following:

> You are in Madrid working on the creation of a subsidiary division of your company. In the middle of a meeting you are handed a note to call your brother in Detroit immediately. You excuse yourself to call and find out that your mother is critically ill. Your four months of work in Madrid has reached a crucial point. You wonder how serious your mother's illness is and decide to wait three days before you return to Detroit. You feel badly about this decision and are experiencing considerable anxiety and worry. (DeFrank et al. 2000: 59)

In spite of the high potential of new technologies to connect people across the globe, leaders need to invest in face-to-face meetings, convening and connecting people, building social capital (Beechler and Javidan 2007), and integrating dispersed efforts and energies (Kanter 2010). Travelling may also facilitate global leaders' development and contribute to fostering a global mindset (Oddou et al. 2000), requiring a 'managing by flying around' approach, which is one that is tolerant of travelling frequently across time zones and facing non-routine issues via physical presence (Kanter 2010). Presence is necessary to start and improve relationships with customers and suppliers, to energize employees around the world, to increase the visibility of the organization in general, and to develop corporate diplomacy.

When excessive courage results in vice

Courage, as with other virtues, represents a middle way between two extremes: cowardice and foolhardiness. When global leaders express excessive courage, the result is not courageous actions and decisions but rather recklessness, obstinacy, and stubbornness. Excessive bravery may lead global leaders to neglect the risks of investing in problematic countries, to underestimate the veiled threats of corrupt governments or environmental and union activists, to accept international assignments for which they have insufficient skills or preparation (Otazo 1999), or to travel excessively, damaging psychological and physical health as well as work–family balance.

Excessive persistence may give rise to intemperate or stubborn obstinacy (Mendonca 2001) ('stubbornness and stupidity are twins': Bennis et al., in Goleman et al. 2008: 48), turning the global leader into someone unable to learn from mistakes and who persists in investments and actions that are not feasible, thus damaging company interests and reputation, and harming stakeholders around the world. The Digital Equipment Corporation (DEC) suffered from this problem when it was the second largest computer company in the world. According to Keough, what brought the company down

> was the conviction that they had the *one right approach*. Everything they did was 'DEC-centric', very proprietary. For all their brilliance, the DEC founders simply refused to adapt to the new, broader-based structure of the computer business. Piece by piece the company was sold off, the last of it in 1998, though I understand the logo survived for a short while in an IT company in India. Inflexibility is a very crippling disease. (Keough 2008: 34–35, italics in original)

Excessive vitality may lead global leaders to pursue an excessive number of projects and investments, and to exceed the amount of long international trips, experiencing restlessness and burn-out. Global leaders with excessive vitality may also become workaholics, neglecting work–family balance, with negative consequences for work–family balance and personal well-being.

Finally, excessive integrity may lead to 'pure' but impractical (Brenkert 2009) and, at the end, ethically questionable solutions. Global leaders suffering from such a syndrome risk losing touch with reality and adopting paltry behaviours, for example refusing to pay for a customer's lunch for fear of being accused of bribery, or firing a lifetime textile worker for taking home a damaged shirt (Morrison 2006). Excess of zeal may be anything but ethical.

More importantly, excessive integrity may lead global leaders to disinvest in a poor country where human rights are violated, thus creating still more difficulties for the poor people they allegedly aim to protect. As Brenkert suggested, referring to Google's initial decision to self-censor the Internet to remain in China, companies do not infringe the integrity principle when they adopt moral compromises, when they are compelled to violate important values or principles for prosecuting higher values or principles. In Brenkert's view (2009: 471),

> [V]iolating a human right, under the circumstances Google faces, does not mean that wrong is not done. It does mean that Google is not pure. It has compromised. (...) [T]hough its integrity has been sullied, it is mistaken to contend that one's integrity demands purity. Rather, the integrity of those involved in business, political, and social action must be focused on an inner core of values over the long run. Consequently, Google might well better view its mantra, 'Do not be evil,' more as an ideal, rather than a directive that can never be violated. Only the moral saint may be able to realize this ideal in all his or her activities. However, the integrity of ordinary humans and businesses does not require that they act only at the ideal (or supererogatory) level.

Conclusion

Cognitive and energizing virtues allow global leaders to pursue several important endeavours: (a) learning and understanding the complexities of the cultural, economic, and political mosaic; (b) interacting and networking positively with a wide range of stakeholders worldwide; (c) making wise and challenging decisions in a glocal context characterized by significant amounts of diversity, uncertainty, and complexity; (d) facing global and local problems honestly and energetically. These endeavours may be facilitated by the other virtues, as we discuss in the following chapters.

It is also important to recognize that virtue is in the middle. When performed excessively, cognitive and energizing 'virtues' become perverse, both for global leaders, organizations, and stakeholders. For example, an excess of creativity may cause global leaders to lose realism. An excess of curiosity may lead them to adopt inconvenient behaviours in idiosyncratic cultural contexts and to follow dangerous adventures. Excessive love of learning may make them obsessive learners unable to put learning into practice. Having the virtues discussed in the next chapters may help in reducing these risks and adopting genuinely virtuous behaviours.

4

Amiability and Citizenship Virtues

The best business decisions are the most human decisions. And, all other talents being even, the greatest managers are also the most human managers.

The #250 management and leadership lesson from Bill Hewlett and Dave Packard, founders of HP.

(Malone 2007: 400)

One of the most compelling questions outstanding in the field of international management is, How can a multinational motivate subsidiaries' top managers to comply with corporate strategic decisions? (...) We provided evidence that the exercise of procedural justice in a multinational's strategy-making process induces commitment, trust, and outcome satisfaction in subsidiary top managers.

(Kim and Mauborgne 1993: 502)

Strengths of justice: making life fairer

The virtue of justice refers to 'that which makes life fair' (Peterson and Seligman 2004: 36). It is expressed in three major human strengths: citizenship, fairness, and leadership (Table 4.1). Citizenship refers to the development of a sense of obligation towards the common good in a way that transcends self-interest (Peterson and Seligman 2004). Individuals with this strength consider themselves as responsible for improving the life of others, including distant communities.

Fairness refers to the individual's treatment of other people in similar ways, where one seeks to avoid one's feelings or issues biasing decisions so that they have specific and particularistic consequences for others (Peterson and Seligman 2004). Fairness is a liberal value; it is the core value behind Weber's notion of bureaucracies as systems that function without regard for persons: treating each case as a case, according to the

Table 4.1. Character strengths through which justice is displayed

Strength	How individuals with this strength behave (examples)	Opposites	Excess
Citizenship (social responsibility; loyalty; teamwork)	• They have a sense of duty to the groups they belong to, which may include the entire human race. • They have an inner drive to do what a group member, a 'true citizen', should do. • They are loyal to the friends and the groups they belong to. • They feel responsible to improve the world in which they live. • They help others who are in difficulty.	Selfishness; self-centredness; egotism.	Forgetting oneself; megalomaniac 'altruism'.
Fairness	• They give everyone a fair chance. • They consider that the same rules may be applied to everyone. • They consider that everyone deserves respect. • They treat people as ends in themselves (not merely means or instruments to reach other ends). • They are sensitive to social injustice.	Favouritism; one-sidedness; prejudice; caprice; iniquity; unfairness.	Insisting on equality when equity is due; exceeding in equity (i.e. creating excessive wage dispersion).
Leadership	• They articulate an appealing vision that motivates others. • They lead by example. • They show individualized consideration for people around them. • They promote intellectual stimulation. • They are able to inspire others.	Clumsiness to influence/inspire others toward collective action.	The dark side of charisma; cultism.

norms of rational-legality, seeks to ensure that neither favouritism nor prejudice flourishes.

Fairness is the product of moral judgement, that is, the process through which people feel what is morally right or wrong, and what is morally proscribed. It refers to the individual's treatment of other people in similar ways. Fair individuals do not let their personal feelings or issues bias decisions and actions towards others; they try to be kind to everyone; they consider people as ends in themselves and respect them, as well as having a sense of what is right and wrong, even where their views may not accord with the norms of specific social orders. For instance, managers in fundamentalist Islamist regimes do not have to accept some prevalent views about the treatment of women.

The virtue of leadership refers to an integrated set of cognitive and emotional attributes that favours the inclination to influence and help other people so that their behaviours and choices will benefit the collective (Peterson and Seligman 2004). Peterson and Seligman considered this quality as typical of transformational leaders (Bass 1999; Tichy and Devanna 1986), a construct covering dimensions such as articulating a vision, providing an appropriate model of behaviour, showing individualized consideration, promoting intellectual stimulation, and inspiring others.

Although the three strengths have similarities (all being relevant to the optimal interaction between the individual and the group or community) and reveal reciprocal influences (e.g. good citizens tend to be fairer, and fair people tend to adopt more citizenship behaviours), they may make unique contributions to the global leaders' positive performance (for a synthesis, please refer to Table 4.4).

Considering that both justice and humanity are interpersonal strengths, a brief note is necessary before proceeding. Whereas justice is a virtue related to impartiality, humanity refers to the willingness to do more than what is merely fair (Peterson and Seligman 2004). Practising one's humanity sometimes implies disregarding fairness or equity principles, and acting with justice may require treating individuals with less kindness and humanity ('justice is blind', as is often said).

Citizenship and a cosmopolitan approach

Global leaders can make a real difference in tackling major world problems, including poverty, climate changes, access to fresh water, and the scourge of HIV/AIDS. They make a difference if they care for the needs of other people and are committed to making the world better (Maak and Pless 2009). The strength of citizenship (involving social responsibility, loyalty, and teamwork) may make global leaders more willing to carry out such endeavours; moreover, such leaders can mobilize the resources to make a difference: people, money, networks, and materials.

Leaders with the strength of citizenship build more sustainable and responsible organizations, being sensitive to their impact on communities (Fort and Schipani 2004), receptive to social accountability norms and standards (e.g. SA8000), and more likely to follow policies and strategies that do no harm to the planet or humanity. Respecting the natural environment helps in preventing conflicts and violence in underprivileged societies. Peace and stability are valuable per se, but also a condition for businesses to operate and prosper (Fort and Schipani

2004). Max de Pree, former CEO of Herman Miller, remarked (Damon 2004: 29):

> [F]or me, one of the very important things that happened in the course of a business career was the slow discovery that business and businesspeople have to be a positive part of society, and that I had to be very serious about the human side of all that was happening in the business world.

Citizenship may lay the foundations of a genuine concern for customers' needs and well-being. Lars Kolind, CEO of Oticon, expressed this strength (Damon 2004) when considering clients as 'whole persons', and in making considerable efforts to produce hearing aids serving the holistic needs of hearing-impaired people. He required employees to serve in multiple roles (e.g. engineers as marketers, accountants in customer service) as a strategic way of sensitizing them to the integral complexity of the clients' needs.

Citizenship also helps global leaders to perform corporate diplomacy (Fort and Schipani 2004; Ordeix-Rigo and Duarte 2009), a role especially important in difficult countries. Corporate diplomacy helps to explain how HSBC opened more branches in China than any other foreign bank (Paine 2010). Every year, HSBC China's CEO Richard Yorke or his deputies visit authorities in each city where the bank operates or would like to operate. Contacts offer feedback about the company performance and plans, as well as information about impending policy directives. The bank is able to get valuable data and provide regulators with information—which facilitates a common understanding of priorities. It also offers HSBC support for pursuing its strategy in a context where multinational companies are expected to contribute to China's development, not only to their own goals.

By building a base of relationships with customers, government officials, public intermediaries, and other relevant stakeholders (including the public), global leaders with the strength of citizenship may enable their companies to thrive in diverse and complex geographies and political jurisdictions, ensuring alignment of agendas, contributing to the benefit of countries, and developing goodwill (Kanter 2010).

Corporate diplomacy increases the company's legitimacy or license-to-operate, reduces risks of misunderstandings, and fosters endorsement by governments and citizens, which, in turn, improves the company's credibility and power within the social system in which it operates. As argued by Ordeix-Rigo and Duarte (2009: 556), at best, multinational companies are revealing and understanding that their presence in society is only sustainable if and only if they are able to satisfy expectations from multiple stakeholders. They understand that they create consequences on many third parties beyond those more directly involved with the value chain of the corporation and try to regulate those consequences. They try to allocate resources with a certain amount of accountability to be able to show their citizenship and their responsibility toward society. Sometimes they are also trying to achieve other benefits, but generally they are not concerned with short-term outcomes but with long-term gains. To this regard, corporations are taking some of the roles that have been generally associated with governments because the scope of their dimension means that their political surroundings (the sphere of all those affected by the corporation's decisions) are comparable in dimension and economical or social power.

One example of a corporate diplomat is Samuel Palmisano, Chairman of the Board and CEO of IBM. He circumnavigates the globe six or seven times a year to meet with authorities and discuss with them how to help a specific country achieve its goals. Such behaviour has been described as a high-level type of conversation that signals the company's interest in contributing to a country in an institutional and enduring way (Kanter 2010).

Global leaders carrying out corporate diplomacy in developing countries may also be asked to advise on emerging issues that are relevant for the country's successful future—situations in which they must find ways to show that they are ready to act or advise in the interests of the community and to serve humanity rather than just the company's narrow, albeit legitimate, interests (Kanter 2010).

Rosabeth Moss Kanter offered several examples of leaders who carried out citizenship-cum-diplomatic roles: a leader, in India, who was frequently invited to present the company's agenda to the minister of commerce, thus helping the country to recognize and anticipate trends and to develop the country's future competitiveness; the leader of IBM for Europe and the Middle East who encouraged IBM employees in Egypt to volunteer to work on the *Building bridges to the Arab World* initiative, which combined technology (a Web portal for Arab women), community service, diversity and women's empowerment goals, and government relations opportunities; the chairman of IBM China who, in 2007, organized his own diplomatic mission to the US, meeting with high-level authorities to build metaphorical bridges. Kanter (2010: 582) concluded:

> Claims of serving society are made credible and tangible when leaders allocate time, talent, and resources to national or community projects without seeking immediate returns, and when they encourage people from one country to serve another.

Yvon Chouinard, founder and owner of Patagonia, also demonstrated citizenship. After realizing that the cotton raised by industrial means had perverse environmental consequences and harmed the health of farmers, he experienced what was described as 'another crisis of conscience' (Csikszentmihalyi 2003: 16). Despite several obstacles, he decided, in the early 1990s, to begin using organically grown cotton for the company's fabrics, despite it being more expensive (Ingram 2002; Rarick and Feldman 2008). The demand increased and encouraged growers to cultivate more organic cotton, and other companies (including Nike, Levi Strauss, and Gap) ended up following Patagonia's example.

In 2001, along with Craig Mathews, owner of West Yellowstone's Blue Ribbon Flies, Chouinard started the '1 per cent for the Planet' initiative, an alliance of businesses that contribute at least 1 per cent of their net annual sales to groups on a list of researched and approved environmental organizations (Rarick and Feldman 2008). Chouinard practises several sports and open-air activities, a demonstration of vitality, which shows that several virtues may be interconnected within the same individual, with positive consequences for him/herself and for society.

Manifestations of citizenship can also be found, for example, in those leaders who infuse their practices and organizational philosophy with the Japanese concept of *kyosei* (Boardman and Kato 2003). The term comes from two Japanese characters that mean working together (*kyo*) and life (*sei*). Ryuzaburo Kaku (1997), former CEO of Canon, defined *kyosei* as 'a spirit of cooperation', in which individuals and organizations live and work together for the common good.

A company that practises *kyosei* 'establishes harmonious relations with its customers, its suppliers, its competitors, the governments with which it deals, and the natural environment' (Kaku 1997: 55). The Caux Round Table initiative saw a group of Japanese, European, and United States leaders develop a set of principles for business behaviour rooted in the ethical idea of *kyosei* coupled with a concern for human dignity (Boardman and Kato 2003; Cavanagh 2000; Goodpaster 2000; Waddock and Smith 2000). Two main purposes of the initiative included improving commercial and social relationships among nations, and reducing social and economic threats to peace and world stability. Other initiatives, such as the United Nations Global Compact, the Equator Principles, the Global Business Oath, or the World Business Council on Sustainable Development also constitute the foundations of genuine citizenship endeavours (see a summary of these and other initiatives in Table 4.2).

It is easy to be sceptical about such initiatives and to see them as 'window dressing', but they set a standard by which behaviours can be judged. Although these citizenship purposes may be endorsed by all

Table 4.2. Global citizenship initiatives

United Nations Global Compact (UNGC)
(www.unglobalcompact.org)

Initiative main features. UNGC is a voluntary initiative comprising 4,000 of the world's most important leaders in business, government, non-governmental organizations, labour, foundations, academia, and international corporate social responsibility. It has been described as the largest corporate citizenship and sustainability initiative in the world.

Principles/objectives. UNGC seeks to advance ten principles (in the areas of human rights, labour, environment and anti-corruption) through the active engagement of the corporate community, in cooperation with civil society. It is expected that, observing such principles, companies (as a primary driver of globalization), can help ensure that markets, commerce, technology and finance advance in ways that benefit economies and societies everywhere.

Caux Round Table (CRT)
(www.cauxroundtable.org)

Initiative main features. CRT is an international network of principled business leaders working to promote a more moral capitalism. Frederick Phillips, former President of Philips Electronics, and Olivier Giscard d'Estaing, former Vice-Chairman of INSEAD, founded it in 1986 as a means of reducing escalating trade tensions. Under the influence of Ryuzaburo Kaku, then Chairman of Canon, the CRT began focusing attention on the importance of global corporate responsibility in reducing social and economic threats to world peace and stability. The CRT Principles for Business were formally launched in 1994, and presented at the UN World Summit on Social Development in 1995.

Principles/objectives. The CRT principles are rooted in two basic ethical ideals: 'kyosei' and human dignity. The Japanese concept of 'kyosei' means living and working together for the common good, enabling cooperation and mutual prosperity to coexist with healthy and fair competition. 'Human dignity' refers to the sacredness or value of each person as an end, not simply as a means to the fulfilment of others' purposes or even majority prescription. The seven core principles are: (1) respecting stakeholders beyond shareholders; (2) contributing to economic, social and environmental spheres; (3) building trust by going beyond the letter of the law; (4) respecting rules and conventions; (5) supporting responsible organization; (6) respecting the environment; (7) avoiding illicit activities.

Equator Principles (EPs)
(www.equator-principles.com)

Initiative main features. The EPs are a voluntary set of standards for determining, assessing and managing social and environmental risk in project financing. They were launched in Washington D.C. on 4 June 2003, and were initially adopted by ten global financial institutions: ABN AMRO Bank, N.V., Barclays plc, Citigroup, Inc., Crédit Lyonnais, Credit Suisse First Boston, HVB Group, Rabobank Group, The Royal Bank of Scotland, WestLB AG, and Westpac Banking Corporation.

Principles/objectives. The EPs are considered a financial industry benchmark for determining, assessing and managing social and environmental risk in project financing. Principles focus on aspects such as (a) social and environment assessment, (b) applicable social and environmental standards, (c) grievance mechanism, (d) independent review, and (e) independent monitoring and reporting.

(*continued*)

Table 4.2. Continued

World Business Council on Sustainable Development (WBCSD)
(www.wbcsd.org)

Initiative main features. WBCSD is a CEO-led, global association of some 200 companies dealing exclusively with business and sustainable development. It works as a platform for companies to explore sustainable development, share knowledge, experiences and best practices, and to advocate business positions on these issues in a variety of forums, working with governments, non-governmental and intergovernmental organizations. Members are drawn from more than 30 countries and 20 major industrial sectors (October 2010).

Principles/objectives. The WBCSD objectives are: (a) being a leading business advocate on sustainable development; (b) participating in policy development to create the right framework conditions for business to make an effective contribution to sustainable human progress; (c) developing and promoting the business case for sustainable development; (d) demonstrating the business contribution to sustainable development solutions and sharing leading edge practices among members; (e) contributing to a sustainable future for developing nations and nations in transition. One relevant initiative is the 'Tomorrow's Leaders group', focusing on four significant global issues—poverty, environmental degradation, demographic change and globalization (see, on website, the 'Manifesto for Tomorrow's Global Business').

Global Business Oath—Young Global Leaders
(www.globalbusinessoath.org)

Initiative main features. The Oath emerged as a response to the global financial crisis of 2008. It was recognized that: (a) the ultimate purpose of management is to serve society; (b) the effects (good and bad) of managerial decisions on the welfare of society are amplified by the accumulation of resources under corporations.

Principles/objectives. Principles focus on global leaders' actions, including principles/values such as (a) companies must serve the society at large; (b) companies must respect and protect the human rights and dignity of all people who are affected by their operations, and will oppose all forms of discrimination and exploitation; (c) companies must respect and protect the right of future generations to enjoy a clean and resourceful planet; (d) bribery or any other forms of corruption are not tolerated; (e) leaders must actively engage in efforts to find solutions to critical social and environmental issues that are central to their companies; (f) leaders must invest in their own professional development as well as the development of other managers.

CERES principles
(www.ceres.org)

Initiative main features. Ceres was launched six months after the Exxon-Valdez oil spill (1989). The initiative brings investors, environmental groups and other stakeholders together to encourage companies and capital markets to incorporate environmental and social

Principles/objectives. Ceres aims that business and capital markets promote the well-being of society and the protection of the Earth's biological systems and resources. The principles are: (1) protection of the biosphere; (2) sustainable use of natural resources; (3) reduction and disposal of wastes; (4) energy conservation;

challenges into their day-to-day decision-making.

(5) risk reduction; (6) safe products and services; (7) environmental restoration; (8) informing the public; (9) management commitment; (10) audits and reports.

Global Sullivan Principles
(www.globalsullivanprinciples.org)

Initiative main features. Reverend Leon Sullivan developed the Sullivan Principles in 1977 as a code of conduct for human rights and equal opportunity for companies operating in South Africa. They are acknowledged to have contributed to the dismantling of apartheid. To further expand human rights and economic development to all communities, Reverend Sullivan created the Global Sullivan Principles of Social Responsibility in 1997.

Principles/objectives. The objectives are (a) to support economic, social and political justice by companies where they do business; (b) to support human rights and to encourage equal opportunity at all levels of employment, including racial and gender diversity on decision-making committees and boards; (c) to train and advance disadvantaged workers for technical, supervisory and management opportunities; (d) and to assist with greater tolerance and understanding among peoples—thereby, helping to improve the quality of life for communities, workers and children with dignity and equality.

Business Leaders Initiative on Human Rights (BLIHR)
(www.blihr.org/)

Initiative main features. BLIHR was launched in June 2003 to create a space for business representatives to share common questions on human rights with other businesses and with human rights' experts. Founding companies were ABB, Barclays, National Grid, MTV Europe, Novartis, Novo Nordisk, and The Body Shop International. Later, Alcan, AREVA, Ericsson, General Electric, The Coca-Cola Company, Zain and Newmont joined. The initiative developed practical tools and methodologies for helping companies to implement the principles of the Universal Declaration on Human Rights, both within their companies and in their stakeholders.

Principles/objectives. The vision and mission statement of BLIHR for the period 2003–2009 was the following: 'Our intention is to find practical ways of applying the aspirations of the Universal Declaration of Human Rights within a business context and to inspire other businesses to do likewise'. The initiative recommended several steps to respect human rights, including those related to non-discrimination, life, liberty, freedom to choose residence, privacy, freedom of thought and expression, association, fair, safe and healthy conditions of work, a fair wage and decent living, social security, and education.

Global Responsible Leadership Initiative (GRLI)
(http://www.grli.org/)

Initiative main features. The Board of Directors of the European Foundation for Management Development (EFMD) initiated GRLI in early 2003. It is 'a global multicultural community of action and learning. It operates with a fully transparent and unique governance model with all partners participating. It is legally set up as a foundation of public interest in Belgium'.

Principles/objectives. 'GRLI's mission is to "develop a next generation of responsible leaders" through collective and individual actions'.

Sources: websites of each organization or initiative

leaders, with positive consequences for the common good, the impact of global leaders and global organizations is much more intense and extensive, not only directly, on these organizations themselves, but also indirectly over all entities with which global organizations have social, economic, or political relationships. Citizenship also positively influences the capacity of global leaders to develop other people, to foster team building, to motivate others, to deal with conflict constructively, to build partnerships around the world, and to lead and participate in multicultural teams: all competencies that several authors have suggested as crucial for global leaders' effectiveness (Conner 2000; Osland et al. 2006; Mendenhall 2006).

Fairness to foster justice

Justice is a topic widely treated in the organizational and management literatures. Employees with positive perceptions of organizational justice develop a wide range of positive attitudes and behaviours, including job satisfaction, organizational commitment, organizational citizenship behaviours, and productivity (Fassina et al. 2008; Li and Cropanzano 2009; Viswesvaran and Ones 2002).

In the leadership context, justice refers to a form of responsibility that dynamically balances the rights of a company's stakeholders, including the owners (Mendonca 2001). Maak and Pless (2009: 544–5) argued that a cosmopolitan ethos includes the sense of global justice:

> [Business global leaders] do not need to be human rights experts but as leading citizens of the world they need to have a distinct sense of global justice to determine in deliberation processes with fellow citizens (e.g., in stakeholder dialogue) who owes what to whom on a global scale, what it requires to take a stand in human rights issues, and to determine the moral duties of businesses and their leadership to engage as agents of (social) justice on a global scale.

One may thus expect that role modelling and social learning, fuelled by the policies and practices global leaders adopt, create a character with a strong sense of right, one that seeks to behave fairly and foster justice in their organizations, with positive consequences for employees' attitudes and behaviours (Viswesvaran and Ones 2002). Kim and Mauborgne (1993, 1996) found that procedural justice promotes subsidiary top managers' compliance with corporate strategic decisions and inspires subsidiary top managers to adopt extra-role behaviours on behalf of the organization.

By practising justice, global leaders may better bond individuals and organizations that are geographically separated and promote enhanced cooperation among the members of global networks. Practising justice can also lead to positive consequences for customers (Clark et al. 2009; George 2003) and suppliers (Hornibrook et al. 2009). Justice may improve corporate social responsibility and compliance across the global supply chain (Boyd et al. 2009; Griffith et al. 2006), stimulate cooperation in strategic alliances (Luo 2008), and decrease opportunism in international joint ventures (Luo 2007).

Global leaders possessing the strength of justice are more likely to impel their companies to stay away from countries with poor human rights records, to refrain from exploiting oppressed cheap labour in the Third World, and to respect minorities in cultural contexts in which they are discriminated against (Bragues 2006). By practising justice, global leaders are able to minimize violence and conflicts and to foster peace—an important condition for businesses to operate and prosper (Fort and Schipani 2004).

One may also consider that global leaders with commitments to higher levels of justice are better positioned to understand the standards of justice (e.g. equity, need, equality) that prevail in different contexts (Greenberg 2001; Morris and Leung 2000; Murphy-Berman et al. 1984), adjusting decisions and policies accordingly. For example, although the desire for equity principles is strong in highly individualistic cultures such as the US, it is weaker in collectivistic cultures such as Japan, where equity is seen very much in terms of cohorts, tenure, and job-tracks. Therefore, when expanding to America, Toyota needed to create a system that team members believed to be fair but that also met Toyota Production System's requirements for teamwork and support beyond the boundaries of the narrowly defined jobs more typical of American companies. Toyota's leaders need to possess justice qualities to implement such an integrative approach.

Fairness was absent in Toshiba more than a decade ago when the company's image was tarnished in China following a biased double standard for dealing with American versus Chinese laptop users (Ip 2007; Pu and Que 2004). In March 1999, the company paid US $1.05 billion to all American users of one of its laptops which had defects related to the floppy disk controller. One year later, however, Toshiba's leaders refused to compensate Chinese customers who purchased the same laptops (Fort and Junhai 2002). In consequence, several Chinese consumers filed a lawsuit in the Beijing No 1 Intermediate

Court, claiming compensation (Ip 2007). A national rage erupted on the Internet and in other media, not only against Toshiba, but also against Japan and the Japanese. Chinese media said the company treated the Chinese as second-class customers (People's Daily 2000). China Central TV broadcasted a 30-minute special programme on Toshiba's behaviour. When Toshiba vice-president, Masaichi Koga, travelled to Beijing to explain the company's position, he was 'bombarded with angrily worded statements from reporters', at a news conference (People's Daily 2000). A substantial portion of senior managers' time had been spent in handling the case. Consumer confidence in Toshiba products decreased. The company suffered from a number of adverse market impacts, including a fall in sale volumes and a steep plunge in its share price (Ip 2007). Fort and Junhai (2002) noted that what they call the 'Confucian approach' makes the avoidance of litigation desirable.

Leadership, energizer of citizenship and fairness

A crucial character strength for global leaders is leadership by which leadership we refer to the capacity to influence without controlling or without resorting to dominance. If one considers role complexity, the wide range and diversity of stakeholders global leaders need to interact with, as well as the need to coordinate fluid and collaborative work relationships and to promote trust and speed of decision-making throughout a global network (Beechler and Javidan 2007), leadership is of great relevance. Articulating a tangible vision and strategy, clarifying values, and catalysing cultural and strategic change have been suggested by several authors (Mendenhall 2006; Mendenhall and Osland 2002; Osland et al. 2006) as important competencies for global leaders.

Leaders, especially those whose leadership is marked by the strengths of prudence, vitality, and love of learning, may face such challenges in a more effective way. They are able (a) to adjust their influence behaviours to the economic, social, and cultural idiosyncrasies of their interlocutors (Javidan et al. 2006); (b) to adopt integrative leadership efforts for making these different approaches work in ways consistent with the global organization strategy; and (c) to act as role models for the employees working worldwide.

More importantly, global leaders with this strength act as corporate citizens, adopting a cosmopolitan and responsible leadership approach (Maak and Pless 2009) for dealing with the world's most pressing problems (e.g. poverty, access to clean drinking water, and global warming). They are also more likely to address the needs of the base of the pyramid

(Prahalad 2005). A good illustration of a product addressed to the base of the pyramid is the Nano, a cheap car produced by Tata, designed to be bought by the millions of people with modest means but with the need for this type of transportation, who might previously have used less safe and more polluting motorcycles for personal mobility (Sehgal et al. 2010).

Another example is VisionSpring (London 2009), a venture employing a micro-franchising model to provide eyeglasses and vision screening that operates in Bangladesh, El Salvador, India, Indonesia, and South Africa. Several stakeholders benefit from this venture. Sellers (i.e. vision entrepreneurs) are able to increase income, develop communication and management skills, and improve family conditions and relationships within their communities. Local consumers increase productivity and income, improve professional reputation, become less dependent on others, and develop self-esteem. Communities benefit from higher economic activity, people develop a sense of dignity and respect, women acquire stronger status, and gender equality increases.

Shoktidoi, literally, 'yoghourt which makes one strong', produced by Grameen Danone, a joint venture between the Grameen Group and Danone, created in 2006, offers another example of a successful innovative product addressed to satisfy the needs of base of the pyramid markets (Sugawara 2010; Yunus et al. 2010). Grameen Danone is considered the world's first consciously designed multinational social business, an international business with a social mission, although run as a for-profit organization. Shoktidoi (a nutritious and inexpensive yogurt for Bangladesh, priced approximately at €6 cents) contains calcium and proteins essential for children's growth and bone strength, favouring locally available ingredients, thus reducing raw material costs, minimizing fossil energy consumption, and countering rural exodus.

When powerful global leaders using the strength of leadership decide to tackle the needs of the base of the pyramid, they can make a real difference. They are potentially more able (a) to develop human capabilities of underprivileged people (so that they learn to help themselves), (b) to assist in eradicating world poverty, (c) to improve the well-being of billions of people, (d) to diminish the imbalance between wealthy and poor nations and, thus, (e) to reduce the floods of economic and political refugees, illegal immigration, and ethnic and civil wars. This way, they are able to foster conditions favourable for social peace— a valuable outcome per se and one that is also crucial for business building and prospering (Fort and Schipani 2004). Cosmopolitan and socially responsible leaders are conscious of the sort of problems that affect people all over the world, even the distant world, and care for the needs of others (Maak and Pless 2009).

In short, the citizenship and fairness initiatives referred to in the previous sections of this chapter are more effective when global leaders express the true force of leadership, rather than the formal power associated with hierarchical position. Leadership works as a catalyst of citizenship and justice strengths. Leadership mobilizes other strengths in pursuit of the common good (Maak and Pless 2009). Its strengths do not translate into cosmopolitan responsible leadership if global leaders are devoid of citizenship and justice strengths. With these three strengths, global leaders are more able to create and establish sustainable relationships with a multitude of stakeholders, fostering stakeholder social capital worldwide (Maak 2007; Maak and Pless 2006) and making their organizations act as global and responsible citizens (Maak and Pless 2009).

Table 4.3. Cosmopolitan leadership principles and how global leaders may sustain them

Principle	Explanation
Recognition of equal worth and dignity	Global leaders ought to recognize and actively promote each person's equal worth and dignity.
Active agency and care	Global leaders ought to actively demonstrate a caring attitude toward others, matters of ethics and justice, and the world's most prominent problems (e.g. poverty, global warming).
Personal responsibility and accountability	Global leaders ought to be aware of their impact (either through their actions or omissions) on the globalized world, thus acting conscientiously, carefully, and responsibly, both at home and in all countries where they operate.
Stakeholder engagement and dialogue	Global leaders ought to work to make certain that the concerns of all stakeholders are considered, and develop a participative dialogue with them to ensure an inclusive approach to cosmopolitan problem solving.
Deliberation on matters of global fairness and justice Inclusiveness and subsidiarity	Global leaders' decisions, mainly in matters of fairness and assistance, ought to be informed and legitimated by a process of conjoint (leaders with stakeholders) moral deliberation. Global leaders' decisions must include and consider all whom the issues at hand may concern, through a process of shared leadership. They must also actively enable others to lead and act responsibly.
Assistance in creating a decent life in the world and building human capabilities	Global leaders ought to bear co-responsibility in promoting human and social rights, assisting people in urgent need, being active supporters of decent living conditions in countries where they operate, and fostering human capabilities (i.e. helping people to help themselves).
Sustainability and stewardship	Global leaders ought to act as stewards of the planet's natural resources and preserve the cosmopolitan right of future generations to lead a decent life.

Built from Maak and Pless (2009)

Cosmopolitan responsible leadership is more effective if global leaders are supplied with further virtues and strengths. Maak and Pless proposed a list of eight cosmopolitan leadership principles, which we summarize in Table 4.3. Several virtues and strengths may sustain these principles. For example, the stakeholder engagement and dialogue principle is more likely to be implemented if global leaders are equipped with gratitude, open-mindedness, social intelligence, and integrity.

When excessive justice is not virtuous

The strengths of justice are drivers of global leaders' positive performance, but one should not neglect possible negative effects of an excessive justice orientation. Once again, virtue is in the middle. Excessive citizenship (e.g. spending too much in philanthropic initiatives without strategic considerations: Porter and Kramer 2002) may make global leaders lose sight of the economic and financial health of the company. Several citizenship actions of Levi Strauss, when headed by Robert E. Haas (Mullins 1990), were criticized by analysts, due to their costs. Some analysts were dissatisfied with the idealism of Haas's decisions (Cavanagh and Bandsuch 2002).

Excessive fairness may also have some negative consequences. An excessive focus on equity (i.e. rewarding individuals according to their merit and the contribution to the organization) may give rise to excessive wage dispersion, with negative consequences for employees' productivity, satisfaction, and cooperative behaviours, and for team and organization performance (Carpenter and Sanders 2004; Cowherd and Levine 1992; Mahy et al., forthcoming; Pfeffer and Langton 1993; San and Jane 2008). The lines delimiting the right balance between cooperation, justice, meritocracy, rivalry, and competition may actually be difficult to draw, and good intentions may produce not so good results. Maintaining equilibrium is both necessary and difficult.

Negative consequences may also result from fairness practices when culture is not taken into account. In fact, the conceptions of justice and the effects of justice on individuals' attitudes and behaviours are contingent upon culture (Brockner et al. 2001; Gelfand et al. 2007; Greenberg 2001; Leung and Kwong 2003; Lind et al. 1997; Morris and Leung 2000; Morris et al. 1999; Tata et al. 2003). If global leaders force the application of equity principles in collectivistic cultures (where equality may be preferred), negative consequences for employees' satisfaction and commitment may arise. In contrast, corporations characterized by low wage dispersion cultures may experience difficulties in individualistic countries

101

Table 4.4. Justice assisting several global leaders' activities

Citizenship	• Being more sensitive to the impacts that the company has on communities and the natural environment. • Being more receptive to social accountability norms and standards (e.g. SA8000). • Following policies and strategies that do not harm the planet or humanity. • Developing genuine concern for the customers' needs and well-being. • Building more sustainable and responsible organizations. • Performing corporate diplomacy, thus increasing the company's legitimacy or 'license-to-operate', reducing risks of misunderstandings, and obtaining endorsement by governments and citizens. • Building a base of relationships with customers, government officials and public intermediaries, and other relevant stakeholders (including the 'public'), thus enabling companies to thrive in diverse geographies and political jurisdictions. • Advising developing countries on emerging issues that are relevant for their more successful future. • Developing and/or joining to initiatives like Caux Round Table, UN Global Compact, and World Business Council on Sustainable Development. • Aspiring to make the world a better place.
Fairness	• Behaving fairly and fostering justice, thus engendering positive consequences for employees' attitudes and behaviours across the worldwide organizational network. • Improving corporate social responsibility compliance across the global supply chain. • Stimulating cooperation in strategic alliances. • Impelling the company to stay away from countries with poor human rights records, to refrain from hiring cheap labour in the Third World, and to respect minorities in cultural contexts in which they are discriminated against. • Understanding the justice standards (e.g. equity, need, equality) that prevail in different contexts, thus adjusting decisions and policies accordingly.
Leadership	• Articulating a tangible vision and strategy, clarifying values, and catalysing cultural and strategic change. • Adjusting influence behaviours to the economic, social and cultural idiosyncrasies of their interlocutors. • Acting as role model for the company's employees working worldwide. • Adopting a cosmopolitan and responsible leadership approach for dealing with the world's most pressing problems (e.g. poverty, access to clean drinking water, and global warming). • Addressing the needs of the base of the pyramid, thus developing human capabilities of underprivileged people, assisting in eradicating world poverty, improving well-being of billions of people, and diminishing the imbalance between wealthy and poor nations. • Nourishing citizenship and fairness initiatives.

where the equity rule prevails. Ikea experienced problems with US managers, who considered that individual achievement was not sufficiently rewarded due to the Swedish avoidance of pay discrimination (Grol et al. 1998; Jackson 2002).

An excess of the strength of leadership may also produce negative consequences. For example, charisma may create excessive centralization (Conger 1990, 1999; DeCelles and Pfeffer 2004; Howell and Avolio 1992) and forms of blind obedience that reduce the ability of the rest of the organization to evaluate decisions coming from the top critically and to send feedback upwards. Lee Kun Hee, chairman of the Samsung Group, a man with a strong personal affection for cars, 'a billionaire car buff' (Kraar 1997), and a desire to 'prove his leadership credentials' (Lee and Lee 2007: 494), decreed that the company would become a car producer in 1994. He was a victim of his own obsessions and power (Hoon 1998; Useem 2003). The target was to make 1.5 million cars per year by 2010. The automobile industry was already an overcrowded field. Analysts questioned the investment (Burton 1999; Lee and Lee 2007). Even worse, in spite of disagreeing with the investment, many of Samsung's top managers were unable to question the strategy of their powerful chieftain, a common organizational problem (Useem 2003). The consequence was that Samsung was forced out of the business (Burton 1999; *Financial Times* 1999; Len 1999; Useem 2003), and Lee had to reach into his own pocket for more than $2 billion to placate irate creditors—not without having told his top managers that he was puzzled that none had openly expressed their reservations (Useem 2003)! Leadership requires reflexivity and openness as well as boldness and a bias for action.

If Lee Kun Hee had acted wisely and more prudently, and his followers had been more courageous, the possibilities of failure would have been less. To develop flourishing organizations and teams, virtuousness is an ingredient that needs to be present on both sides of the leader–follower relationship. When the skills of leadership are used in excess, a fair amount of prudent and courageous followership may be a good antidote. Paradoxically, followers' prudence and courage have fewer opportunities to blossom when their leaders are not well equipped with these virtues themselves.

Strengths of humanity

Whereas justice is a virtue related to impartiality, humanity manifests in caring relationships with others, a virtue displayed via three main

Table 4.5. Character strengths through which the humanity virtue is displayed

Strength	How individuals with this strength behave (examples)	Opposites	Excess
Love	• They share aid, comfort, and acceptance. • They develop strong positive feelings, commitment, and even make sacrifices in favour of others. • They are able to develop bonds of intimacy.	Alienation; estrangement; loneliness; aloofness; spite; envy; selfishness.	Over-zealousness; sentimentality; 'incompetent do-goodism' (Solomon 1999); paternalism.
Kindness (generosity; nurturance; care; compassion; altruistic love)	• They are compassionate and concerned about the welfare of others. • They do favours for others. • They help others in an altruistic way. • They are generous.	Stinginess; mean-spiritedness; wrath; coldness; indifference.	Intrusiveness; unctuousness (Solomon 1999); mawkishness.
Social intelligence (emotional intelligence; personal intelligence)	• They are able to perceive, understand, and assess their own and others' emotions and motives. • They use emotional information to facilitate cognitive activities. • They are emotionally self-controlled. • They use social information to get others' participation. • They act wisely in relationships.	Inaccurate self-understanding and social and emotional inability in social relationships; cluelessness; self-deceit.	Intrusiveness; manipulation; chameleon-like behaviour.

character strengths (Table 4.5): love, kindness, and social intelligence. Love refers to the capacity to develop and maintain reciprocal relationships, emotional bonds between teammates and co-workers, and mentoring relationships. It is a virtue marked by the sharing of assistance, comfort, and acceptance. Kindness means a tendency to be compassionate and concerned about other people's welfare, to demonstrate compassion for their problems and difficulties, to do honest favours for them, and perform good deeds. Social intelligence is the capacity to process *hot* information: motives, feelings, and other domains directly relevant to individual well-being and survival. It involves personal (intrapersonal) intelligence, social intelligence, and emotional intelligence.

A cosmopolitan ethos requires that global, responsible leaders demonstrate not only a sense of global justice but also a sense of care for the basic needs of others and a desire to fulfil their duty of assistance to the needy (Maak and Pless 2009). Both elements may benefit from global leaders' humanity strengths. A caring attitude should not be restricted to those close at hand; rather it requires caring and empathy towards the distant needy, 'based on mutually shared feelings of flourishing and humanity' (Maak and Pless 2009: 545). Peter Singer argues that all human beings, especially those in better economic and social positions, have the duty to contribute to the creation of a fairer *one community*. He proposed the following public policy aimed at producing good consequences (Singer 2002: 194):

> [A]nyone who has enough money to spend on the luxuries and frivolities so common in affluent societies should give at least 1 cent in every dollar of their income to those who have trouble getting enough to eat, clean water to drink, shelter from the elements, and basic health care. Those who do not meet this standard should be seen as failing to meet their fair share of a global responsibility, and therefore as doing something that is seriously morally wrong. This is the minimum, not the optimal, donation. (...) To give that amount requires no moral heroics. To fail to give it shows indifference to the indefinite continuation of dire poverty and avoidable, poverty related deaths.

Singer was not referring specifically to global leaders and multinational corporations. However, considering the *power*, the *privilege*, and the *potential* of global leaders and corporations (Maak and Pless 2009), they are not morally exempt from the duty of nourishing a fairer *one community*—not necessarily just through monetary donations, but mainly via responsible and cosmopolitan citizenship actions and decisions, where the strengths of humanity and justice meet to generate positive organizational and social performance. Humanitarianism (i.e. humanity and citizenship) was what, reputedly (Purkayastha and Fernando 2007), guided Anita Roddick in many of the important choices she made in life—at least according to the stories that circulated about her. According to Damon (2004: 75).

> her humanitarian impulses have determined the kinds of relationships she has had with people who have been crucial to The Body Shop's success. First and foremost among these people were women in developing countries whose native methods of bodily care became Roddick's signature product. Roddick's admiration for these women, and her fascination with their culture, enabled her to learn from what they were doing and establish highly generative business relationships with them. Listening to, learning from, and conducting successful business with indigent tribal women from many parts of the world requires a number of capacities that spring directly from a humanitarian orientation: deep interest in people from all backgrounds, respect for people with different knowledge and skills than yourself, humility

with respect to the wisdom of people without formal education, and trust in their capacities to deal honestly and responsibly with an outsider.

Prudence is however necessary in interpreting this enlightened portrait: as we have remarked in the previous chapter, Anita Roddick and the Body Shop were controversial in terms of the relation between the rhetoric and reality (Purkayastha and Fernando 2007). Some of the stories about Roddick's wanderings in the wider world were clearly clever marketing, as Entine suggests, quoting her public relations director: 'I think Anita Roddick is a very brilliant woman.' She paused. 'You know, Anita's gone over the top. We used to joke that I've created this Frankenstein. If you start believing all this stuff that is written about you, you have got to go dotty, haven't you? She started to believe her own publicity and this is always the death knell to anybody' (Entine 2002).

The acquisition of the company by L'Oréal in a deal from which she reaped great benefits, a company whose practices were often criticized by Roddick, reinforced the accusations of hypocrisy and empty rhetoric addressed to Body Shop, its founder and figurehead. Critics argue that Body Shop was no different from other companies in its pursuit of profit, made from exploiting consumer sentiment, and that a huge gap existed between the appealing image projected by the company and its practices. More benevolent views suggest that Roddick's humanitarian driving force was relatively powerless in the face of the business world's 'hard' reality, and that the desire of L'Oréal to 'buy' into corporate social responsibility meant that L'Oréal was genuinely interested in organizational learning from the humane and socially responsible Body Shop and its founder.

In considering how Body Shop's commitment to the virtue of humanity is laudable, two things are important. First, (the image of) humanitarianism was greeted by numerous customers and humanitarian and environmental activists worldwide, with positive consequences for the Body Shop's reputation, growth, and profitability, at least in its first decade. Second, the acquisition by L'Oréal damaged the Body Shop's reputation and led customers to 'forsake' the company for allegedly having renounced its virtue. Consistency and coherence between rhetoric and reality is clearly of long-term importance.

Next, we explore with more detail why the three humanity strengths (i.e. love, kindness, and social intelligence) may help global leaders to pursue positive organizational performance (synthesis in Table 4.6). Considering that love and kindness are strictly related (e.g. love nourishes kindness; kindness promotes reciprocal relationships that may give rise to love feelings and actions; altruistic love is one component of kindness), both are treated together—and we sometimes will use the term 'humanity' while referring to both.

Love and kindness: caring for employees and other stakeholders

Caldwell and Dixon (2010: 93) defined love as 'the unconditional acts of respect, caring and kindness that communicate the worth of others and that promote their welfare, growth, and wholeness'. It is at the core of the servant leadership (Greenleaf 1998) approach, and is increasingly thought of as a responsibility of leaders in organizations (Batten 1999; Caldwell and Dixon 2010; Damon 2004). Empirical and theoretical research has shown that expressing care and concern for others is crucial to leadership success (Reave 2005). Grant (2008a) suggested that compassionate leaders foster followers' self-efficacy and productivity. James Autry pointed out that good and proper management to a great extent embodies love and caring (Autry 1991).

Max DePree, of Herman Miller, also argued that leaders have the duty of demonstrating to their employees that they care about their welfare and are committed to their success, as well as to the success of the organization (DePree 2004). Caldwell and Dixon (2010) also stated that great leaders acknowledge that investing in others via the expression of commitment to their interests reinforces not only relationships but also the organization itself.

Love and kindness have both been considered crucial for leader effectiveness (Barbuto and Wheeler 2006; Dennis and Bocarnea 2005; Fry 2003; George 2003; Grant 2008a, 2008b; Liden et al. 2008). They have been at the core of the lasting success of companies such as Southwest Airlines, Kimberly-Clark and DaVita (Nirenberg 2001; Pfeffer 2007), and there are reasons to believe that one of the main sources of the organizational cultures of these unusual firms is the virtuousness of their founders and leaders who set a powerful and inspiring example.

According to Csikszentmihalyi (2003), leadership must accept that worker well-being should come before products, profits, and markets. In his view, few CEOs have adopted such an approach as deeply as Anita Roddick, founder and former CEO of The Body Shop. Roddick observed that she loved the relationships she had with her franchises and her employees ('my most treasured, loved friends'; 'my extended family') (Csikszentmihalyi 2003: 149). During the period before the L'Oréal takeover, this love was often not reciprocated as disgruntled franchises were bought back by the parent company. Body Shop 'paid out more than GBP100 million to settle 14 franchisee suits and buy out dissident franchisees . . . Although details in each case are different, franchisees broadly contend that financial problems reflect deterioration in BSI's operating ethics. Product supply and quality of its cosmetics, which franchisees must source from the parent company, top their list' (Entine 2002). While Csikszentmihalyi is a respected researcher, on this occasion the rhetoric, rather than the reality, of the Body Shop might have been uppermost in gaining his attention.

Several global leaders have used love and kindness to leverage the growth and sustainability of their enterprises. Love and kindness are crucial for developing networking skills (Jokinen 2005) and fostering worldwide networks. A global leader with the strengths of love and kindness is more apt to respect people from different cultures 'as they are'. Instead of being distracted by their imperfections (Delbecq 2008), he/she may develop more sophisticated cultural intelligence. If one looks at different cultures with love and respect, one may discover riches where others see poverty, and local wisdom where others see ignorance (Diamond 1998).

Love and kindness allow global leaders to instil a sense of community (thus promoting peace: Fort and Schipani 2004) and to build and develop mentoring relationships (Delbecq 2008; George 2003; Ragins and Cotton 1999). Mentoring allows for the transmission of knowledge rapidly across global networks, increasing people's capacity to make decisions where they need to be taken (and as soon as possible), and thus develops social capital. Narayana Murthy, the founder of India's Infosys, calls himself Chairman and Chief Mentoring Officer (Kanter 2010). Mentoring is also a common practice at IBM (Kanter 2010).

Through mentoring, an expatriate leader may develop local country employees' competencies and strong local management teams, thus helping the company to 'localize' its staff, decrease expatriation costs, and motivate local country employees (Law et al. 2004; Mezias and Scandura 2005; Selmer 2003, 2004). Both strengths may also allow a global leader to mentor impatriates (Harvey and Novicevic 2004) and individuals who are preparing for international assignments (Jassawalla et al. 2006), in this way helping their cross-cultural and psychological adjustment and also helping them to be more effective.

Love and kindness are more appreciated where collectivistic and feminine orientations rather than individualistic and masculine ones are valued. Thus, global leaders may need other virtues such as curiosity, wisdom, self-regulation, and social intelligence for discovering how to adopt different levels of love and kindness in different cultural contexts.

However, it is more important to show love and kindness differently in different contexts, which is why curiosity, perspective, self-regulation, and social intelligence may also be crucial.

Martinez and Dorfman (1998) suggest that outstanding Mexican leaders tend to be involved in the private lives of their employees (e.g. helping a family member of an employee who is hospitalized). According to the authors, although similar behaviour may also be valued and seen as an expression of care in other collectivist societies, it can be interpreted as an invasion of privacy in less collectivist ones, as a form of paternalism. In individualistic contexts, a more appropriate expression of compassion might be enquiring after the situation or allowing a temporary reduction of job duties so that the employee may be able to care for her relative. Those examples suggest that behaviours that are appropriate and that signal consideration and compassion vary across contexts, even though consideration and compassion may be evaluated positively in most cultures (Den Hartog 2004; see also Den Hartog et al. 1999).

Therefore, although the value ascribed to manifestations of love and kindness in organizations may be contingent on the cultural context, its value cannot be disregarded in individualistic cultures. Bill George, former CEO of Medtronic, the world's largest manufacturer of implantable biomedical devices such as pacemakers, heart valves, defibrillators, and neuro-stimulators, pointed out that, by 'leading with heart', a leader is more competent in establishing closer relationships with colleagues, thus building teams whose collective business knowledge is superior to that of the leader (George 2003: 24). Building such ties is especially challenging for leaders working with culturally diverse teams and with teams whose members operate in different locations.

'Leading with heart' is also important in caring for customers and making the world better (Delbecq 2008). Overcoming some internal resistance, Daniel Vasella, from Novartis, gave proofs of such strength when deciding to provide Gleevec for free for anyone with an income below $40,000, and at a reduced price for patients with incomes up to $100,000 (George 2003).

Leading with heart may also help global leaders to build organizational healing (Powley and Cameron 2008) and create a sense of community within the organization. Jeffrey Pfeffer provides an example of how demonstrations of compassion by global leaders are important in making companies more similar to communities, and in attracting employees (scholars, in this case) and customers (students) from around the world (Pfeffer 2007). As visiting professor at IESE, he observed how the caring culture of the organization contributed to making the school an attractive place to work:

> When my wife, Kathleen, came down with a severe earache from flying with a cold, the dean, Jordi Canals, arranged for an appointment first at a clinic and subsequently with a famous ear specialist, sent an English-speaking employee in a taxi to accompany her to both appointments, and paid for the taxi and the doctors' visits (. . .). This was neither required by the terms of my visit at IESE nor even expected, and naturally earned the undying gratitude of both my wife and myself. For Jordi Canals and his goal of building a community, it was almost automatic to offer help to someone who was having difficulty, even if that individual was just a temporary part of the organization. (Pfeffer 2007: 20–21)

It is not easy to identify the real motivation underlying the IESE's dean's behaviour. However, his care created a sense of gratitude. A receiver of gratitude potentially develops affective reasons to deepen affective commitment to the organization.

Humanity may also help to mitigate the consequences of crises. Toyota and its leaders revealed this strength during the 1997 Asian financial crisis. Toyota's Thailand operation weathered four straight years of losses, but an order had come down from then President Hiroshi Okuda: 'Cut all costs, but don't touch any people' (Takeuchi et al. 2008: 102). The prudent decision to create a preventive safeguard (e.g. a large cash reserve) for riding out rough times is also rooted in humanity, in the wise and prudent values of the company's founding leaders (Liker and Hoseus 2008). These strengths appear to have been in shorter supply during the massive recall scandal of 2010, in which US government officials have said that Toyota did not tell them about problems with faulty accelerators until it exploded as an issue in the media.

Global leaders rich in strengths of humanity are also more likely to deal effectively and to adopt citizenship and responsible actions for facing complex issues related to human rights violations in underprivileged countries. Robert E. Haas, former chairman and CEO of Levi Strauss, demonstrated citizenship virtues when dealing with suppliers who used child labour (Canavagh and Bandsuch 2002; Donalson and Dunfee 1999). The company was ahead of other apparel makers in taking measures against the use of child labour. In 1992, noticing that many seamstresses at Bangladesh suppliers were 11, 12, and 13 years old, Levi's first inclination was to force the suppliers to fire them. However, after having found that these young girls were the sole support of their families' survival, the company agreed to send them to school and to pay for tuition, books, and uniforms on condition that the suppliers agreed to pay the children's regular wages and to hire the girls back when they attained the legal working age of 14.

Haas also withdrew $40 million worth of sewing work from China, due to this country's violations of human rights. Some outside analysts claimed that the decision had nothing to do with ethics but only with public relations aimed to lure more customers and raise profits. However, Beaver held that there was no pressure on US firms to leave China, and that the withdrawal could lead Levi's to 'pass the chance to clothe an increasingly affluent China' (Beaver 1995: 37). Mitchell (1994: 46) argued that Haas 'believes the corporation should be an ethical creature—an organism capable of both reaping profits and making the world a better place to live in'.

Love and kindness are also relevant for global leaders to have a balanced and rich personal life, a relevant source of social and emotional capital necessary for dealing with the rough demands of working in global landscapes. A flourishing and balanced family life helps global leaders to carry out their international assignments, either if the family stays at home or goes with them. Work–family balance and family emotional support are important predictors of expatriates' success, including for dual-career couples (Fischlmayr and Kollinger 2010; Grant-Vallone and Ensher 2001; Harvey 1995; Harvey and Wiese 1998; Lee 2007; Lee and Liu 2006).

Social intelligence: emotional and social radar

Social intelligence, a combination of intrapersonal intelligence, interpersonal intelligence, and emotional intelligence, has been referred to as a predictor of leader effectiveness (Goleman 1998; Hopkins and Bilimoria 2008; Riggio and Reichard 2008; Wong and Law 2002) and as a relevant competency of global leaders (Alon and Higgins 2005; Brownell 2006; McCall and Hollenbeck 2002). For some authors, emotional intelligence can be thought of as a principal dimension of global leadership (Jokinen 2005).

A global leader with social intelligence demonstrates a sincere interest in and concern for others, a heightened ability to listen to employees, customers, suppliers, authorities, partners, and other stakeholders from different contexts, and a deep capacity to understand different viewpoints, and to interpret emotions and verbal and non-verbal communicational cues in different cultures. As a consequence (Alon and Higgins 2005; Black et al. 1999; Den Hartog 2004; Goleman 1998; Jokinen 2005;

Morrison 2000; Riggio and Reichard 2008), such a person tends to be more:

- Competent in understanding local markets, customers, competitors, and governments quickly;
- Effective in overcoming barriers to communication that separate people across cultures and vast geographic distances;
- Able to emotionally connect with people from various backgrounds;
- Equipped with a higher capacity to understand the emotional tone within cross-cultural teams and thus channel such emotions in a more appropriate way;
- Apt to understand and manage others' emotions, thus being more effective in influencing others and in managing conflict and negotiating in diverse contexts;
- In emotional control when facing unfamiliar situations in challenging cultural contexts;
- Able to know in which contexts it is appropriate or not to express emotions in public;
- Capable of identifying and mentoring future leaders;
- Able to articulate appropriate messages and convincingly communicate a vision to a multicultural and highly diverse workforce and implement it in an uncertain environment.

In large organizations, top leaders frequently have difficulties developing an accurate sense of the company's affairs. Reports often mask real problems, and people are afraid to report unpalatable hard facts. To keep one's finger on the pulse it is necessary to create and develop positive, open, frank, and honest social relationships, with social intelligence being necessary to develop and support these positive networks. Csikszentmihalyi (2003: 125) described the following strategy used by the head of a large multinational corporation:

> Two weeks ago, I spent one entire week (...) traveling to seven different cities and having meetings with employees. I talked to two to three hundred employees twice a day (...) for maybe an hour, giving them my views and then leaving an hour and half for them to ask me any questions they had. That's how you keep your finger on the pulse. (...) I've got to get out and be with customers and be with employees and be in the field and watch what goes on and provide motivation. Last week I was in Asia all week. (.....) I was visiting our staff, visiting our plants, showing an interest in what they are doing. That's how you do it. You don't do it sitting here.

John Reed, former CEO and chairman of Citicorp (Csikszentmihalyi 2003), met at least twice a year personally with the heads of the major world banks, and, more frequently, with CEOs of companies such as General Motors, General Electric, or IBM. He also spent at least half the morning talking on the phone with tens of people from his inner network in the company, his major decisions always being taken after consulting some of them. Of course, this is no guarantee of making the right decisions, as Citicorp learned to its costs during the GFC (when Reed was no longer CEO, to give him his due). The CEO of Citigroup, as it became, who led the bank merrily into the global financial crisis, was clearly a man of limited ethical values (Madrick 2011), who mired the bank deep into a decade in which vast sums of money flowed through Wall Street, 'directing capital on the basis of financial chicanery, outrageous compensation packages, and bubble-infected stock price valuations' (Krugman and Wells 2011).

Strengths such as vitality for travelling across borders and time zones, as well as humility, curiosity, and prudence are important for developing worldwide networks, but the emerging social contacts are only effective in providing and receiving useful feedback if the leaders have enough social intelligence. With social intelligence, global leaders (a) become better active listeners, (b) are more able to 'catch' the true facts around the world and thus make more accurate decisions, (c) reveal emotional self-control for avoiding cultural mistakes in psychologically distant places, (d) empathize with people from different cultural contexts, and (e) understand the meaning of verbal and non-verbal messages in high-context cultures (Hall 1981). In such cultures, typically Eastern ones, the meanings of a message depend on the external environment, situational factors, and non-verbal behaviour.

In short, social intelligence is crucial for developing and maintaining networks around the world that help global leaders to provide and receive feedback, to be well informed, and make more accurate decisions. Mike Hackworth, co-founder and chairman of Cirrus Logic, leading supplier of signal-processing components for audio and energy applications, described how empathy helped him (Csikszentmihalyi 2003: 164):

> I think that one of the things that helped me tremendously in my career is that I could put myself in the other guy's shoes. So whether it's in a negotiation, or in motivating people on a team to get a job done, to accomplish an extraordinary task in a short period of time (...) my being sensitive to their issues and helping them get through their issues, was due, I believe, to my empathetic nature, and that then dramatically increased their commitment

Table 4.6. Humanity assisting several global leaders' activities

Love and kindness	• Fostering a sense of community within the company. • Developing networking skills and sustaining worldwide networks. • Building and developing mentoring relationships, thus transmitting knowledge fast through the global network, and increasing people's capacity to make decisions where they need to be made. • Caring for customers and other stakeholders, and making the world a better place. • Mitigating the consequences of crises (e.g. plants' closing) for employees. • Adopting citizenship and responsible actions for facing complex issues related to human rights violations in underprivileged countries. • Having a balanced and rich personal/family life—a relevant source of social and emotional capital necessary for dealing with the rough demands of working in the global arena.
Social intelligence	• Demonstrating sincere interest in and concern for others. • Listening to employees, customers, suppliers, authorities, partners, and other stakeholders from different contexts. • Understanding local markets, customers, competitors, and governments quickly. • Understanding the emotional tone within cross-cultural teams, thus channelling such emotions in a more appropriate way. • Understanding different viewpoints, and interpreting emotions and verbal and non-verbal communicational cues in different cultures. • Overcoming barriers to communication that separate people across cultures and vast geographic distances. • Keeping self-emotional control when facing unfamiliar situations in psychologically distant cultural contexts. • Managing conflict and negotiating in diverse contexts. • Articulating appropriate messages and convincingly communicating the company's vision to a multicultural and highly diverse workforce. • 'Catching' the true facts around the world and thus making more accurate decisions.

to want to achieve the goals. They redoubled their energy and put more into it, and you could accomplish uncommon results.

When excessive humanity becomes problematic

If virtue is in the middle, excessive humanity may produce negative consequences for global leaders, their organizations, and their stakeholders. Excessive love may lead global leaders to lose bravery or to avoid difficult but necessary decisions. Excessive love and kindness may also lead them to lose the 'sacred' component of leadership, the healthy separation between the roles of leading and following (Grint 2010), and render them unable to take hard and difficult, although necessary, measures (e.g. closing a plant; firing a friend who is also an incompetent leader). They may also lose the psychological distance necessary to be impartial and to implement fair practices and policies.

When mentoring or coaching organizational members, global leaders with excessive humanity may develop too much social proximity, thus preventing them from acting with professionalism and creating difficulties in developing the protégés' autonomy. In some cultural contexts (e.g. those characterized by low humane orientation and high masculinity), an excessively humane leader may be interpreted as weak, thus losing credibility and respect, and thus the capacity to make things happen (Javidan et al. 2006; Muczyk and Holt 2008). Even when performed at a reasonable level, individualized consideration, a dimension of transformational leadership, may lead to followers' dissatisfaction in individualistic and masculine cultural contexts where such behaviour may be seen as favouritism or inequity (Vandenberghe 1999).

Excessive social intelligence may also negatively influence the performance of global leaders. A global leader with excessive proficiency in managing others' emotions may end up manipulating others and pursue unethical ends and means (Austin et al. 2007; Dougherty and Krone 2002; Grieve and Mahar 2010). Therefore, emotional intelligence may also be detrimental to global leaders' positive performance if they are not strong in terms of other strengths, such as integrity, justice, and humanity.

Conclusion

Amiability and citizenship virtues allow global leaders to pursue several important endeavours, including: (a) adopting a cosmopolitan and responsible leadership approach that promotes human dignity and development; (b) adopting, implementing and facilitating a sustainable and responsible management strategy, thus contributing to the common good; (c) performing corporate diplomacy, thus increasing corporate legitimacy in different and difficult social, economic, and political contexts; (d) adopting a respectful leadership approach, and fostering trust, justice, and fluid cooperative work relationships between diverse stakeholders within the global network; (e) fostering a sense of community within the company; (f) building and developing mentoring processes; (g) managing conflict and negotiating constructively in diverse contexts. Reaching these positive effects requires the observation of the *golden mean*. When justice and humanity give rise to leniency, and a humane orientation renders the leader unable to make difficult although necessary decisions, the consequence may not be virtuous but actually perverse.

5

The Virtues of Transcendence

A core component of any classic definition of character is composed of an individual's ability to constrain their personal appetites on behalf of the supposed needs of a greater societal good.

(Wright and Goodstein 2007: 931)

The practice of the virtue of temperance enables leaders to exercise restraint and discipline in order that irrational expression of emotions does not cloud their judgment and prevent them from viewing persons, things, and events in their proper perspective.

(Mendonca 2001: 271)

Strengths of temperance: resisting temptations, delaying self-gratification

Temperance has become inexorably associated with the attitudes of those who would seek to abolish the consumption of alcohol. In fact, as a virtue, temperance is much wider than this singular prohibition. The virtue of temperance refers to control over excess, including any form of auspicious self-constraint or self-control. It means 'the exercise of self-control that, in general, would lead one to avoid and resist the temptation to overindulge in hedonistic behaviours' (Mendonca 2001: 270). Bastons (2008: 398) characterized temperance in the following way:

The use of control—temperance—guarantees that intention is fuelled only by the true good that is beyond apparent good, and according to the true knowledge. The development of this competence could be expressed as follows: the more a person is able to moderate his passions the more able he is to value real good; and therefore, his intentions will be of greater quality. Put in a negative form: the more somebody values apparent good, the more difficult it will be for him to value real good, and so the quality of his intentions will diminish and, therefore, his capacity to correctly evaluate his decisions.

Individuals who are consistently temperate, guarding against excesses and who exercise self-control, it has been argued, tend to be happier, more productive, and more successful (Peterson and Seligman 2004). Temperance is manifest in four main character strengths: forgiveness and mercy, humility and modesty, prudence, and self-regulation (Table 5.1). Forgiveness refers to relinquishing resentments or claims to retribution against an offender. It does not mean ignoring the injuries: rather, it 'cleanses the spirit from the poison of hate and anger' (Malloch 2010: 757). Humility can be viewed as consisting in the realistic appreciation of one's contribution and of the contribution of others (Solomon 1999). Modesty refers to the estimation of one's merits or achievements with moderation (Peterson and Seligman 2004). Prudence is a form of practical reasoning that consists in the careful consideration of the long-term consequences of two types of actions, those that are taken and those that are not (Peterson and Seligman 2004). Prudence helps individuals to manage the connection between other strengths. For example, a prudent individual is able to temper hope with realism, open-mindedness with accurate reasoning, bravery with self-regulation, persistence with perspective. Self-regulation is the ability to exert control over one's own responses (e.g. thoughts, emotions, impulses, performances, and other behaviours) so as to pursue goals and live up to standards (ideals, moral injunctions, norms, performance targets, others' expectations). The capacity to delay self-gratification is one of the main features of self-regulated individuals.

Temperance has been demonstrated by level-5 leaders, that is, those who are simultaneously modest and wilful, shy and fearless (Collins 2001), with characters such as Darwin Smith of Kimberly-Clark, and Colman Mockler of Gillette being mooted as candidates. Not seeking glory for themselves, they sacrificed personal gain for the good of their companies. Combining humility with courage, they did not hesitate to fight for the company. For example, Gillette was the target of a hostile takeover from Ronald Perelman, who aimed to break the company into pieces to finance other takeover raids. Although losing the opportunity for substantial personal gain, Colman Mockler, the company's CEO, did not sell his own shares (Barbe and Kleiner 2005; Collins 2001).

Goffee and Jones described Darwin Smith as 'shy, unpretentious and even awkward'. They considered that

'Smith looked more like a small-town hick than a corporate titan—an image he used to his advantage, both to stay close to the business, and to deflect

Table 5.1. Character strengths that express temperance

Strength	How individuals with this strength behave (examples)	Opposites	Excess
Forgiveness	• They respond positively (in a benevolent, kind and generous way) to transgressions by offering mercy instead of vengeance, avoidance or malevolence. • They do not develop bad feelings when people make them angry. • They do not hold a grudge for very long.	Unforgivingness; mercilessness; vengeance; spitefulness.	Sanctimoniousness.
Humility/ modesty	• They have an accurate sense of their abilities and achievements. • They let their accomplishments speak for themselves. • They do not seek the spotlight. • They acknowledge mistakes and imperfections. • They regard themselves as fortunate to be in positions when good things happened to them.	Immodesty; grandiosity; pomposity; pride; arrogance; vanity; bragging.	Self-mortification; unctuousness.
Prudence	• They choose judicious goals. • They demonstrate farsighted concern for the consequences of their actions and decisions. • They resist impulses that satisfy shorter-term goals at the expense of long-term ones. • They have a flexible and moderate approach to life. • They balance the multiple plans, aims, and aspirations that motivate them. • They are reflective, deliberate, and practical.	Imprudence; recklessness; irresponsibility; carelessness.	Timidity; risk aversion.
Self-regulation (self-control)	• They are able to delay gratification. • They are able to avoid doing things that they think they should not do. • They are able to regulate or control excesses of all types. • They are morally disciplined. • They avoid things that are bad for them in the long run, even if they are fun in the short run.	Intemperance; impulsiveness; explosiveness; wildness; out of control; libertinage; lust.	Rigidity; anal-retentiveness.

unwanted outside attention. Smith was a geek before geeks became fashionable. Yet, under his quiet rule, Kimberly-Clark outperformed not only competitors like Procter & Gamble, but also GE, Hewlett-Packard, Coca-Cola, 3M and every other star of corporate America'. (Goffee and Jones 2006: 34)

Jim Collins (2001: 68) referred to Darwin Smith as follows:

Compared with [CEOs like Iacocca, Dunlap, Welch, and Gault, who make headlines and become celebrities], Darwin Smith seems to have come from Mars. Shy, unpretentious, even awkward, Smith shunned attention (. . .). But if you were to consider Smith soft or meek, you would be terribly mistaken. His lack of pretense was coupled with a fierce, even stoic, resolve toward life.

The reference to stoicism is relevant here: neither humility nor prudence and temperance should be equated with submission, self-abasement, weakness, or softness. Humility is a realistic evaluation of one's contribution as well as the recognition of the contribution of others and the role of circumstances (Solomon 1999). Donald Keough, former CEO of The Coca-Cola Company, suggested that temperance is especially relevant for contemporary leaders, who manage in a scrutiny-intensive world. In his view, some leading executives go to great lengths to reach the status of celebrities, a temptation that may have very serious ethical implications (Keough 2008). Courting the limelight and seeing one's name in print and oneself on television is hardly conducive to a focus on the more humdrum details of running an organization effectively. Moreover, there is always the problem of routinizing the charisma that can be manufactured around a celebrity CEO. Australian Zoo founder, Steve Irwin, the 'Crocodile Man', built a charismatic and colourful image around his adventures with wildlife, through a television show that was extremely popular around the world. However, in an accident, a sting ray killed him while he was filming and diving off the Barrier Reef, getting closer to dangerous nature than was prudent. As the face of the Australian Zoo, this posed an immediate problem for the surviving leader of the business, his widow. She resolved this by pushing her young daughter, Bindy Irwin, into the limelight as the new 'face' of the business. What had previously been seen as clever marketing by many observers now became seen as excessively manipulative of a vulnerable young person. The same problem of the routinization of charisma will also face other businesses, such as the Virgin empire, which rely on celebrity CEO branding.

If intemperance (i.e. hubris, narcissism, arrogance, selfishness) may have catastrophic consequences for domestic leaders themselves, their organizations, and society (Kellerman 2004), the impact is stronger when global operations and cross-cultural issues need to be dealt with (Vera and Rodriguez-Lopez 2004). In a boundaryless world characterized by 24-hour communication, the intemperance of a global leader in one part of the world may trigger a worldwide chain reaction, undermine the company's reputation, weaken trust between employees and the firm and its leaders, and damage the company's market value.

Next we discuss how temperance contributes to the global leaders' positive performance (synthesis in Table 5.2). Although the four strengths have similarities (they all represent any form of auspicious self-constraint or self-control), and reveal reciprocal influences (e.g. prudence and forgiveness tend to require some level of self-regulation), they make unique contributions to the global leaders' positive performance.

Forgiveness and mercy for building social capital

Forgiveness is an almost neglected topic in management studies (Bright 2006; Bright et al. 2008). However, together with love and trust, forgiveness is a critical value of virtuous leaders (Caldwell and Dixon 2010). Forgiveness has several benefits at the individual and collective levels. Individuals experience physiological and psychological healing, less illness and stress, greater creativity and learning, enhanced cardiovascular fitness, emotional stability, better social relationships and happiness. Forgiving another person does not mean *forgetting* or excusing him/her from being accountable but allows that person to regain self-esteem and to restore his/her ability to work together comfortably with the other (Bright 2006; Bright et al. 2008). As Enright suggested, forgiveness benefits the forgiver far more than the person being forgiven (Enright 2001; see also Bright 2006).

At the collective level, forgiveness helps to repair workplace relationships, to develop cooperative efforts, to restore relations and positive emotions, and to create a safe culture (Edmondson 1999) where risk-taking and creativity are encouraged, and individuals feel that they can pursue their potential in spite of committing mistakes and failures. Nelson Mandela, who was in jail for twenty-seven years, forgave his jailers and enemies, fostering national reconciliation.

Global leaders with strong forgiveness are more prepared to develop social connectedness and richer social capital (Beechler and Javidan 2007; Bono and McCullough 2006; Bono et al. 2008; McCullough et al. 2009; Tsang et al. 2006). They are potentially more prepared to resolve conflicts constructively, to foster cooperation and to promote justice, thus developing better relationships and managing conflicts more effectively. They are more tolerant when facing misunderstandings resulting from cross-cultural differences and conflicts, thus being able to develop positive cross-cultural interactions and global organizational networks, and are better able to express cultural adaptability when carrying out international assignments. Global leaders with strong forgiveness are also more likely to experience better physical and psychological health, and well-being, optimism, and self-efficacy (Bono and McCullough 2006; Bono et al. 2008; Cameron and Caza 2002; McCullough et al. 2009)—thus facing challenges with more vitality, a strength that helps them to deal effectively with the demands of their role and promotes their positive performance. Through contagion effects, global leaders may also promote forgiveness within the companies with which they interact, thus buffering and amplifying positive effects (Bright 2006; Cameron and Caza 2002; Cameron et al. 2004; Grant 2008b) across a wide range of organizations. Forgiveness relates to agreeableness and emotional stability (Peterson and Seligman 2004), both referred to by Caligiuri (2006) as important resources for global leader effectiveness.

Humility: the light of hidden gems

The word 'humility' comes from the Latin *humus*, meaning earth or ground (Gunn and Gullickson 2006). To be humble is to be grounded. Several authors have considered humility a noble quality of any effective and strong leader (Bright 2006; Ferch 2004). To make wiser decisions about where to invest his money during the dotcom boom, a venture capitalist visited the corporate offices and the personal neighbourhood of the entrepreneur seeking funding (Delbecq 2008). The aim was to perceive the degree to which the funding demander was grounded or narcissistic. Humility is the mid-point between two negative extremes: arrogance and lack of self-esteem (Vera and Rodriguez-Lopez 2004). Damon considered humility, one's willingness to admit imperfections, and to correct them, as the private side of integrity. In his view, honesty and humility are critical aspects in the business world. Honest and humble people tend to learn more and to cause no harm in the long run (Damon 2004).

Humility, an 'admirable virtue' (Damon 2004), is often seen as being embodied by Nelson Mandela, perhaps the closest contemporary example of a secular saint (Stengel 2008). Individuals with humility thrive intellectually and emotionally, because it provides them with an open-mindedness enabling them to continue learning and build a sense of teamwork with other people. Empirical studies have shown that humility is connected to leadership effectiveness (Reave 2005), with Vera and Rodriguez-Lopez (2004: 393) presenting it as a source of competitive advantage:

> Humility is frequently associated with shyness, lack of ambition, passivity, or lack of confidence. We argue quite the opposite—that humility offers strategic value for firms by furnishing organizational members with a realistic perspective of themselves, the firm, and the environment. In fact, we propose that humility is a critical strength for leaders and organizations possessing it, and a dangerous weakness for those lacking it.

Developing humility is a necessary virtue for global leaders, especially when they operate in cultures where individualistic values and the 'great person' views of leaders and leadership prevail (Delbecq 2008). The powerful position and notoriety of 'great leaders', as well as the symbolic apparatus that surrounds them, makes such people vulnerable to temptations of hubris and dominance, with perverse consequences for strategic decision-making and the development of fruitful and transparent relationships with stakeholders. Humble leaders tend to be better listeners, to develop healthier social relationships, and to surround themselves with talented people (Gunther and Neal 2008). Humility is also important to hold one's ego in check.

Such signs of respect may be relevant, for example, when cross-country mergers and acquisitions occur. After Publicis (Paris) acquired Saatchi (London), in the first meeting of executives of both companies, Saatchi's chairman, who was British, made his opening speech in French, although he was not fluent and Publicis' executives were English-speakers (Kanter 2010). After acquiring a French company, the leaders of an Indian company suspended their no-alcohol rule to serve French wine, including in their headquarters in India (Kanter 2010).

When combined with courage, prudence, and self-regulation, humility may be a powerful source of personal and organizational resilience. Anne Mulcahy never planned or expected to become CEO of Xerox (Caminiti 2005). Knowing and assuming that she lacked financial expertise, she turned humbly to the experts to educate her about balance-sheet management (George 2009). She stayed away from the media spotlight (Collins 2009), avoiding stock analysts and reporters, and eschewed fame and publicity (Caminiti 2005; Adams and Shook 2008). With such strengths, she led the rescue of Xerox from near bankruptcy, leading by example, flying anywhere to meet a customer (Adams and Shook 2008), and developing trust bonds among tens of thousands of people working worldwide. She was described as a 'hidden gem' (Adams and Shook 2008).

Vera and Rodriguez-Lopez (2004) pointed out several features of humility with relevance for global leadership. For example, being open to new paradigms is crucial for understanding different social, economic, political, and cultural contexts, and for adopting new approaches when dealing with diverse markets, people, and entities. Humility feeds the ability to listen and learn (Gunn and Gullickson 2006). By acknowledging one's own limitations and mistakes, and attempting to correct them, global leaders are better prepared to face different contexts with interest and respect, and to learn from cultural mistakes.

Asking for advice is crucial when entering new markets and interacting with diverse employees, customers, suppliers, and authorities. It is also important in being able to accept criticism and bad news, especially those about one's mistakes and failures, as well as to incorporate the insights of others into decisions (Delbecq 2008). During World War II, Winston Churchill created a special office whose duty was to bring him bad news, in order to know the truth, no matter what it was (Keough 2008). On the contrary, Hitler was surrounded by good news messengers, the consequence being that he thought he was still winning the war when defeat was imminent. Keough stressed that, to be an effective leader, it is necessary 'to find ways to break out of the isolation and bunker mentality that many bosses find so tempting' (Keough 2008: 51). Hubris will encourage leaders to conduct their managerial manoeuvres in the dark, sure of their own judgement and thus needing no advice from others (Gunther and Neal 2008).

Encouraging others may be essential for increasing human capital in developing countries and thus reducing expatriation costs. Sharing honour and recognition with employees is crucial to being accepted and respected in unfamiliar contexts. By recognizing organizational members' efforts worldwide, a global leader provides them with opportunities for performing meaningful work and experiencing feelings of higher purpose (Damon 2004). Through their example, humble leaders are also able to promote organizational humility and, indirectly, competitive advantage, because humility is a VRIN resource: valuable, rare, irreplaceable, and non-imitable (Vera and Rodriguez-Lopez 2004). Humility may foster organizational learning, service, and organizational resilience.

A humble global leader is in principle more willing and prepared to accept and be comfortable with the ambiguity surrounding international and cross-cultural activities, than one who is less humble (Distefano 1995). (S)he is also more able to look at what customers are saying and what competitors are doing (Mulchay, in Gunn and Gullickson 2006). Having less reason to protect self-esteem (Peterson and Seligman 2004; Vera and Rodriguez-Lopez 2004), the humble leader may be more cautious and more able to conserve emotional and psychological resources when dealing with complex and ambiguous cross-cultural issues. Such psychological resources may help him/her to avoid intemperate, unrealistic, or dangerous ambitions, and to develop more positive relationships with their interlocutors from diverse cultural contexts.

Humility may also help global leaders focus on developing people's commitment and dedication to the organization and its mission rather than seeking their dedication to the leader him/herself. Global leaders must accept that the organization is larger than any of its members. As a consequence, people will not be following a leader but a set of values that result from the organization's identity (Kanter 2010). When Percy Barnevik, former CEO of ABB, selected executives to act as pillars of a new global company (Vera and Rodriguez-Lopez 2004), he ascribed higher relevance to humility and respect for other cultures than to language acquisition and international experiences. Humility is important for leaders and its absence is a weakness for those who lack it (Vera and Rodriguez-Lopez 2004) because humble leaders develop more adequate views of the world, including an awareness of the limitations of their representations about the world.

Various business leaders, such as Sam Walton (Wal-Mart), Herb Kelleher (Southwest Airlines), Ingvar Kamprad (Ikea), Mary Kay Ash (Mary Kay Inc), Norberto Odebrecht (Odebrecht Organization), William Pollard (ServiceMaster Industries), Darwin Smith (Kimberly-Clark) and Konosuke Matsushita (Matsushita Electric), have all been touted as humble. For example, in an international meeting of the organization's executives, after explaining that the corporation was delivering outstanding performance, Odebrecht warned about the risks of being dazzled by success and forgetting the qualities—particularly humility—that promoted such success in the first place. Matsushita was known for his determination to eradicate complacency and arrogance in the company.

Humility may be especially important when operating in countries where this strength is greatly valued. For example, Khaliq Ahmad (2001: 96) suggested the following advice for leading in Malaysia:

> Do not adopt an elitist attitude, but learn to be modest and humble. Avoid magnifying differences in status by downplaying one's symbols of achievement (car, big office, etc.) and by reducing one's 'distance' from others. (. . .). A humble leader is often respected by subordinates as he/she comes across as being an approachable person who is able to communicate in the language of dignity. This is illustrated in the saying: 'Mengikut resmi padi makin berisi

makin tunduk, bukan seperti lalang, makin tinggi makin melayang', which in English means 'Be like the paddy (rice) plant, the heavier it gets, the lower it bows; be not like the hay grass, the taller it gets, the more the seeds get wafted away.'

Prudence: practical wisdom for wiser decisions

Kane and Patapan (2006: 711) defined prudence as 'the ability to make sound decisions under complex, ever-changeable conditions. (...) A truly prudent person judges thoughtfully and acts decisively, reconciling the demands of the most important with those of the most pressing'. Aristotle (1999) observed that one cannot strive for good without practical wisdom. Nor can one be practically wise in the absence of moral virtue. It is prudence, in this sense, that ensures the rightness of the means we adopt to reach virtuous aims.

Prudence enables individuals to choose wise means for reaching valuable aims, to be careful about their choices and consequences, and to avoid making and saying things that may later be regretted. Prudence may be considered the result of combining intellectual capacity with all other virtues (Kane and Patapan 2006). Its small role in management theory notwithstanding, prudence is crucial for ethical decision-making (Bastons 2008). Domènec Melé (2010: 643), a business ethics professor, noted that prudence

> helped by respect and benevolence for persons and a real contribution to the common good, not only determines what alternatives are not ethically acceptable but also helps to solve dilemmas and above all, identifies which alternative can bring about the greater human good. [Prudence] should be the main driver for decision making.

Prudence is an important feature of virtuous and excellent leaders in general (Collins 2001; Flynn 2008; Kane and Patapan 2006; Mendonca 2001; Tredget 2010; Whetstone 2003). However, the greater uncertainty, complexity, and diversity that global leaders face when operating worldwide makes this virtue especially relevant for fostering their performance and helping them to improve the condition of the world (Kanter 2010). Prudence helps global leaders to consider the merits of alternate paths when facing ethical dilemmas.

A typical dilemma may emerge when a company considers leaving a country in protest against human rights abuses, thus protecting the company's reputation and pressuring authorities of such a country, rather than investing in the country in order to preserve actual and future organization interests, although hurting its reputation in doing so (Beaver 1995). In such situations, global leaders may be forced to adopt moral compromises in such a way that, in order to protect one set of relevant values, it is necessary to sacrifice another important set of values (Brenkert 2009).

Prudence is also crucial for developing cultural intelligence (Alon and Higgins 2005; Earley et al. 2007; Ng et al. 2009), a concept that captures a person's capability to adapt effectively to new cultural contexts and to interact within diverse teams or organizations (Kanter 2010). With prudence, global leaders avoid jumping to conclusions when dealing with distant cultures. They may make better decisions when working abroad, be more inclined to accept coaching before starting an international assignment (Otazo 1999), and they are more effective in dealing with non-democratic or corrupt governments.

Prudence is also indispensable for being cautious in reacting to alarming news in the media and to NGO protests and claims (George 2009; Swartz 2010). Jeff Swartz, President and CEO of Timberland, expressed prudence when he had to deal with '65,000 angry activists', supporters of Greenpeace, who sent e-mails (1 June 2009) to the company protesting against its alleged use of leather sourced from animals from deforested areas of the Amazon. In fact, only about 7 per cent of the leather used by the company was sourced from Brazil. On the other hand, deforestation tops the list of the environmental priorities of Timberland: 'We've planted a million trees in China; we host community regreening events in cities all over the world. Our logo is a tree, for crying out loud. How much more ridiculous could this campaign be?' (Swartz 2010: 40).

Swartz's first response was anger, but he soon realized that he did not want to be portrayed as a corporate bully or as a victim (Swartz 2010). Although feeling angry about the large amount of protest messages and their content, Swartz adopted a careful way forward, preserving the company's reputation and interests, without battling against Greenpeace. He eventually admitted that: (1) Greenpeace was asking a good and legitimate question: where did Timberland leather come from? (2) Timberland did not know the answer to this question; (3) the company might learn and benefit from outside perspectives, which could help its sustainability-oriented culture.

One of the first of Swartz's frustrations came from the leather supplier not knowing where the ranchers grazed their cattle. However, some weeks later, in a context in which there were mounting pressures from other companies (e.g. Nike) on leather suppliers, Timberland reached an agreement with its supplier according to which the supplier would certify that the hides did not come from deforested areas. Meanwhile, the company started to reply to Greenpeace e-mailers in different languages, according to the nationality of their Internet address. Some protesters replied in a positive tone. At the end of July 2009, Timberland issued a statement, praising Greenpeace for bringing the matter to the industry's attention. In return, Greenpeace issued a statement ('as gratifying as praise' said Swartz (2010: 43)), saying that Timberland had taken a leadership position on the issue (http://www. greenpeace.org/international/press/releases/greenpeace-praises-timberland; press release, 29 July 2009; retrieved 12 September 2010).

Swartz summarized the lessons learned: (1) 'when angry activists come at you, don't stand there with your arms folded and your mind closed', rather look at possible common goals and admit that the issues raised may be legitimate; (2) 'don't greet them naively with open arms', since that for every common goal, other personal and unwanted goals are at play; (3) 'in times of tension, watch and listen.' When one reads Swartz's 2010 *Harvard Business Review* article, where the story is reported, his prudence clearly emerges: Swartz acknowledges the effectiveness of what he called Greenpeace's 'guerrilla tactics' but is cautious about pointing out its flaws. The contribution of stakeholders such as Greenpeace helped Timberland renew its engagement in becoming a more responsible and sustainable organization.

In contrast, Tony Hayward, former CEO of BP, when dealing with the Deepwater Horizon platform catastrophe, followed an imprudent path. *Newsweek* (14 May 2010) quoted him as having said that the Gulf of Mexico 'is a very big ocean. The amount of volume of oil and dispersant we are putting into it is tiny in relation to the total water volume.' He not only undervalued the extent of the catastrophe, and appeared to have ignored safety warnings before the rig exploded (Mason and Roberts 2010), but he made several other gaffes and mistakes—including spending a weekend watching a yacht race in Britain, as workers continued to clear up the spill when it already covered an area the size of Luxembourg (Eden 2010; Mason and Roberts 2010), and saying that he would 'like to get his life back', an extremely insensitive remark given the loss of eleven lives in the rig accident. While Jacquelin Magnay argued that Hayward's sailing day may have offered the CEO a fresh new appreciation for the beauty of sea that his firm's exploding rig had despoiled, this might be little consolation for those whose lives and livelihoods suffered from the oil spill (Magnay 2010). *The Economist* (2010a) also wrote:

> When Tony Hayward said 'I'd like my life back' on May 30th, losing his job as boss of BP was probably not what he had in mind. But on July 27th he

accepted the inevitable. On his watch, zillions of gallons of oil spilled into the Gulf of Mexico. When the microphones were on, gaffes gushed from his lips. He was a walking public-relations disaster and had to go.

Imprudent actions and words also forged the hostility of the US government authorities against Hayward and BP in a demonstration of how the relationship between politicians and multinational companies is delicate (Kanter 2010). Ben Heineman, former general counsel for GE, argued that companies need their own 'foreign policy' (Kanter 2010), a mode of life that requires not only prudence but also a combination of wisdom, open-mindedness, courage, and social intelligence (i.e. diplomacy). Some authors suggest that imprudence may be a 'stain' in BP's culture, considering that the company has failed to learn from the long list of crises and accidents in its history, being arrogant and seemingly unable to learn from mistakes. Success may blind companies to some very real dangers (Lyall et al. 2010).

Hayward is but a recent case in a long and dishonourable line of corporate clowns. In an unguarded moment, while making a 1991 speech to the British Institute of Directors, Gerald Ratner, the owner of a family firm of UK high-street jewellers, Ratners, referred to the products he sold in the following terms: 'We also do cut-glass sherry decanters complete with six glasses on a silver-plated tray that your butler can serve you drinks on, all for £4.95. People say, "How can you sell this for such a low price?" I say, "because it's total crap"'. He then went on to say that some of the earrings his shops sold were 'cheaper than an M&S prawn sandwich but probably wouldn't last as long' (*The Telegraph* 2007). The company almost collapsed into bankruptcy as its stock plummeted after this speech was widely reported. It may have been an honest observation, if a little colourful, but it was hardly temperate. In contrary cases, global leaders' temperance, especially in crisis situations (Powley and Taylor 2006), may have a strong symbolic value in consolidating and cohering the efforts and energies of company stakeholders operating in different and distant cultural contexts.

Self-regulation to develop personal and organizational discipline

Self-regulation has also been suggested as important for global leaders (Jokinen 2005), the alleged intemperance of Dominique Strauss-Kahn, the former International Monetary Fund chief, with respect to sexual impulses, being emblematic. For global leaders self-reflection is crucial (a) to avoid being dazzled by the media spotlight, (b) to practise self-restraint rather than make megalomaniac decisions just because one can, (c) to make decisions that respect the interests and rights of poor communities in developing countries, (d) to respect partners with fragile power positions in developing countries (Tavis 2000), (e) to self-restrain from exploiting the absence of effective regulatory checks in some contexts (Fort and Schipani 2004), (f) to avoid unethical opportunities when working in remote cultures where human rights are disregarded, and (g) to avoid consumption habits that may appear extravagant, ostentatious, and disrespectful when working in poor communities and interacting with people from deprived economic contexts.

Self-regulation was not evident when German and American managers blamed each other reciprocally with regard to DaimlerChrysler's debacle (Adler 2002). American managers blamed the company's 50 per cent drop in value on the 'bull-headed, dominant, and just plain dishonest' German managers. German managers blamed their American counterparts whom they described as 'unworldly and too focused on the bottom line' (Adler 2002: 256). Intemperance may also explain Green Giant's move from California to Mexico. The company transferred agricultural and food-packaging operations from the Salinas Valley in California (wages being $7.50 per hour) to Irapuato in Mexico ($0.62). In spite of the economic development the move brought to the area, a perverse consequence of the relocation was an extreme diminution of the water table, which created environmental devastation and social resentment (Fort and Schipani 2004).

Self-regulation may prevent global leaders from making Napoleonic-style acquisitions (Kroll et al. 2000) fed by hubris and driven by personal self-aggrandizement (Bollaert and Petit 2010; Hayward and Hambrick 1997; Morck et al. 1990; Roll 1986; Seth et al. 2000). Warren Buffett ironically argued (1981 Berkshire Hathaway Annual Report) 'that many corporate acquirers think of themselves as beautiful princesses, sure that their kisses can turn toads into handsome princes. The acquirers pay substantial premiums over market value, believing that they can release the imprisoned princes. (. . .) But (. . .) we've observed many kisses but very few miracles' (Hayward and Hambrick 1997: 103). One possible consequence of this kind of acquisition is what has been called 'diworsification' (Orfalea et al. 2008), as exemplified by the cases of Daimler and Chrysler, Time Warner and AOL, Kmart and Sears, Quaker Oats, and Snapple (Keough 2008: 95).

An example of potential corporate hubris was the buy-out of Word-Perfect by Novell, in March 1994 (Kroll et al. 2000). Observers suggested that, behind the deal, there was an attempt to build an empire comparable to Microsoft's. Raymond Noorda, Novell's CEO, offered $1.4 billion for WordPerfect. However, Novell's rude managerial approach toward Word-Perfect led to a haemorrhage of managerial and technical talent in the acquired company. The consequence was that the performance of Word-Perfect fell off, and Novell was forced to sell WordPerfect for less than 10 per cent of what it paid to buy it.

In contrast, self-regulation may be crucial in making a successful corporate turnaround. Lou Gerstner showed self-regulation when taking the helm of IBM. In opposition to HP's Carly Fiorina, who promoted her media image as a celebrity CEO (Malone 2007), he stayed away from the media, 'never allowing hype to precede results' (Collins 2009: 165). Adopting an attitude of personal discipline (e.g. by self-regulating), engaging in the practice of under promising and over delivering (Collins 2009), and fostering a culture of discipline, he led the restoration of the greatness of IBM. Jim Collins referred to him in the following terms: 'Gerstner came in as a savior CEO yet clearly had the discipline to make difficult decisions (and to resist making panicky decisions). (...) In the end, Gerstner was clearly ambitious for IBM first and foremost, beyond himself' (Collins 2009: 162).

In contrast, a lack of self-regulation may lead global leaders to intemperate decisions with perverse consequences at the global level. Behaviours such as those of Denis Kozlowski, former CEO of Tyco, who spent $2 million in a week-long birthday party for his wife and used company resources to support a sumptuous life (Bragues 2006; Collins 2009; Kellerman 2004; Vera and Rodriguez-Lopez 2004), damaged employees' commitment worldwide. *Business Week* (28 May 2001) once lauded Kozlowski as the most aggressive CEO in the US but eventually came to describe him as a 'scoundrel' (Ketchen et al. 2008) in spite of their earlier endorsement of his bravery and vitality. Intemperance may lead to fraudulent accounting, dishonest procedures, and to legal problems with negative personal and organizational impact. Virtues need to be both coherent and consistent; those who were once heroes can readily become villains.

In many Asian cultures, displaying emotions is interpreted as a lack of self-control, and thus as a sign of weak leadership, something that requires global leaders working as expatriates to watch closely: in such contexts, self-regulation is crucial for managing emotional expression (Den Hartog 2004; Forster 2000; Hendon 2001; Weiss and Stripp 1998). Self-regulation helps in developing cultural intelligence (Earley and Mosakowski 2004; Earley et al. 2007) and in adopting behaviours and attitudes that accord with the norms of different cultural contexts. Forster (2000: 64) explained the process:

For the Chinese, displaying emotion violates face-saving norms by disrupting harmony and causing conflict. In the West, a smile is usually a sign of happiness or friendly affirmation; in Japan, this can also be used to avoid answering a question or to mask an emotion. Sitting with crossed knees in the West is socially acceptable; in many Arabic cultures it is deeply offensive as it shows the sole of your foot. In Vietnam, men often express friendship by touching each other during conversations; in the UK, America or Australia this would be considered inappropriate. In many Muslim countries, touching the head is deeply offensive whereas touching the shoulders is seen as a sign of brotherhood. In Korea, young people are socially forbidden from touching the shoulders of their elders.

In negotiating with Thais, Hendon (2001: 47) recommended:

Farangs [i.e. foreigners] should never lose control of their emotions, and they should not be overly assertive. This is considered poor manners. Because Thais avoid confrontation at all costs, they will usually try not to say 'no' (This is similar to the Japanese negotiating style). Instead of saying 'no', they often make implausible excuses or pretend they do not understand English. They may tell you they must check with higher authorities, even when such precedent does not exist. Likewise, Thais find it difficult to accept a direct negative answer from you. So when you have to say 'no', say it indirectly whenever possible.

The above examples show how leaders from both East and West need to adjust their behaviours to fit local cultural norms. Self-regulation is necessary to avoid cultural mistakes and to preserve good business and personal relationships. Without self-regulation, how can a global leader from Europe or the US deal with a Thai (or Arab) partner who, during a negotiation process, takes his hand and holds it? How could (s)he refrain from expressing irritation after perceiving that his/her Japanese partner responds to an offer with a lengthy silence or with an ambiguous 'yes' (Fujio 2004)? How could a global leader used to a monochronic culture refrain from expressing annoyance after observing that his Portuguese partner arrives at an important business meeting twenty minutes after the time scheduled with a smile, without showing any signs of discomfort (Cunha and Cunha 2004; Schuster and Copeland 1999)? How can an assertive leader from the US, accustomed to saying 'yes' when she means 'yes' and 'no' when she means 'no', constrain her habitual assertiveness in dealing with partners from more indirect, non-assertive cultures? How can a global leader from Thailand or China learn to behave assertively towards Western business partners?

Table 5.2. Temperance assisting several global leaders' activities

Forgiveness and mercy	• Developing social connectedness and social capital.
	• Fostering cooperation and promoting justice.
	• Facing misunderstandings resulting from cross-cultural differences and conflicts. Resolving conflicts constructively.
	• Developing better cultural adaptability when carrying out international assignments.
	• Promoting forgiveness in stakeholders worldwide, thus facilitating buffering and amplifying positive effects across a wide range of organizations.
	• Experiencing better physical and psychological health, and higher well-being, optimism and self-efficacy—thus facing challenges and endeavours with more vitality.
Humility/ modesty	• Being open to new paradigms, thus understanding and respecting different social, economic, political, and cultural contexts, and adopting new approaches when dealing with diverse markets, peoples, and entities.
	• Acknowledging one's own limitations and mistakes, thus being better able to face different contexts with interest and respect, and to learn from cultural mistakes.
	• Looking at what customers are saying and what competitors are doing.
	• Asking for advice, thus being more able to enter new markets and interact with diverse employees, customers, suppliers, and authorities.
	• Hearing 'bad news' and knowing the truth worldwide.
	• Developing others, thus increasing human capital in developing countries and reducing costs with expatriation.
	• Recognizing organizational members' efforts worldwide (instead of gather the laurels for him/herself), thus providing them with opportunities for performing meaningful work and experiencing feelings of high purpose.
	• Promoting organizational humility.
	• Accepting and experiencing comfort with the ambiguity surrounding international and cross-cultural activities.
	• Developing the people's commitment and dedication to the organization rather than to the leader him/herself.
	• Avoiding intemperate, unrealistic, or dangerous ambitions.
Prudence	• Weighting several paths for facing ethical dilemmas in idiosyncratic contexts.
	• Adopting moral compromises.
	• Developing cultural intelligence.
	• Avoiding jumping to conclusions when dealing with culturally distant behaviours and attitudes.
	• Making a wise decision when invited to work abroad.
	• Accepting mentoring or coaching before starting and during international assignments.
	• Dealing effectively with non-democratic governments.
	• Being cautious in reacting to media alarming news and to NGO protests and claims.
	• Performing corporate diplomacy.

Self-regulation	• Avoiding being dazzled by the media spotlight.
	• Practising self-restraint rather than making megalomaniac decisions—just because one can.
	• Making decisions that respect the interests and rights of poor communities in developing countries. Respecting partners with fragile power positions in developing countries.
	• Avoiding 'vices' when working/acting in remote cultures where human rights are disregarded.
	• Avoiding consumption habits that may appear extravagant, ostentatious, and disrespectful when interacting with people from deprived economic contexts.
	• Avoiding 'absurdly' overpriced and 'Napoleonic' acquisitions.
	• Adopting and developing personal and organizational discipline for being successful in a complex corporate turnaround.
	• Avoiding displaying emotions when working in some cultural contexts.
	• Developing cultural intelligence and adopting behaviours and attitudes according to the norms of different cultural contexts.

Potential dangers of excessive temperance

When global leaders' temperance is developed to an excessive extent, their performance may suffer. Excessive forgiveness and mercy may lead global leaders to neglect the real dangers of forgiving and restoring relationships with unethical individuals (McCullough et al. 2009). Although such risks may confront any leader, the dangers are magnified for leaders who interact with individuals from several cultures, with different moral values and ethical compasses. Some extra awareness may be necessary for operating worldwide, including when involved in negotiations with parties from distant cultures.

Excessive humility may lead global leaders to ask for advice too often and, because they recognize their own limitations and mistakes, to lose credibility and trust when working with people from cultures where strong leaders are more valued (Jackson 2002; Javidan et al. 2006; Otazo 1999). Too much humility, especially if unaccompanied by courage, may also lead to a lack of ambition and to passivity, increasing vulnerability to abusive behaviours, especially in cultures with less well-developed humanitarian orientations and where this strength does not fit local implicit theories of leadership. The risks are lower in cultures where modesty is more appreciated (Yifeng and Tjosvold 2008: 145):

> In American society, with its heavy emphasis on the individual, one tends to attribute success to one's own talent and effort. In the Chinese tradition,

> however, individuals are expected to give credit not only to themselves but also to their family, colleagues, or even the whole society for 'personal' success. To the Chinese managers, 'personal satisfaction' may have a smack of selfishness or an unbecoming lack of modesty. (Farh et al. 1991)

Excessive prudence may lead to timid and delayed decisions, to inaction, and to overt risk aversion. Global leaders with excessive prudence may overvalue the risks of investment in some developing countries and disinvest as soon as the first sign of political, economic, or social turmoil emerges, and be excessively cautious when making international deals, thus losing opportunities (Brett 2001). They may be unable to adopt moral compromise proactively when facing serious ethical dilemmas, thus jeopardizing the pursuit of high values (Brenkert 2009). They may also develop excessive fear of accepting a difficult, although necessary, international assignment and wrongly withdraw from informing the media when they ask for data about the company's procedures and strategy. Excessive prudence may even transform into cowardice.

Excessive self-regulation may lead global leaders to be too rigid, unable to take advantage of the good things that being a citizen of the world allows one to experience. A rigid posture towards life may lead to lower well-being and less rewarding interpersonal relationships. Global leaders with an excess of self-regulation may also be unreasonably demanding towards employees, requiring undue sacrifices from people unwilling or unable to make them. Excessive self-regulation may be especially negative when global leaders operate in cultures that value open expression of emotions and feelings, assertiveness and extroversion (Gannon and Pillai 2010; Jordan and Cartwright 1998).

Strengths of transcendence: experiencing meaning in life

Transcendence represents strengths that forge connections with the larger universe and help individuals to experience meaning in their lives, including in the workplace. Meaning is what Medtronic's leaders helped their employees to develop in nurturing their feelings of being part of a heroic cause pursuing a noble purpose (Freiberg and Freiberg 2004; George 2003). Annual events for employees from around the world were held with invited physicians and patients in which the ways that Medtronic products changed and saved lives was promoted. Doing this, the company has been able to instil a noble sense of purpose in employees, helping them ascribe meaning to their jobs, increasing work and organizational commitment. In such moments, employees cognitively and affectively connect their everyday work with a noble purpose. Manufacturing life-saving devices can thus become more than just an ordinary job (Freiberg and Freiberg 2004).

When employees see a connection with a higher purpose (Driver 2005) and experience meaning at work, they are often able to represent their contribution in more positive terms. The janitor working in a hospital can reconstruct herself as helping physicians to save lives; the cleaner at NASA can feel that he is helping to put a man on the moon (Freiberg and Freiberg 2004); a mason, rather than laying bricks, is helping to build a beautiful cathedral or temple to inspire worship and faith. Connections with purpose may work as the ties that bind employees and managers operating in different locations around the world (Den Hartog 2004).

Transcendence as a core virtue expresses itself in five character strengths (Table 5.3): appreciation of beauty and excellence, gratitude, hope, humour, and spirituality. Appreciation of beauty and excellence represents the ability to recognize and appreciate the existence of goodness in the world (Peterson and Seligman 2004). Its defining feature is the emotional experience of awe or wonder when the individual is in the presence of beauty and excellence. Gratitude is the sense of thankfulness and joy in response to a gift (e.g. a tangible benefit from a specific other; a moment of peaceful bliss evoked by natural beauty), and involves experiencing the transcendent emotion of grace. Hope refers to the process of thinking about the future with the expectation that the events one expects will materialize (Peterson and Seligman 2004). Humour involves several facets, such as the recognition that incongruity exists and can be approached playfully, a cheerful view on adversity that helps one to look on the bright side of life, and the desire to make others smile (Peterson and Seligman 2004). Humour makes our human condition more bearable (Peterson and Seligman 2004). Spirituality, the prototype of this category, refers to one's belief in a transcendent dimension of life (Peterson and Seligman 2004), which may involve religiousness, faith, and sense of purpose.

A common thread that connects strengths of transcendence is that each allows people to establish connections to a larger universe, instilling meaning in their lives. Appreciation of beauty and excellence connects the individual to excellence. Gratitude connects the individual with goodness. Hope connects the individual with the future. Humour connects the individual to troubles and contradictions in a way that produces pleasure. Spirituality connects the individual to the transcendent aspects of life. Next, we discuss how

Table 5.3. Character strengths through which transcendence is displayed

Strength	How individuals with this strength behave	Opposites	Excess
Appreciation of beauty and excellence (awe, wonder, and elevation)	• They notice excellence and beauty in their surroundings, and appreciate/admire it profoundly. • They reveal predilection to excitable feelings and actions motivated by broad interests and curiosity. • They appreciate and experience positive emotions when observing physical beauties, excellent skills and talents, and demonstrations of moral goodness.	Mindlessness; insensibility; philistinism; shallowness; triviality.	Bewitchment; 'the optimum is enemy of the good'.
Gratitude	• They appreciate each day they are alive. • They live life more as gift than as burden. • They feel grateful for achieving goals and successes with the help of others, and reciprocate generously. • They are able to feel thankful for bad things that happen. • They feel lucky, fortunate, and graced, often feeling 'I don't deserve this.'	Ingratitude; ungratefulness.	Excessively 'indebted' to everything and anything.
Hope (optimism; future-mindedness; future orientation)	• Despite challenges and difficulties, they remain hopeful about the future. • They look at the bright side of things. • They believe that 'every cloud has a silver lining. • They approach life as if every sad situation has a positive side. • When things are uncertain for them at work, they usually hope for the best. • They are optimistic about what will happen to them in the future.	Hopelessness; helplessness; pessimism; gloom.	Over-optimism; unrealism; neglecting risks.
Humour (playfulness)	• They are able to make others laugh. • They welcome the opportunity to brighten someone else's day with fun and laughter.	Humourless; sourness; tediousness.	Inconvenience; no sense of seriousness; buffoonery.

	• They try to add some humour to whatever they do. • They do not allow a gloomy situation to wash away their sense of humour. • They use amusing stories to defuse conflicts.		
Spirituality (religiousness; faith; purpose)	• They conduct life with a worthy purpose. • They believe in powers that are transcendent. • Their high purpose beliefs help them to understand the meanings of things they experience.	Spiritual emptiness; godlessness; purposelessness.	'Out-of-this- worldliness' (Solomon 1999); undue proselytism.

these different connectors nourish or facilitate global leaders' positive performance (for a summary see Table 5.4).

Appreciating beauty and excellence

Appreciation of beauty and excellence may promote global leaders' effectiveness and positive performance in multiple ways. A leader with this strength is more able to appreciate and learn what is distinctive, efficient, and excellent in certain parts of the world. Kanter noted that many IBMers who have worked across geographic boundaries talk with admiration about cultures such as the Japanese, 'because of team members who are punctual, courteous, and willing to talk in the middle of their night' (Kanter 2010: 601). The appreciation might be somewhat instrumental but it is an opening to the otherness of a different cultural patterning.

An appreciative leader is more likely to see beauty in what might otherwise be seen as the idiosyncratic habits and practices of people from developing countries, instead of adopting such an ethnocentric perspective depreciating different, seemingly less sophisticated, ways of life. (S)he is more likely to connect deeply with other people and to focus on perfecting local language proficiency, instead of assuming that 'English is *the* business language' or resorting to an interpreter. (S)he is also more able to develop a global mindset (Beechler and Javidan 2007) and cultural intelligence (Earley and Mosakowski 2004; Earley et al. 2007).

Appreciative leaders have less rigid views of right and wrong and are more motivated to accept and feel good living with diverse cultures, thus being less prone to experience cultural shock. In this way, they develop flourishing relationships with people from different contexts, including employees, customers, suppliers, joint-venture partners, and authorities. Global leaders with this strength are also able to forge a common identity among units operating worldwide, a common feeling of membership, a greater ability to be communicative, manage conflicts constructively and negotiate effectively, and a sense of community that works against centrifugal forces of fragmentation (Kanter 2010). Appreciation shares some similarity with openness to experience, a personality trait necessary for global leaders (Caligiuri 2006).

When employees in different parts of the world feel that the company's global leader appreciates the uniqueness of each place, they are more likely to develop similar appreciation, thus behaving more respectfully when interacting within cross-cultural teams. Global leaders' modelling and appreciation of differences potentially motivates employees from different cultural contexts to feel free to express more aspects of their identity at work (Kanter 2010), with this expressed diversity being a potential source of tolerance and innovation (Kanter 2010; Rego and Cunha 2008a).

Appreciating excellence in virtuous manners may help global leaders to attempt to achieve excellence, a crucial path to growth, and to compete effectively with strong global players. According to Csikszentmihalyi (2003), there is a transcendent motivation for being the best. Norman Augustine, former CEO and chairman of Lockheed Martin, described his motivation (Damon 2004: 117):

> [I]n truth, what I was trying to build was the greatest aerospace company in the world, and I thought that if we did that, maybe that would increase shareholder value. But to me you have to have a more lofty goal than making money.

Gratitude: celebrating goodness

Gratitude refers to having a life orientation according to which one celebrates what is good, and is grateful for what (s)he has, who (s)he is, and where (s)he is in life (Thompson et al. 2008). Gratitude does not mean having less ambition or adopting a passive look towards life. On the contrary, individuals with this strength adopt a 'cup half full' philosophy that offers them an adaptive approach to life. Gratitude

(Ketchen et al. 2008) led Warren Buffett to consider that he won what he called an 'ovarian lottery': being born in the US within a wonderful family and with access to decent schools, which his philanthropic endeavours (Schroeder 2009) acknowledge, 'giving back to society and helping out where governments are failing' (Schwass and Lief 2008: 1). Ketchen Jr, Adams, and Shook (2008: 531) described Buffett as follows:

> Despite Buffett's immense wealth and success, his reputation centers on humility and generosity. Buffett avoids the glitz of Wall Street, and has lived for 50 years in a house he bought in Omaha, Nebraska for $31,000. Meanwhile, his 2006 donation of approximately $30 billion to the Bill and Melinda Gates Foundation was the largest charitable gift in history.

Research shows that gratitude fosters and sustains positive and supportive social relations (Bartlett and DeSteno 2006; Bono and McCullough 2006; McCullough et al. 2002; McCullough et al. 2001; McCullough et al. 2008). Individuals with higher levels of gratitude are also happier, more enthusiastic, interested, hopeful, optimistic, energetic and determined, more satisfied with life, and healthier (Bono and McCullough 2006; McCullough et al. 2004; Polak and McCullough 2006). A grateful global leader can be expected to face 'global life' with more vitality, a strength that serves several global leaders' relevant activities and roles. It is also likely, through reciprocity and contagion effects, that grateful global leaders will spread trust, gratitude, and other positive emotions across the organization, in this way nourishing virtuous spirals (Fredrickson 2003; Fredrickson and Joiner 2002) and promoting extra-role behaviours that improve organizational performance (Organ and Paine 2000; Rego and Cunha 2008b). Gratitude may also make global leaders develop corporate missions and visions with a high purpose.

Grateful global leaders are more able to develop cultural intelligence (Earley and Mosakowski 2004; Earley et al. 2007). Instead of declining a difficult international assignment, they experience enthusiasm and gratitude for having such an opportunity, and these reactions foster their cross-cultural adjustment and performance. They appreciate the opportunities to meet people and work in different places around the world, instead of assuming negative visions of less sophisticated ways of life. Feeling grateful for living abroad and for interacting with people from different cultures, global leaders are more able to respect individuals and entities, thus developing positive global networks, from which knowledge, wisdom, and useful insights can be gathered to make better decisions. Grateful global leaders face cultural difficulties with hardiness and the desire to learn from mistakes, experiencing higher cross-cultural adjustment and performance when working abroad.

They are also more likely to develop humility. As a consequence (Vera and Rodriguez-Lopez 2004), they (a) are more open to new paradigms, thus being more capable of revising ineffective strategies, (b) acknowledge their own limitations and mistakes, thus making efforts to develop leadership competencies, (c) ask for advice, being more effective when difficult decisions need to be made in a context of high ambiguity and complexity, (d) develop others, thus strengthening social and human capital, (e) share honours and recognition, thus increasing psychological capital, motivation, commitment, and performance of other leaders and employees worldwide (Reave 2005) and (f) experience comfort with the ambiguity surrounding international and cross-cultural activities, being more likely to remain calm, vigorous, and resilient. They are also more likely to build and develop mentoring relationships, as a way to give back the benefits experienced in their rich international experience (George 2003; Ragins and Cotton 1999).

Grateful global leaders are better able to recognize the privileges inherent in their position (Maak and Pless 2009). Thus, they are more aware that being a privileged citizen of the world conveys responsibilities, especially taking into account the interests and well-being of the multitude of individuals and institutions they employ, contract, and influence. Gratitude may also reduce the materialistic strivings of global leaders (Polak and McCullough 2006). Such attitude may free them from the materialistic obsessions that have fed executives whose compensation packages defy economic logic (Kirkland 2006) and that contribute to widespread loss of public confidence in the institutions of capitalism, corporations, and their leaders (Child 2002). Marc Gunther, senior writer of the *Fortune* magazine, answered as follows when asked about the role virtues play in organizational leadership (Gunther and Neal 2008: 276):

> They are crucial. Look at the obvious and very important issue of executive pay. A greedy CEO who takes home $10 or $20 million a year sets a terrible example. He is a poor steward of shareholder money. He has an inflated sense of his own self importance. By contrast, a more modest pay package indicates that a CEO is working for the good of the enterprise, not to enrich himself, and that he or she understands that success belongs to everyone, and that the fruits of success should be distributed fairly. Which CEO would you want to follow?

Hope: being optimistic and expecting the best

Csikszentmihalyi (2003: 6) argued that as humans, 'we cannot survive without hope'. Global leaders are no exception. Hope may help leaders to face the uncertainty and complexities of the globalized world with optimism and a strong focus on discovering pathways to solve problems and to benefit from opportunities (Luthans et al. 2007). Hope nourishes willingness to face opposition, hardships, and suffering, to achieve goals, and it feeds conviction that the organization's vision, purpose, and mission will be fulfilled (Fry 2003; Fry et al. 2011). Hope stimulates the search for new possibilities in a way that generates excitement (Markovits and Donop 2007). Bill Pollard claimed that, when confronted with the challenges of the job, he followed what he called a mindset of solvability (Csikszentmihalyi 2003: 157):

> While I often don't state that, mentally that's the way I come. There has got to be a solution. There is a way to solve this. There is an answer here. There's no problem that's insolvable or too big to solve. So it comes with a mind-set of solvability. And that's probably the most important [strategy].

Hopeful global leaders maintain optimism (Csikszentmihalyi 2003; Jokinen 2005), self-confidence, and a future orientation when facing unprecedented obstacles and problematic assignments, especially when experiencing the first months of an international project in a completely novel culture. They are also potentially more creative (Rego et al. 2009; Rego, Sousa, Marques, and Cunha 2012). Hope may also help global leaders to develop effective corporate diplomacy (DeFrank et al. 2000; Kanter 2010) and to adopt positive efforts to perform track two diplomacy (Fort and Schipani 2004; Montville and Davidson 1981–1982; Ordeix-Rigo and Duarte 2009).

Hope is especially important when errors mount and the realization strikes home that the response to these has been inadequate. The leaders of Toyota would have needed to draw on deep well-springs of hope to emerge with credit from the safety recall of 2010, in which government officials have said that Toyota did not tell them about the problem until media exposure; that Toyota decided the fault was not a safety issue when it received the first reports over a year before, and that, initially, the twenty-six cases across Europe in the winter of 2008/09 were treated as 'a quality issue'. Only when the problem recurred one year later, did they treat it as a safety issue. Similarly, in the US, it was only after government pressure that Toyota admitted the extent of their liability and was forced to recall over eight million cars worldwide. Saint Augustine (as quoted in Brown 1998: 136) said that hope 'has two beautiful daughters. Their names are Anger and Courage, Anger that things are the way they are, and Courage to make them the way they ought to be.'

Humour: making work and life more enjoyable

Humour connects the individual to troubles and contradictions in a way that produces pleasure. It makes the human condition more bearable (Peterson and Seligman 2004). Humour may be the most controversial inclusion in the virtues and character strengths framework. It is normally excluded from taxonomies of virtues (Solomon 1999). However, as Solomon pointed out, this strength has been recognized as essential to life in every age and in every culture; thus, it may be viewed as universal. Some management researchers have noticed the importance of humour previously. Warren Bennis, for instance, argued that effective leaders 'tend to be curious, energetic, and gifted with an acute sense of humor'. To realize the benefits of leading a diverse workforce successfully, leaders must have 'understanding, humor, honesty, and integrity' (McCuiston et al. 2004: 89). Warren Buffett, in addition to being a successful investor, is a good writer with a strong sense of humour, as shown in his letters to shareholders (Wong 2009). Companies such as Southwest Airlines, Ben & Jerry's Ice Cream, and Sun Microsystems have in part attributed high levels of employee commitment, cohesiveness, and performance to their leaders' use of humour and its positive contagious effects on followers (Avolio et al. 1999; Box and Byus 2009; Hof et al. 1996; Katz 1996). An organization composed of clowns would be dysfunctional, but an individual with an exceptional sense of humour makes work more enjoyable. The consequences for flexibility and resilience may also be relevant (Solomon 1999).

A study focusing on the effects of leadership on humour and individual and unit performance (Avolio et al. 1999) revealed that: (a) the use of humour by leaders was positively related to individual and unit performance; (b) transformational leaders used humour more frequently; (c) transformational leadership was more positively related to unit performance for leaders who used humour more frequently. Other studies have revealed that the use of humour in organizations is associated with higher morale among workers, enhanced group cohesiveness, greater employee satisfaction and more positive emotions, increased individual and group creativity, motivation and productivity (Bates 2007; Hill 2008; Hughes 2009; McManus and Delaney 2007; Vecchio et al. 2009).

Leaders may use humour to alleviate status differentials and decrease social distance between themselves and followers, to cope with stress, to relieve frustrations, to reduce tensions in their relations with and among employees and other interlocutors, to connect with an audience, to help people deal with their problems more effectively, to signal to followers that they can handle difficult problems, to foster identity and more positive relationships within teams (Terrion and Ashforth 2002) and to cultivate employees' trust, positive emotions, and creativity.

There is reason to believe that humour may help global leaders to achieve positive performance (Greger and Peterson 2000; Jokinen 2005; Schell and Solomon 1997; Yoosuf 2005). With humour, they are able to relieve tensions that emerge in uncertain, ambiguous, and stressful situations. Jim Firestone described Anne Mulcahy from Xerox in the following terms: 'Even though we're in serious situations with serious business opportunities, at the end of the day she doesn't take herself too seriously' (Gunn and Gullickson 2006: 10).

Global leaders with a good sense of humour are able to deal positively and with fair play when interacting with people from polychronic cultures, where time is *not* money, and from countries where wealth, leisure, and communication infrastructures are less developed than in the wealthiest nations. They may react with playfulness when making cultural *faux pas* and observing behaviours which, in light of their culture, appear strange.

If humorous global leaders are also characterized by strong gratitude and love of learning, it is more likely that they will face diversity and adversity with positive feelings instead of complaints about the toughness of the job. They are more likely to establish positive relationships with employees, customers, authorities, and other partners in culturally distant places, to adopt more effective and constructive strategies (e.g. through ice breaking) for handling conflict and negotiations, and to develop better cross-cultural adjustment when working abroad. They may create positive emotions, flexibility, creativity, and resilience in the subsidiaries' managers and employees.

By being humorous, global leaders are more prepared to support coaching cultures (e.g. Virgin, IKEA, Semco) characterized by features such as fun, trust, energy, support, psychological safety, and learning (Solomon 1999). Richard Branson, of Virgin, sought to create a friendly, egalitarian, non-hierarchical, fun, exciting, and convivial atmosphere in all of his companies, an ambience in which people enjoy themselves (Dearlove 2007; Kets de Vries 1998). Virgin's culture has a lot to do with Branson's sense of humour, as is evident from the title of his book, *Losing my virginity: How I've survived, had fun, and made a fortune doing business my way* (Branson 1998). Branson has been considered the 'world's greatest brand builder' (Dearlove 2007). He launches and advertises new brands in unusual ways as readers have probably noticed. These glamorous events may include military tanks in parade, well-dressed (well, undressed) models, and so on. Virgin, as a global conglomerate, is distinguished only by its style, which flows directly from Branson.

Humour may also be important for communicating effectively in press conferences attracting the attentions of local and global media. Gerald Ratner though that he was cracking a joke when he referred to his products as crap—but it was a joke misjudged. Many global leaders are public figures, and their impact in the media should not be neglected. Beyond integrity, temperance, and courage, humour may also be of good value. If people at the top do not express a sense of humour, they can be represented as 'just another middle-aged-man-in-a-suit-CEO' (Jackson et al. 2003: 244).

Humour involves risks, however. On the one hand, the public and the media may adopt a jeering approach that undermines leaders' credibility and reputation. The line separating humour from imprudent exhibitionism is often thin. Richard Branson sparked outrage among Australian cricket fans after beaming a huge image of himself onto Sydney Harbour Bridge backing England in the Ashes (MailOnline, 10th July 2009; www.dailymail.co.uk; retrieved 14 October 2010). One fan said that Richard Branson should be arrested and punished. And a Virgin public relations representative received a call from an Australian journalist who said: 'Get your rich Pom off our bridge'. Branson ended up apologizing.

Spirituality: there's more to life than making money

Spirituality is the prototype of the virtues of transcendence, referring to beliefs and practices grounded in the conviction that there is a transcendent (i.e. non-physical) dimension to life. Although religion may sustain spiritual values and purpose, spirituality is distinct from religion, and a leader does not have to espouse religious beliefs to provide spiritual leadership to followers (Reave 2005). Theoretical and empirical evidence suggests that spirituality associates individuals with meaningful or transcendental accomplishments (Sanders III, Hopkins and Geroy 2003), and that spiritual leadership has positive impacts on leaders, followers, and organizational performance, well-being, and flourishing (Fry 2003, 2008; Fry and Matherly 2007; Fry and Slocum 2008; Fry et al.

2005; Reave 2005). Spirituality may impel leaders to see that there's more to life than making money.

Fry and Slocum (2008) suggested that spiritual leadership might contribute to maximizing a firm's triple bottom line, and to improving employee well-being, sustainability, and social responsibility, without sacrificing economic and financial performance. While such relations are notoriously difficult to establish empirically in the short term, they tend to manifest themselves in long-term survival. A review of 150 studies showed that there is a clear consistency between spiritual values and practices, and effective leadership (Reave 2005).

Spiritual leadership inspires workers by means of a transcendent vision and corporate culture founded on altruistic values that seek to develop a committed and productive workforce (Fry and Slocum 2008). Leaders displaying these qualities are relevant for every organization. However, a transcendent, meaningful, or higher purpose vision, together with a virtuous organizational culture, is especially fruitful for developing international flows of organizational learning, and for bringing together efforts and initiatives emerging in different locations and diverse social, political, economic, and cultural environments (Den Hartog 2004).

In a context of high complexity, ambiguity, and uncertainty, where the potential for fragmentation and dissipation is high (Den Hartog 2004; Kanter 2010), leaders able to foster a sense of community (thus developing the bonds that allow integrating efforts and energies of diverse and geographically dispersed people and units) will flourish. If a virtuous or high purpose vision and a positive and transcendental culture serves to clarify the general direction of change, to simplify hundreds or thousands of more detailed decisions, and helps to coordinate the actions of many different people quickly and efficiently (Fry 2003), it also serves to simplify, unify, and integrate the daily decisions and to coordinate the actions of diverse people and entities worldwide. When appropriately communicated and accepted, such vision promotes identification and commitment among people working in diverse environments (Den Hartog 2004).

Virtuous visions and actions emerging within global organizations disseminate throughout a wide network of partners globally. In this way, contributing to making the world better (George 2009) becomes a more realistic endeavour. Csikszentmihalyi argued that, even if one discounts certain self-serving aims of visionary leaders, it appears that these leaders are effective in advocating their vision because of their genuine conviction that the efforts they are proposing will indeed have a positive impact. Their message, in other words, is effective because it comes from the heart (Csikszentmihalyi 2003).

A genuine conviction (the authenticity of which has been greeted with great scepticism by critics, as discussed in previous chapters) may have mobilized Anita Roddick to found The Body Shop in 1976, on a model taken from a small chain in San Francisco, and to turn the company into a global giant (Den Hartog 2004. See also Damon 2004, and Csikszentmihalyi 2003. On the contested origins of the Body Shop model, see Entine 2004). Roddick's vision was expressed in terms of environmental and social issues, opposing the testing of cosmetics on animals, the need for excessive packaging, and promoting fair trade. As expressed in a text from the AnitaRoddick.com website (http://www.anitaroddick.com/aboutanita.php; retrieved 14 October 2010):

> Businesses have the power to do good. That's why The Body Shop's Mission Statement opens with the overriding commitment, 'To dedicate our business to the pursuit of social and environmental change.' We use our stores and our products to help communicate human rights and environmental issues.

The effectiveness of the vision in providing direction and 'glue' greatly depends on how the leader *lives* the vision, acts as a role model, and expresses virtuous leadership (Den Hartog 2004). By giving proof of courage, integrity, bravery, and persistence, global leaders can communicate and implement their visions. On the contrary, when the leader's integrity is dubious, his/her vision, no matter how well-crafted and communicated, will be received with scepticism and loose vigour (Mendonca 2001). This what happened when the Body Shop was sold to L'Oréal.

Social intelligence and wisdom are important in articulating a persuasive vision. Moreover, vitality is necessary for feeding the efforts, energy, and great amounts of time that global leaders spend travelling around the world to explain the vision and its meaning, as did ABB's Barnevik and Philips' Jan Timmer (Den Hartog 2004).

In the global-multicultural arena, open-mindedness, curiosity, love of learning, and perspective are also relevant for enabling global leaders to develop and articulate the vision appropriately in different contexts. On the one hand, differences exist among cultures about the preference for consensual versus leader-centred visions (Den Hartog 2004). On the other hand, great differences also exist across cultures in the preferred use of language, style of communication, and non-verbal messages. For example, while it has been suggested that Confucian values make the Chinese more receptive to visions expressed in nonaggressive manners (Redding 1993), Americans, and other people from what are collectively seen as more masculine and direct cultures, are generally seen as being more receptive to assertive styles.

The strengths of humanity and wisdom may also help global leaders define and articulate a passionate vision, as suggested in the following excerpt from a speech by Anita Roddick (Den Hartog and Verburg 1997: 373):

> What we do well at The Body Shop is communicate with passion because passion persuades. We also know that in this decade, to educate and communicate you have to be daring, enlivening and different. We go into the highway with our messages; our lorries are like moving billboards. I believe in promoting our products through global culture and linking them to political and social messages. These anecdotes have a dramatic effect because people feel they are part of the planet. (...) We see any empty space as an opportunity to create an atmosphere, deliver a message, make a point. Allow me to leave you with a favorite ethos printed on a T-shirt, given to members of staff: head in the clouds, feet on the ground, heart in the business.

The spirituality of global leaders may promote organizational spiritual capital and social capital across and within units around the world (Malloch 2010). A global leader with an appreciation of strong spirituality is also able to understand the spirituality or religiosity of employees. For example, Joaquin, the Colombian leader of a Malay branch of a Japanese company discussed in Chapter 3, recognized the importance of the *Haj*, the sacred journey to Mecca, and created a system allowing ten employees to go there each year without having to take vacation days (Otazo 1999).

When people look for avenues for expressing spirituality in the workplace, spiritual global leaders may be inspirational and a source of well-being, motivation, and performance of followers working in different countries (Reave 2005). Csikszentmihalyi (2003) argued that when a leader's vision embraces goals such as doing the best possible job, helping humankind and the environment, or obeying a cosmic purpose, the organization becomes invested with a soul, existing as part of a large whole. He concluded that if a vision is widely believed to be genuine, it becomes a magnet for the energies of the organization.

Spirituality may also increase leaders' internal locus of control and vitality for dealing with strong ambiguity, complexity, and stressful contingencies (Sanders III et al. 2003). Bob Miller, President and CEO of Envirotest Systems, acknowledged that the prayer and reflection he developed when attending the 'Spirituality for Business Leadership' seminar at Santa Clara University, helped him create serenity that made him feel he was a better leader, able to listen, be innovative, flexible, calm, and decisive during crises (Miller 2000). Ricardo B. Levy, then the successful President and CEO of Catalytica, who attended the same course and who has also been characterized as a spiritual leader (Gunther and Neal 2008), said (Levy 2000: 1309):

> [The course] made me recognize that spirituality goes far beyond the times set aside for religious practice, that spirituality is inside me, that it is the compass in everything I do. (. . .). I gained an appreciation that at the root of the connection between spirituality and business leadership is the recognition that we all have an inner voice and that it is the ultimate source of wisdom in our most difficult business decisions. (. . .) We are challenged with the need to reach deeper, the need to draw from our spirituality to find the right course. (. . .) [W]hat enables the leader to carry out the decision with a measure of dignity that preserves his or her balance, tempering the debate with compassion so that the organization's members also preserve their dignity? (. . .) The answer is in a quiet zone that transcends outside inputs and can give us strength and direction, a quiet zone that helps us overcome our ever-present weakness, biases, and fears. This zone of quiet in the midst of chaos is where our inner voice speaks.

Leaders' spirituality is frequently, although not necessarily, grounded in religious faith and principles (Damon 2004; Reave 2005), or on what might be called secular humanism (Csikszentmihalyi 2003). Damon argued that many business leaders extract their creative inspiration from strongly held beliefs, with faith instilling work with a sense of purpose that energizes imagination and gives them the courage to take risks (Damon 2004). One example is that of Jeff Swartz, of Timberland. Community service is a bulwark of Swartz's faith, and all employees at Timberland get 40 hours a year off to volunteer at the charity of their choice (Conlin 1999).

Another example is Bill Pollard, former chairman and CEO of Service-Master, a company with more than 12 million customers in the USA and 44 other countries (Malloch 2010). The reason behind the growth and success of ServiceMaster, according to Pollard, is its commitment to honouring God and to developing people (Malloch 2010). People work better for a cause rather than just for a salary, he thought (Csikszentmihalyi 2003: 143–65):

> For me, it has been clearly the whole process of the development of the person. And that is what has brought meaning to my work. I've seen people grow as individuals, grow in who they're becoming as well as what they're doing, grow as parents, grow as contributors in their community or contributors in their churches or places of worship, grow as healthy citizens. All those things are fulfilling to me and bring meaning to the fact that work results in that. What

other activity could I be involved with where so many people had an opportunity to produce something, to achieve a result, and in all that, to also develop as persons?

Dedication to his faith also helps to explain (Damon 2004) how and why Sir John Marks Templeton was a successful global investor and mutual fund pioneer, whose financial gains allowed the creation of several philanthropic initiatives (e.g. the John Templeton Foundation; the Templeton Prize for Progress toward Research or Discoveries about Spiritual Realities; the Templeton Library in Sewanee, Tennessee, and the Templeton College of the University of Oxford, endowing the Oxford Centre for Management Studies to become a full college of the university with a focus on business and management studies). Damon (2004) stated that Templeton devoutly believed in the love of all humanity, and argued that leaders' spiritual faith is frequently the source of a generative morality, giving rise to an ethical imagination and creative business concepts, encouraging leaders to build philanthropic initiatives with genuine concern for the community benefits and the company itself.

Table 5.4. Transcendence assisting several global leaders' activities

Appreciation of beauty and excellence	• Appreciating and learning what is distinctive, efficient, and excellent in certain parts of the world. • Avoiding an ethnocentric perspective that depreciates less sophisticated ways of life and damages cross-cultural adjustment. • Connecting deeply with other people and focusing on perfecting local language proficiency (instead of assuming that 'English is *the* business language' and resorting to an interpreter). • Accepting and feeling good living together with diverse cultures—thus increasing cultural intelligence and cross-cultural adjustment. • Forging a common identity among unities operating worldwide, a common feeling of membership, and a sense of community that works against centrifugal forces of fragmentation. • Communicating, managing conflicts and negotiating more effectively in different cultural contexts.
Gratitude	• Diffusing trust, gratitude, and other positive emotions throughout the organization. • Promoting employees' extra-role behaviours that foster organizational performance. • Facing 'global life' with more vitality. • Developing high purpose corporate missions and visions. • Experiencing enthusiasm and gratitude for having the opportunity for working abroad—thus experiencing greater cross-cultural adjustment and performance in international assignments. • Respecting individuals and entities—thus developing positive global networks, from which knowledge, wisdom, and useful insights can

(continued)

Table 5.4. Continued

	be gathered for taking better decisions and establishing better strategies. • Facing cultural difficulties with hardiness and the desire to learn from mistakes. • Developing humility. • Feeling gratitude for having the power and the 'privilege' inherent in the position, thus assuming reciprocal citizenship responsibilities toward stakeholders (including communities and society). • Reducing materialistic strivings and adopting fairer executives' compensation packages.
Hope	• Facing uncertainty and complexities of the globalized world with optimism and a strong focus on discovering pathways for solving problems and taking advantage of opportunities. • Nourishing the conviction that the organization's vision, purpose, and mission will be fulfilled. • Maintaining optimism when experiencing the first months of an international assignment in a completely novel culture. • Developing creativity to face the idiosyncrasies of markets and cultures, to negotiate more effectively. • Developing effective corporate diplomacy.
Humour	• Relieving one's own and others' tensions emerging in uncertain, ambiguous, and stressful situations. • Dealing positively and with fair play when interacting with people from different cultures. Establishing positive relationships with employees, customers, authorities and other partners in such places. • Reacting with playfulness when making cultural faux pas. • Facing diversity and adversity with positive feelings instead of with complaints about the difficulties of the job. • Adopting more effective and constructive strategies for handling cross-cultural conflict and negotiations. • Engendering positive emotions, flexibility, creativity, and resilience in the subsidiaries' managers and employees. • Supporting coaching cultures. • Communicating effectively in press conferences.
Spirituality	• Developing a sense of community. Bringing together efforts and initiatives emerging in different locations and diverse social, political, economic, and cultural contexts. • Developing high purpose visions and transcendental cultures that simplify, unify, and integrate daily decisions and coordinate the actions of diverse people and entities operating worldwide. • Building enduring organizations that contribute to making the world a better place to live in. • Understanding and respecting the spirituality or religiosity of employees from different cultures, promoting the organizational spiritual capital and, thus, social capital across and within unities operating worldwide. • Promoting well-being, motivation, and performance of followers working in different countries who are looking for avenues for expressing their spirituality in the workplace. • Developing an internal locus of control and vitality for dealing with strong ambiguity, complexity, and stressful contingencies of the global arena.

Drawbacks of excessive transcendence

As with the other virtues, the virtue of transcendence resides in a golden mean. Excessive appreciation of beauty and excellence may lead global leaders to look for optimal solutions and strategies, neglecting that the optimum is enemy of the good and losing opportunities for making and implementing possible or viable decisions and strategies. The search for excellence may make global leaders unable to understand that what is thought excellent today may be considered ordinary tomorrow. An excessive appreciation of beauty may lead one to lose contact with rude or vulgar realities. And an excessive appreciation of excellence may lead to the articulation of visions of perfection that do not show much correspondence with reality.

Excessive gratitude may lead global leaders to become fascinated with their achievements and privileges, neglecting bad events and prospects, and losing ambition. Excessive hope may lead global leaders to unrealistic optimism that, in turn, leads to neglect of risks and problems, and commitment to solutions, decisions or strategies that are not feasible. One may consider the former CEO of BP, Tony Hayward, who acted imprudently and displayed an excess of optimism when dealing with the Deepwater Horizon platform catastrophe (Mouawad and Krauss 2010). He maintained that the company had been extraordinarily successful in response to the spill, which was clearly an overstatement (Helman 2010).

Global leaders with an excess of humour may be inconvenient and disrespectful when dealing with individuals of different cultures, thus hurting personal relationships, trust, negotiations, and their own credibility. Jokes that work well in some contexts may be offensive in other contexts. Cultures differ in the degree to which humour is used and accepted in social relationships (Gannon and Pillai 2010; Imahori and Cupach 1994; Martin 2002; Nevo et al. 2001; Sueda and Wiseman 1992).

Too much investment in spirituality may lead to the articulation of high purpose visions that do not adhere much to reality, thus being unrealistic and demobilizing. Global leaders with excessive spirituality may mentally navigate transcendent worlds that divert them from the tough realities of the global business. If global leaders with strong religious beliefs are not prudent and wise when sharing their convictions, but rather adopt authoritarian and proselytizing behaviours (Peterson and Seligman 2004), they may alienate the commitment and trust of employees and other stakeholders who do not share the same beliefs.

The dark side of workplace spirituality (e.g. manipulation, subjugation) should not be discounted (Driscoll and McKee 2007; Lips-Wiersma et al. 2009; Cunha et al. 2006).

Conclusion

Transcendence virtues may help global leaders to contribute to positive organizational performance in several ways, including: (a) being prudent and humble, and making wise decisions; (b) respecting and adjusting to other cultures, and developing social connectedness and social capital; (c) being open to new paradigms, thus understanding the *glocal* complexity and adopting new approaches when dealing with diverse markets, people, and entities; (d) acknowledging one's own limitations, and facing cultural mistakes with dignity, and learning from them; (e) avoiding intemperate, unrealistic or dangerous ambitions; (f) appreciating, learning with, and feeling grateful for the splendid diversity of the world; (g) pursuing excellence, sustainable management practices and policies; (h) articulating positive and meaningful visions and missions, thus making people feel they perform meaningful work, and forging a common identity among units operating worldwide, a common feeling of membership, and a sense of community that works against the forces of fragmentation.

6

The Virtues of Global Leaders: An Integrative Research Perspective

My point is that the coalescence of virtue and profit is possible only when daring, creative and insightful business leadership is practiced in society. Such leadership should take cognizance of the psychological, social and spiritual values, and associated needs, of individual workers and their families, thereby placing business at the service of society as a whole. It is incontrovertible that ethics plays an important role in the creation of a business environment in which virtues and values are brought into relationship for the good of all. In this regard, character and, in particular, the character of leaders is paramount.

(Flynn 2008: 359–360)

The happy life is thought to be virtuous; now a virtuous life requires exertion, and does not consist in amusement.

(Aristotle 1999: 173)

Greed is for wimps.

(Wilkinson and Omidi 2010: R7)

Bridging character strengths and virtues

As the previous chapters suggested, different groups of strengths (i.e. core virtues) tend to support different roles, activities, and competencies (Table 6.1). Wisdom and knowledge help global leaders to learn and understand the complexities of the cultural, economic, and political mosaic as well as to interact positively with diverse stakeholders worldwide. Courage allows global leaders to make challenging decisions and face global and local problems honestly and energetically. Justice helps global leaders to cultivate a cosmopolitan ethos, to lead respectfully, to

Table 6.1. Core virtues sustaining global leaders' activities and competencies

Wisdom and knowledge
Learning and understanding the complexities of the cultural, economic, and political 'mosaic', and interacting/networking positively
- Learning, understanding and taking advantage of the global market and the complexities of the cultural, economic, and political mosaic.
- Developing glocal savvy for working both abroad and in the global arena.
- Developing global business and global organization expertise.
- Developing strategic plans and creating services and products that take local and global issues into account.
- Developing passion for and respecting cultural differences, and developing positive interactions with diverse stakeholders.
- Developing positive interactions with diverse stakeholders (e.g. negotiation partners, employees, local authorities, impatriates, expatriates, communities).
- Finding ways to make the world a better place.

Courage
Taking challenging decisions and facing global and local problems honestly and energetically
- Keeping integrity when ethical and human rights problems need to be approached in different cultural, economic, social, and political contexts.
- Being honest with stakeholders worldwide.
- Adopting moral compromises when necessary.
- Facing with vigour the hassles of frequent travelling, working in different time zones, and working in cultural, political, social, and economic adverse conditions.
- Assuming mistakes and preserving the company's reputation worldwide.
- Defining ambitious strategies and goals, and energizing stakeholders worldwide.
- Pursuing and nourishing high purpose visions with courage and integrity.
- Creating the trust necessary to develop and nourish fluid and collaborative relationships with stakeholders worldwide.

Justice
Pursuing a cosmopolitan ethos, leading respectfully, fostering trust and cooperation, and promoting human dignity and development
- Adopting a cosmopolitan and responsible leadership approach that promotes human dignity and development, and makes the world a better place.
- Adopting, implementing, and facilitating a sustainable and responsible management strategy ('people, planet, profits'), thus contributing to the common good.
- Performing corporate diplomacy, thus increasing the corporate legitimacy in different and difficult economic, social, economic, and political contexts.
- Acting as role model, and adopting a respectful leadership approach, and fostering trust, justice, and fluid cooperative work relationships between diverse stakeholders within the global network.
- Adopting integrative leadership efforts for making different approaches to work in ways consistent with the global strategy.

Humanity
Promoting trustful and cooperative relationships, caring about and developing others, and having a more accurate emotional and social sense of what happens in the local and global arenas
- Fostering a sense of community within the company.
- Developing networking skills and fostering positive worldwide networks.
- Building and developing mentoring (e.g. expatriates, impatriates, local country nationals).
- Caring for customers and other stakeholders, and making the world a better place to live in.

- Empathizing with and listening to employees, customers, suppliers, authorities, partners, and other stakeholders from different contexts.
- Keeping self-emotional control when facing unfamiliar situations in idiosyncratic cultural contexts.
- Managing conflict and negotiating constructively in diverse contexts.
- Knowing the truth.

Temperance

Being prudent and humble, making wise decisions, respecting and adjusting to different cultures and people, learning from mistakes and adopting a level-5 leadership approach

- Respecting and adjusting to other cultures, and developing social connectedness and social capital.
- Being open to new paradigms, thus understanding glocal complexity and adopting new approaches when dealing with diverse markets, people, and entities.
- Listening to and asking for advice, thus being more able to enter new markets and interact positively with diverse stakeholders.
- Accepting bad news and knowing the truth worldwide.
- Acknowledging one's own limitations, and facing cultural mistakes with elevation, and learning from them.
- Developing others and recognizing their efforts.
- Adopting prudent decisions and moral compromises, and preserving the company's reputation.
- Promoting organizational humility (a valuable, rare, irreplaceable, and difficult to imitate resource).
- Making decisions that respect the interests and rights of poor communities in developing countries.
- Adopting and developing personal and organizational discipline.
- Avoiding the media spotlight.
- Avoiding intemperate, unrealistic, or dangerous ambitions.

Transcendence

Appreciating, learning with, and feeling grateful for world diversity, and pursuing excellence, sustainable management practices and policies, and meaningful visions and missions

- Appreciating and learning from the richness of the world cultural mosaic. Promoting organizational learning within and across unities, branches, and organizations.
- Articulating positive and meaningful visions and missions, thus making people feel they perform meaningful work, and forging a common identity among unities operating worldwide, a common feeling of membership, and a sense of community that works against centrifugal forces of fragmentation.
- Feeling grateful for having the opportunity to experience diversity, and for having the power and the 'privilege' inherent in the position, thus spreading trust, gratitude, and other positive emotions across the organization.
- Reducing materialistic strivings and adopting fairer compensation packages.
- Pursuing excellence in the company and the global network of which it is part.
- Facing adversity, uncertainty, and the complexities of the globalized world with humour, optimism, and a strong focus on discovering creative pathways for solving problems and taking advantage of opportunities.
- Building enduring organizations that contribute to making the world better.

Adapted from Rego et al. (2012)

nurture trust and cooperation, and to promote human dignity and development. Humanity makes them able to promote trustful and cooperative relationships, to care about and develop others, and to have a more accurate emotional and social sense of what happens in the local and global markets. Temperance helps them to be prudent and humble, to make wise decisions, to respect and adjust to different cultures and people, to learn from mistakes, and to adopt a level-5 leadership approach (Collins 2001). Transcendence facilitates appreciating, learning with, and feeling grateful for the splendid diversity of the world, and pursuing excellence, sustainable management practices and policies, and meaningful visions and missions.

Considering the complexity of global leadership, different character strengths and virtues may be necessary to support a global leader's activities. The case of Mectizan is illustrative of how high purpose actions of leaders may articulate the combination of several virtues and strengths, such as prudence, citizenship, spirituality, justice, and humanity (Mendonca 2001; Spreitzer and Sonenshein 2004). Mectizan is a drug that Merck, one of the world's largest pharmaceutical companies, decided to donate for the treatment of onchocerciasis, or river blindness, a case we discuss next.

Combining prudence, citizenship, high purpose, justice and humanity

In 1978, Merck & Co. discovered that Mectizan, a veterinary antibiotic, was a potential cure for river blindness, an endemic disease in tens of countries, mainly in West Africa and Latin America. The disease causes painful itching, progressive blindness, and reduction in life expectancy. The company leaders faced and debated three issues (Mendonca 2001; Michaelson 2008; Spreitzer and Sonenshein 2004). First, the people who desperately needed the medicine were unable to pay for it, meaning that the company would never recover its research or distribution costs for the drug. Second, if the company donated the drug, an expectation of future donations could follow. Such expectations might discourage future research in the area in a profit-oriented company. Third, the company risked bad publicity and potential added costs for any unexpected adverse side effects of the drug that, in turn, could damage the drug's reputation as a veterinary antibiotic.

The debate ended when Merck decided to manufacture and distribute the drug for free in the developing world, a decision that amounted to millions of dollars foregone revenue. The decision resulted in the

Mectizan Donation Program, which played a pivotal role in the control of onchocerciasis (Peters and Philips 2004). In 1950, George W. Merck, then the company's president, in a speech to the Medical College of Virginia, addressed the decisive factor in making this prudent, humane, and higher purpose decision (Merck & Co. 2005: 57):

> We try never to forget that medicine is for the people. It is not for the profits. The profits follow, and if we have remembered that, they have never failed to appear.

The Mectizan Donation Program, involving the World Health Organization, the World Bank, UNICEF, Ministries of Health, the Task Force for Global Health, non-governmental development organizations, and local communities, became a successful public–private partnership in the health sector and was considered a model for addressing other serious cases in development and international health (Peters and Philips 2004). In this way, Merck helped to eradicate river blindness, at its own expense. Since 1987, the company has donated more than 2.5 billion tablets of Mectizan in more than thirty countries worldwide (www.merck.com). Glynn and Jamerson (2006) argued that Vagelos' *principled leadership* saved many lives and was a source of reputational capital for Merck. For such efforts and good deeds, Merck and its executives won formal recognition (e.g. awards from the Business Enterprise Trust and Harvard Business School) as well as considerable informal kudos.

Prudence recommends that we, as authors and readers of this book, should be cautious when interpreting the motivations of Merck's leaders. As Spreitzer and Sonenshein (2004) pointed out, it is possible that Merck acted simply out of self-interest, rather than a higher moral purpose (Michaelson 2008); however, these authors also noted that there is reason to believe that Merck's behaviour could be thought of as an example of positive deviance: (1) Mectizan had no foreseeable profits, but an estimated $250 million price tag; (2) besides development, manufacturing, and distribution costs, the company also risked damaging its corporate reputation; (3) it faced a huge distribution problem, with logistical difficulties costing Merck a significant amount of money and involving additional risks; (4) it was not possible to predict the strategic implications of Merck's decision, and no one could anticipate with reasonable certainty that the decision to donate the drug would have a positive impact on long-term profitability. Spreitzer and Sonenshein (2004: 835) concluded:

One might propose that Merck's decisions were guided by a long-term profitability strategy, tied to publicity or some other benefit. But this kind of post-hoc analysis is tautological. Skeptics might assume that Merck's actions were guided by self-interest, because why else would it donate the drug? But we can also interpret Merck's behaviors as a function of the organization's mission to promote public health. The fact that Merck's decision was a long-term strategic success does not necessarily imply that its motivation was based exclusively on self-interest.

In short, there are reasons to believe that, beyond self-interest, the leaders of Merck were also guided by human, social, and ethical considerations. Integrating self-interest into virtuous decisions made by leaders is not negative but rather a virtue. Leaders undertaking the difficult and noble mission of providing high quality drugs to patients, investing in researching new drugs, and assuring a company's reputation and survival in the long run cannot be blind to self-interest: they have to make profits to pay wages and make investments. In being virtuous, one need not discount self-interest—sometimes it can serve broader purposes as well as those closer at hand, as appears to be the case on this occasion (Damon 2004; Kanter 2010; Solomon 1999).

Clusters of strengths assisting global leaders' activities

Global leaders' competencies, actions, or roles may require the combined contribution of several strengths. For example, curiosity, open-mindedness, love of learning, social intelligence, and citizenship may be crucial for developing cultural adaptability and being able to build positive interactions with diverse stakeholders. Curiosity, open-mindedness, and love of learning help global leaders to be inquisitive about other cultures and peoples, and to accept differences without prejudice. Social intelligence helps them better to capture and interpret behaviours and attitudes of those others whom they encounter. Citizenship is useful for adopting a cosmopolitan and responsible ethos towards different others.

A combination of citizenship, gratitude, fairness, leadership, persistence, and spirituality may be necessary for global leaders to develop and adhere to global initiatives such as the Caux Round Table, the United Nations Global Compact, the World Business Council on Sustainable Development, or the Business Leaders Initiative on Human Rights. Citizenship, gratitude, and fairness help global leaders to develop a cosmopolitan ethos. Leadership and persistence are necessary for conducting the process in spite of difficulties and risks. Spirituality may help pursuing the citizenship initiatives in light of a high purpose. And there is always self-interest: to sit at the table with the global captains of industry and to wear an ethical smile while doing so is not bad for either personal or organizational reputation.

Integrity in ethically complex contexts is more likely to be practised if the global leader is also rich in wisdom, bravery, persistence, vitality, hope, citizenship, self-regulation, and prudence, as well as more usual forms of capital. For example, in facing issues related to violation of human rights and dignity in certain contexts, wisdom is necessary to make sense of several potentially competing facets of the issue. Bravery, persistence, vitality, and hope help the leader to stay focused, resilient, and optimistic in the face of obstacles and risks. Citizenship is crucial for understanding the dignity of all human beings, including the distant needy (Maak and Pless 2009). Self-regulation and prudence help the global leader to transcend personal interests, to be disciplined, and cautious when acting, deciding, or speaking.

The combination of humility, vitality, bravery, persistence, love, and kindness may be necessary to make difficult decisions that keep personal credibility intact and do not destroy interpersonal bonds but foster trust and cooperation among employees and other stakeholders, allowing the salvation of a company from bankruptcy, as happened in Xerox, headed by Anne Mulcahy. The force of Warren Buffett, both as a widely admired executive and philanthropist, also comes from a crucible of strengths that include wisdom, prudence, citizenship, gratitude, humility, integrity, humour, self-regulation, and generosity.

When virtues and strengths are not combined, their effects may be perverse. A courageous leader without integrity and humanity may make profitable deals in corrupt contexts, putting the reputation of the company and its long-term development in serious trouble. For instance, BAE Systems is a well-known organization that, over forty years, has fostered British arms sales to countries as diverse as Qatar, Chile, Czech Republic, Austria, Tanzania, South Africa, Romania, and Saudi Arabia (Leigh and Evans 2010). Sir Dick Evans, Managing Director and subsequently Chairman of BAE between 1990 and 2004, was clearly a courageous man: he was instrumental in delivering the largest arms deal in British history, known as the al-Yamamah sales to Saudi Arabia. It was in 2006 that the Blair government blocked legal inquiry from the Serious Fraud Office into this Saudi arms deal, citing 'national security' interests as its reason for doing so. BAE Systems has been a hugely profitable company but it could not be claimed to be virtuous: it is not only the trade that it is involved in that is problematic but that it has been alleged that its weapons systems have been sold through bribes, commissions, and kickbacks. On 26 June 2007, BAE announced to the London Stock Exchange that the US Justice Department had initiated an investigation under the 1977 Foreign Corrupt Practices Act. The Washington authorities opened an investigation into the very Saudi deals that had been declared off-limits in Britain.

Courage without humility can make leaders rash (Vera and Rodriguez-Lopez 2004) and unable to develop positive and fluid interactions in the global network. A brave leader without prudence (Irwin 1997) may make extremely risky investment decisions, thus jeopardizing effectiveness. The might and power of the Saudi regime worked to protect BAE and the governments that sponsored it and, while such protection might be efficient, it is extremely difficult to claim it was virtuous.

In certain cases, the 'strength' of bravura may even nourish or facilitate vices such as intemperance and dishonesty. Allegedly and apparently, it was 'bravura' that fed or facilitated the intemperance and dishonesty of some leaders of the *News of the World* newspaper. Perverse consequences have rebounded on the newspaper itself (surgically closed, in the meantime), some of its leaders, especially the Murdochs, James and Rupert, and News International and the parent company, News Corps, itself. Employees without any apparent fault lost their jobs—not to mention all the victims the newspaper harmed through illegal phone hacking, corrupting the police, and other wrongdoings (Sonne et al. 2001; *The Economist* 2011a, 2011b; Whalen and MacDonald 2011).

Love of learning without integrity may give rise to unacceptable uses of the knowledge (Gaut 1997) for manipulating employees, and authorities or customers in poor countries. A global leader with strong wisdom needs courage and prudence to put wisdom and knowledge at the service of difficult but wise decisions. Prudence in the absence of courage, humanism, and justice may lead global leaders to behave cowardly (i.e. to shut their eyes) when facing human rights infringements (Singer 2002). Humanity without justice may impel global leaders to adopt favouritism and partiality, thus damaging the motivation and performance of those who, showing high merit, are harmed for not being a part of the leader's in-group.

In short, global leaders' effectiveness and positive organizational performance require a combination of forces. Table 6.2 shows how different activities and roles of global leaders may be facilitated by a combination of strengths. Neither list of activities and strengths is intended to be exhaustive but is rather illustrative. Understanding strengths' interrelationships may be useful for selecting global leaders according to the roles they have to carry out.

Table 6.2. How combinations of strengths may assist several global leaders' activities

Global leaders' activities	Strengths
Developing and nourishing innovative and successful strategies that take advantage of the actual stage of globalization and the inherent properties of international exchanges.	Bravery; creativity; curiosity; hope; integrity; open-mindedness; persistence/perseverance; perspective/wisdom; prudence; self-regulation; vitality
Being open to new paradigms, thus understanding different social, economic, political and cultural contexts, and adopting new approaches when dealing with diverse markets, people, and entities.	Appreciation of beauty and excellence; citizenship; curiosity; gratitude; humility; love of learning; open-mindedness; perspective/wisdom
Developing motivation and willingness to enter and confront unfamiliar situations (e.g. accepting international assignments).	Appreciation of beauty and excellence; bravery; curiosity; hope; love of learning; open-mindedness; persistence; prudence; self-regulation; vitality
'Catching' the true facts around the world, knowing the 'truth', and thus taking more accurate decisions.	Appreciation of beauty and excellence; curiosity; fairness; humility/modesty; humour; kindness; leadership; love; love of learning; open-mindedness; persistence/perseverance; prudence; self-regulation; social intelligence
Facing complex, difficult, and unavoidable ethical situations/dilemmas in the global arena, adopting moral compromises when necessary.	Bravery; citizenship; fairness; hope; integrity; leadership; open-mindedness; persistence/perseverance; perspective/wisdom; prudence; self-regulation; vitality
Performing corporate diplomacy and track two diplomacy.	Appreciation of beauty and excellence; bravery; citizenship; creativity; fairness; kindness; leadership; love; open-mindedness; persistence/perseverance; perspective/wisdom; prudence; self-regulation; social intelligence
Negotiating globally with partners of different cultures.	Bravery; creativity; fairness; hope; humour; integrity; kindness; leadership; love; open-mindedness; persistence/perseverance; perspective/wisdom; prudence; self-regulation; social intelligence
Developing cultural intelligence.	Appreciation of beauty and excellence; citizenship; curiosity; gratitude; humility/modesty; integrity; kindness; love of learning; love; open-mindedness; persistence/perseverance; perspective/wisdom; prudence; self-regulation; social intelligence; spirituality (high purpose); vitality
Identifying and adopting leadership behaviours that are more appropriate in different contexts.	Curiosity; humility/modesty; integrity; leadership; love of learning; open-mindedness; perspective/wisdom; prudence; self-regulation; social intelligence

(continued)

Table 6.2. Continued

Global leaders' activities	Strengths
Creating the trust necessary for stimulating, fluid, and collaborative work relationships with stakeholders from many different economic, legal, political, social, and cultural systems.	Appreciation of beauty and excellence; bravery; citizenship; fairness; forgiveness/ mercy; gratitude; humility/modesty; humour; integrity; kindness; love; self-regulation; social intelligence; spirituality (high purpose)
Developing others (e.g. coaching and mentoring other leaders, impatriates and expatriates).	Humility/modesty; humour; integrity; kindness; leadership; love; open-mindedness; persistence/perseverance; perspective/wisdom; prudence
Forging, pursuing, and nourishing high purpose visions.	Bravery; citizenship; gratitude; integrity; persistence/perseverance; prudence; spirituality (high purpose); vitality
Adopting a cosmopolitan/responsible leadership approach for dealing with the world's most pressing problems, improving corporate social responsibility compliance across the global supply chain, and building more sustainable and responsible organizations.	Bravery; citizenship; creativity and moral imagination; fairness; gratitude; hope; humility/modesty; integrity; leadership; love; love of learning; open-mindedness; perspective/wisdom; persistence/ perseverance; prudence; spirituality (high purpose); vitality

Contingency factors

The examples referred to above, and the connections between global leaders' activities and strengths illustrated in Table 6.2, also suggest that the relevance of strengths is contingent on the global leaders' roles and missions (Suutari 2002). For example, integrity, bravery, perseverance, prudence, and self-regulation may be more relevant for working and interacting with partners from contexts in which corruption is extensive, and for operating in countries where human rights and dignity are disrespected. Love of learning, open-mindedness, curiosity, appreciation of beauty, and excellence are more necessary for dealing with partners from novel cultures and for leading cross-cultural teams with great diversity. Citizenship, fairness, prudence, love, and spirituality are more relevant for operating in poor countries and communities, where the global company may make a difference in improving life conditions and fostering human and social development.

Vitality is more necessary for leaders who travel frequently and live abroad for long periods. Humanity is more relevant to an expatriate leader who runs a foreign subsidiary in South East Asia in a country with a very different religiosity and set of values, and who needs to develop goodwill with local country employees, than it is to the

American manager in the US headquarters in charge of South East Asia operations, to whom s(he) reports. Of course, the other side of the coin is what leaders are supposed to do when the context that they deal with is decadent, corrupt, and illegal, such as Saudi Arabia, to whom BAE sold arms. On a contingency argument, the global leaders should tailor their actions to the context—which is clearly what BAE did very effectively, bribing and paying commissions all down the line. Does this make their leaders virtuous? Clearly not: effective, perhaps, but hardly virtuous.

Different cultural contexts may require different character strengths (Gelfand et al. 2007; Javidan et al. 2006; Koopman et al. 1999; Muczyk and Holt 2008). For example, love and kindness may be more important for working and leading in cultures that regularly emphasize more feminine, collectivistic, and paternalistic values than those that are more masculine and individualistic. Humour may be more relevant for leading employees and interacting with people from affective versus neutral cultures (Trompenaars and Hampden-Turner 1997, 2004). Humility may produce better effects in cultures where a humble attitude is appreciated (Ahmad 2001; Yifeng and Tjosvold 2008) than in cultures where such strength may be interpreted as weakness and an undesirable trait of effective leaders. Spirituality may be more relevant in cultures where most stakeholders espouse religious values and beliefs (Otazo 1999) than in highly materialistic cultures.

When global leaders work at home

Being located and operating in the home country's headquarters does not decrease the relevance of virtues. For example, integrity is important, not just for those leaders who work in countries with ethically problematic practices and who interact with people from such contexts. It is also crucial for global leaders operating at home who have to support and inspire honest actions and policies of subsidiary managers. Global leaders, who are poor in wisdom and in the knowledge necessary to understand the complex mosaic of cultures and ethical practices around the world, are less able to lead the managers of subsidiaries who work worldwide appropriately. They may adopt policies and practices that collide with certain cultural and ethical contexts, and lose the credibility and trust from those who have to face directly the subtleties of each context.

Open-mindedness and love of learning are important, not only for leaders who travel regularly and interact with people from diverse cultural contexts. They are also important for developing cross-cultural savvy and understanding the cultural, economic, social, and political idiosyncrasies experienced by subsidiary managers. For example, a leader working in the US and supervising an expatriate operating in Asia Pacific must be aware that, when making deals in the region, the expatriate must have personal relationships, and develop the so-called 'family, friends, and favours' approach, whose development may take a long time and slow down decision-making (Otazo 1999). In the absence of such cross-cultural savvy, the American leader may make an inaccurate performance appraisal of the executive and repatriate him/her prematurely, precisely at the moment their relationships with local stakeholders reach the appropriate level for translating into good deals. Appropriate proposals, systems, processes, and approaches that the expatriate leader wants to implement locally may be rejected.

Reciprocal influences between strengths

Strengths may reinforce each other. Bravery and perseverance help global leaders to be honest. It is not to be expected that a global leader will be consistently honest if (s)he is not brave and persistent. Spirituality may foster humility and gratitude, and humility may nourish curiosity (Gunther and Neal 2008). Self-regulation and wisdom may help global leaders to be prudent: it is difficult to be prudent without personal discipline and wisdom. Global leaders who appreciate beauty and excellence are more likely to develop curiosity and love of learning, and vice versa. Global leaders who are grateful are more likely to adopt humane and fair practices. Most citizenship activities will not be feasible if global leaders are poor in the strength of leadership.

The development of one virtue does not necessarily result in developing other virtues. The development of one virtue may actually make more difficult the development of other virtues (Irwin 1997). For example, the development of bravery may create difficulties in acquiring kindness, love, and prudence. The development of love (sometimes implying partiality towards those loved ones) may impede (or, at least, make difficult) fairness (by definition, meaning impartiality). Developing forgiveness may make the development of bravery more difficult. Developing hope may also make developing prudence difficult—optimistic global leaders may be, at least from time to time, imprudent. In some situations, being courageous may require being somewhat imprudent and preserving modesty and forgiveness for other circumstances; otherwise, no leader would accept an international assignment or invest in certain problematic countries.

Being prudent may require putting appreciation of beauty and excellence and spirituality in second place.

Being virtuous is, thus, a complex journey. It will be rare to find all the referred qualities embodied in any single person. A virtuous human being is not a saint. Pursuing some virtues may force him/her to invest less in others. Therefore, expecting to have idealized, pure, virtuous global leaders heading organizations is neither prudent nor wise. In the same way that virtues are *in the middle*, it can be argued that virtuous global leaders are those who *tend* to be virtuous—with strengths and weaknesses, performing good and not so good acts, just like the rest of us. Therefore, the qualities we have identified should be thought of just as elements or dimensions in the ideal type for a good global leader. They may guide researchers and practitioners in their identification of global leaders who may produce more positive organizations. The crusade for pure virtuous leaders is neither realistic nor wise.

The notion of virtuousness is also relevant for framing the interpretation of the next sections. We suggest that human strengths and virtues are facilitators and enablers of global leader development—and development activities may also help in developing strengths. For example, working in tough environments may help develop bravery. Dealing with unprivileged people may grow humility and gratitude (Elkins 1998). Developing virtues and competencies is, thus, a continuing process.

Strengths and virtues as facilitators of leadership development

Cross-cultural and global leadership development experiences are crucial for developing a global mindset (Beechler and Javidan 2007; Caligiuri and Tarique 2009; Gupta and Govindarajan 2002). With an increasing demand for global leaders to carry out global strategies, organizations need to develop global leadership competencies for improving organizational effectiveness (Caligiuri 2006; Mendenhall 2006; Ng et al. 2009; Suutari 2002). Several development methods have been suggested, including (Caligiuri et al. 2005; Suutari 2002) international assignments (expatriation), impatriation, short-term development assignments, individualized coaching and mentoring on cultural experiences, international teams, international training and development programmes, action learning projects, international meetings and forums, and international travel (see Table 6.3).

165

Table 6.3. Methods for developing global leadership competencies

Methods	Comments/considerations
International assignments (expatriation)	• One of the most powerful (although costly, in terms of financial resources, time, family challenges) strategies for developing global leaders' competencies. • Individuals become more able to understand the worldwide operations and capabilities, learn cross-cultural competencies, develop cultural intelligence, and acquire a global mindset. • Individuals develop bonds of trust among people working in several places, and build their networks. • The flows of communication between units become more fluid, and knowledge is transferred. • For producing (better) benefits, the individuals (now repatriates) must have positions, after the mission, in which they can make use of the acquired competencies and experience.
Impatriation (transfer of host-country managers to headquarters, for training purposes)	• Individuals may benefit from the international experience as the expatriates do. • Impatriates bring to headquarters the understanding of the local contexts and cultures from which they proceed. • After impatriation, the individual may be in a good position to represent headquarters in the places where units are established.
Short-term development assignments	• They are sometimes called awareness-building assignments. • The primary purpose may be developing cross-cultural sensitivity and appreciation of the cultural, social, and economic mosaic.
Individualized coaching and mentoring on cultural experiences	• Individuals benefit from being coached by executives (and/or professional coaches) with cross-cultural experience and savvy. • Both coaching and mentoring may be carried out before, during and after international assignments. However, both activities are usually useful whenever the client or protégé needs to carry out international or cross-cultural roles and has not enough competencies.
International teams	• Networks of experts from several fields are developed. • Contrasting views and values can invite members to think globally. • Individuals develop cultural intelligence and a global mindset.
International training and development programmes	• The programmes can be internally or externally organized. The external ones may be necessary if not enough competencies exist in the organization—but the programme must be tailored. • To promote integration, cross-cultural interaction, networking, and cultural intelligence, participants and teaching staff must proceed from different cultures. • The effectiveness of these programmes may be improved when they are combined with action learning components.

Action learning projects/teams	• A multi-cultural team focuses on a specified set of objectives to be completed in a given time frame, which would have an impact on the total business.
	• Participants in these projects are challenged to think beyond their present jobs and to focus on challenges facing their whole business. They learn by doing.
	• A member of senior management must be appointed to coach and safeguard the team against possible criticism and political manoeuvring.
	• Individuals develop personal inquiry and learning, and achieve personal growth.
International meetings and forums	• Individuals know each other and learn, develop trust and networking, share knowledge and experiences, and ask for information from those who may have it.
	• Depending on the time length of interaction, cultural intelligence and global mindset are more or less developed.
International travel	• Trips help individuals to make contact with different cultures and develop cultural sensitivity.
	• The benefits can be enhanced if individuals 'dive' into the local homes, schools, and shops to have a more accurate idea about what real life is.
	• It must be made clear that the purpose of the trips is not just for task accomplishment, but is also developmental.

Built from: Caligiuri et al. (2005); Gregersen et al. (1998); Suutari (2002)

Research indicated that developing cross-cultural competences via developmental cross-cultural assignments was among the top-five organization-wide practices affecting the effectiveness of multinationals (Stroh and Caligiuri 1998). The study's findings suggested that firms' financial success was positively related to their ability to successfully develop global leadership competencies. Other researchers have argued that, more than inadequate or deficient resources, the limitation of global leaders' competencies represents the major constraint to globalization (Bartlett and Ghoshal 1992; Suutari 2002).

However, development costs are high, and even higher are the costs of investing in individuals who later reveal themselves unable to meet the firms' needs (Caligiuri and Tarique 2009). Global experience does not guarantee effective global leadership development (Cohen 2010). One way to increase the chances of success is to select individuals with higher potential and then offer them developmental experiences (Caligiuri 2006; Suutari 2002). Considering that global leadership is a journey of personal learning and transformation (Osland et al. 2006), we suggest that individuals with character strengths and virtues will be more motivated to accept or look for, and to take advantage of development experiences (Figure 6.1).

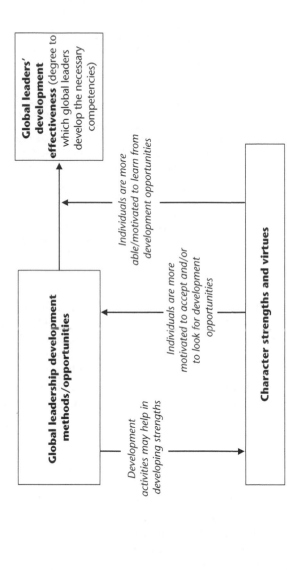

Figure 6.1 Character strengths and virtues as moderators and antecedents of global leadership development methods

Adapted from Rego et al. (2012)

Academic research directions

In contrast with cross-cultural leadership, the topic of global leadership is a nascent field in the organizational literature, having received much less attention than domestic leadership (Beechler and Javidan 2007; Osland et al. 2006; Suutari 2002). Studies of character strengths and virtues of global leaders are scarce, and virtuous leadership deserves more theoretical and empirical attention (Pearce et al. 2008). Therefore, avenues for future research are wide and deep, and countless questions are open to debate and empirical testing.

One of the most important questions is how global leaders' character strength and virtue relate to positive performance via the mediating role of virtuous global leadership. That is to say, it is important to test to what degree global leaders' virtues lead them to perform virtuous global leadership behaviours and, thus, to foster positive organizational performance. Beyond measuring character strengths and virtues (already operationalized through the *VIA Inventory of Strengths*: Peterson and Seligman, 2001; 2003), it is necessary to operationalize the virtuous global leadership and positive performance construct's measurement. We consider that the activities included in Figure 1.1 and Table 6.1 may be a possible departure point for operationalizing the virtuous global leadership's construct.

Measuring positive organizational performance is, however, a more complex endeavour. One may start by considering long-term financial performance (used to build the 'best performing CEOs in the world' ranking: Hansen et al. 2010) as a useful proxy. How do different global leaders' character strengths and virtues interact in predicting organizational long-term financial performance? However, other variables must be taken into account (e.g. organizational presence in rankings such as 'the best places to work for'; social accountability, and environment certifications; fairness of restructuring or downsizing practices; reducing the carbon footprint). Are such rankings dominated by organizations led by more virtuous global leaders? Do they win social accountability certifications more often?

Future studies may also test the relationship between global leaders' character strengths and virtues and their effectiveness, and whether it is mediated by variables such as a global mindset (Beechler and Javidan 2007), cultural intelligence (Earley et al. 2007), and other cognitive, relational and business competencies (Bird and Osland 2004; Mendenhall 2006). For example, one may speculate that global leaders' character strengths and virtues foster positive organizational performance because leaders develop global mindset and cultural intelligence and are thus more effective. Such variables may also act as moderators. For example, global leaders' character strengths and virtues may foster positive organizational performance if global leaders are also supplied with global mindset and cultural intelligence. Mediating variables at the organizational level (e.g. trust, collective self-efficacy) may also be pertinent. That is to say, global leaders' character strengths and virtues may foster positive organizational performance because leaders foster organizational trust and self-efficacy, these organizational features nourishing performance.

Another important research stream would consist in testing whether the relevance of character strengths and virtues for global leaders' performance is contingent on roles and missions. For example, is spirituality more relevant for dealing with people from contexts where spiritual values and practices prevail? Are integrity and bravery more relevant for global leaders who work and interact with partners from deeply corrupt contexts? Are forces such as curiosity, love of learning, and open-mindedness more relevant for dealing with partners from novel cultures and for leading cross-cultural teams with strong diversity? Is creativity more relevant for leading companies aiming to satisfy the needs of the 'base of pyramid'? Is vitality more necessary for leaders who travel frequently and live abroad for long periods? Are bravery, integrity, citizenship, and prudence more relevant for leaders who are charged to carry out track two diplomacy?

A key topic for further analysis is the extent to which global leaders' character strengths and virtues disseminate throughout the whole global organization and its subsidiaries across the world, and become embedded in routines, rituals, and rites that characterize the organization. Leadership in local sustainability programmes, in social welfare initiatives, in setting the pace for labour and management best practices may be considered. Longitudinal studies (Pearce et al. 2008) may test if the virtuousness degree of global leaders is reflected in (a) the kind of leaders they appoint for subsidiaries across the world, (b) the criteria they use for selecting expatriates; (c) the trust bonds developed between headquarters and subsidiaries, (d) the levels of job performance and affective organizational commitment developed by employees working in different subsidiaries across the world; (e) in-role and extra-role behaviour of subsidiaries' managers (Kim and Mauborgne 1996).

Do global leaders with high character strengths and virtues demonstrate better cross-cultural adjustment when working abroad? Are they more competent in carrying out effective track two diplomacy missions? Are they more willing to join initiatives such as the Global Compact,

World Business Council on Sustainable Development, or the Global Business Oath? What is the relationship between the global leaders' character strengths and virtues and the strength, breadth, and depth of the global networks they develop? What kind of visions and missions do global leaders with different degrees of character strengths and virtues develop? How is global leader virtuousness reflected in the relationships between the organization and its customers, suppliers, authorities, and partners? Do organizations led by virtuous global leaders have less exposure to judicial problems with stakeholders?

Future studies may also investigate to what degree the selection criteria for global leaders comprise character strengths and virtues. Do boards, companies, and headhunters consider such criteria when assessing the candidates' potential? Is there any relationship between such orientation and the degree to which companies are vulnerable to corporate scandals? To what extent do virtuous global leaders take into account character strengths and virtues for selecting their successors and expatriates? Is such a practice influenced by the virtuousness of their companies' culture?

Finally, future studies may empirically test the suggestion that character strengths and virtues make individuals more motivated to accept and look for development opportunities, and make them more able to learn from such opportunities. One possibility is to test, with adaptations, the theoretical model proposed by Ng, Van Dyne and Ang (2009). These authors used experiential learning process theory (Kolb 1984) to explain how global leaders may extract positive learning outcomes from experiences with international assignments. They proposed cultural intelligence as a moderating variable (i.e. individuals with higher cultural intelligence are more able to take advantage of international assignments). We suggest that virtues and character strengths may also play an important moderating role.

Experiential learning theory suggests that experience is critical for learning and change. The theory views learning as a holistic process of adapting to the world which requires integrating, perceiving, thinking, feeling, and behaving, as well as interaction between the individual and the environment. The theory proposes a four-stage learning cycle: (a) the tangible episodes or events of the immediate experience (*concrete experiences*) are the basis of (b) descriptive processing (*reflective observations*), which are then assimilated and distilled into (c) conceptual interpretations and symbolic representation of the experience (*abstract conceptualizations*), which become the basis for (d) action, or actual manipulation of the external world (*active experimentations*). Testing ideas in the real world (i.e. *active experimentations*) generates new experiences that trigger new cycles of learning (Ng et al. 2009).

For example, when contacting their Asian partners (*concrete experience*), a European leader operating in Malaysia may make *reflective observations* about the partners' idiosyncratic behaviours during the negotiation. As a consequence, (s)he develops *abstract conceptualizations* about why such behaviours are adopted, and reacts differently (*active experimentation*) to how (s)he usually behaves when negotiating with European counterparts. By adopting such behaviour and observing how Malaysian partners react, the European lives new experiences that facilitate further learning. Three learning outcomes may result from this experiential learning process (Kraiger et al. 1993; Ng et al. 2009):

- *Affective learning* outcomes refer to changes in the individuals' motivation and attitudes resulting from the learning experience with development opportunities. Global leaders tend to develop (a) higher self-efficacy for performing global leadership roles in different cultural contexts, (b) lower ethnocentrism and higher ethnorelativism toward other cultures, (c) stronger respect for distinct cultures, and (d) higher motivation for accepting other international experiences and development opportunities.

- *Knowledge* outcomes refer to the quantity and type of knowledge acquired during the learning experience. Global leaders tend to develop more accurate knowledge about other cultures' idiosyncrasies and the leadership styles more appropriate in different cultural contexts.

- *Behaviour* outcomes refer to the degree to which individuals develop newly learned behaviours for working and operating in other settings. Global leaders tend to develop a flexible repertoire of effective leadership behaviours in different cultural settings.

Future studies may test if character strengths and virtues (a) influence the degree to which individuals are motivated to accept international work assignment experiences and other development opportunities, (b) influence the experiential learning processes, (c) moderate the relationship between international work assignment experiences and experiential learning processes, between experiential learning processes and learning outcomes, and between learning outcomes and development opportunities. The resulting model is depicted in Figure 6.2. Next, we present examples supporting the suggested connections.

- Arrow 1—As previously argued, individuals with high levels of curiosity, open-mindedness, love of learning, leadership, bravery, and vitality are more likely to accept and look for development opportunities.

- Arrow 2—Individuals with higher curiosity and love of learning are more likely to seek cross-cultural experiences (i.e. concrete experiences) during development experiences. Open-mindedness, love of learning, wisdom, and appreciation of beauty and excellence help them to make more appropriate reflective observations. Love of learning, open-mindedness and wisdom make them more able to make appropriate abstract conceptualizations. Creativity, bravery, persistence, vitality, and hope impel them to carry out more active experimentations, and these experimentations are more appropriate if the individuals are also rich in prudence, humility, and social intelligence. Love of learning, open-mindedness, love, kindness, citizenship, justice, social intelligence, and humour help them to develop positive interactions and thus have more cultural contacts (i.e. concrete experiences), instead of separating themselves from direct and meaningful contact with the local culture.

- Arrow 3—Prudent and self-regulated individuals are more likely to adopt culturally appropriate active experimentations from abstract conceptualizations, thus experiencing new fruitful experiences that nourish other concrete experiences. Wisdom helps them to make more appropriate abstract conceptualizations from the reflective observations. Humility helps them to use unsuccessful active experimentations as opportunities for initiating a new cycle of learning.

- Arrow 4—Individuals with higher curiosity, love of learning, bravery, and persistence are more likely to use new knowledge acquired during the development opportunities for carrying out new international missions. Those with higher wisdom and prudence are more likely to select appropriate international missions after acquiring knowledge about other cultures in previous learning experiences. Those with higher gratitude, citizenship, and spirituality are more likely to accept new missions in which the new flexible leadership repertoire may be put at the service of a higher purpose.

- Arrow 5—Individuals with wisdom are more likely to translate active experimentations into useful behavioural leadership strategies for different cultural settings. Bravery, persistence, vitality, and hope may help them to translate such active experimentations into self-efficacy for performing global leadership roles in different cultural contexts. Open-mindedness, citizenship, and appreciation of

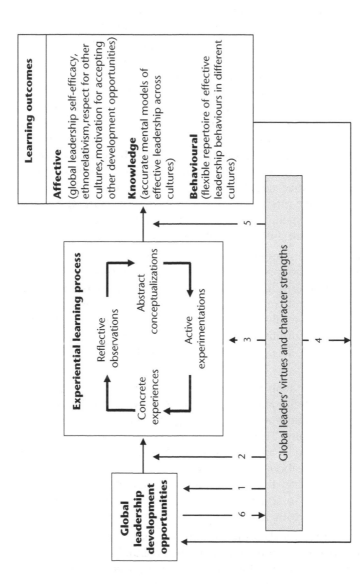

Figure 6.2 Virtues and character strengths as facilitators of the experiential learning process

Adapted from Ng et al. (2009)

beauty and excellence help them translate active experimentations into higher ethno-relativism and respect for distinct cultures.

- Arrow 6—Experiencing global leadership development opportunities help to develop character strengths. For example, an individual working in an international team composed of successful expatriates of countries where humility is valued may learn to develop this force, observing the greatness of his/her humble partners.

Some research suggestions may not be easy to implement. Collecting data on the mediators, moderators, and outcomes of the development opportunities discussed previously requires longitudinal designs and some variables will not be easy to operationalize (e.g., the four stages of the experiential learning process). Collecting data about global leaders' virtues and effectiveness may also be a difficult task. Due to both agenda constraints and desires to protect their image, the expectation that global leaders will participate in research surveys may be too optimistic.

Formal models, while helpful, may be more useful as orienting devices than literal frames for data collection and testing. There is more than a single way to do research, and surveys are only one way of collecting data. Global leaders leave many traces: in-depth analyses of (a) their discourse (interviews; messages in company reports; letters to shareholders; press releases) and (b) the congruence between discourse and practice may allow for the collection of valuable data (Podolny et al. 2010). Moreover, national elites often move in well-defined university circles and can be conversationally questioned as they engage in university life, as members of boards and committees, and as adjunct staff. The structured observation method used by Mintzberg (1971) may also be a useful way to identify global leaders' character strengths and the routes through which they are displayed, for example, in contacts with stakeholders and other interlocutors across the world. Such a method is very demanding but one can expect that the more virtuous leaders will be motivated to contribute to improving scientific knowledge within this unexplored field.

Conclusion

Although character is not 'dead' (Wright and Goodstein 2007), efforts must be made to keep it alive. This chapter points out several research routes through which such endeavour must be pursued. Naturally, writing, teaching, and researching will be in *vain* if practitioners remain sceptical about the virtue of virtues in leadership and organizational life. While cynicism about academic pursuits is a characteristic of a certain tough-minded attitude to business, not all leaders are necessarily cynical or sceptical. Jeff Immelt, the CEO of GE, argued that he wanted GE to be known as a virtuous company, in order to attract and motivate the most talented people (Gunther and Neal 2008). With this book, we expect to help other leaders pursue the same endeavour—not for fashion or folklore reasons, but because developing capacities that enable leaders to become, in their own spheres, virtuosi in virtue, can make organizations, especially multinational ones, crucial engines of social and economic progress (Ghoshal et al. 1999). After the 2011 disclosures about hacking, corruption, and other criminal behaviour at News Corp's News International, the alternatives are quite clear. Not only does an absence of virtue risk character, it also risks profits and criminal conviction. In the next chapter, having explained *why* striving for virtue in leadership deserves to be done, we shall discuss *how* virtuosity in this sphere can be attained.

7

What Is To Be Done?

Far from being villainous or exploitative, management as a profession can be seen for what it is—the primary engine of social and economic progress.

(Ghoshal et al. 1999: 13)

In high school I was complaining about a boring subject. My mother said, 'Donald, there is no such thing as a boring subject. What's boring is your refusal to try to find what makes it interesting.'

(Keough 2008: 176), former CEO of Coca-Cola Company)

The recursiveness of virtues and virtuosity

What is to be done? For leaders schooled in realism, this is *the* important political question. Rewarding virtuous actions can promote organizational virtuousness and positive organizational performance (Pearce et al. 2008). However, it is naïve to suppose that paying people to be virtuous will lead to virtuous leadership. Symbolic compensations, both from corporations and other institutions, may have stronger and more significant power. Publicly praising organizations and leaders for virtuous initiatives and practices may be a powerful enabler of organizational virtuousness (Kanter 2008). Nancy Adler (2008) suggested that the Nobel committee might need to consider private sector initiatives as candidates for future Nobel Peace Prizes, in line with the 2006 Prize to Muhammad Yunus.

Promoting citizenship initiatives similar to those referred to in Chapter 4 (see Table 4.2), fostering conditions for corporations to feel compelled to disclose triple bottom-line reporting (financial, social, and environmental performance), and promoting corporate transparency practices (Kanter 2008; Newton 2006) may also stimulate organizations to select and support virtuous leaders, although such reports risk being mere public relations or exercises in window dressing. Finally, it is important to teach virtues and character strengths in business schools (Allio 2003; Manz et al. 2008). There is an explicit need to counter the implicit MBA ideology of celebrating success in competition, whatever the costs of winning might be. Narratives (e.g. books, movies, and biographies), mentoring relationships, collaborative learning, service-learning, and self-reflection exercises and strategies may help to pursue such an endeavour (Hill and Stewart 1999).

Above all, we believe that social science is an essentially recursive activity. To the extent that its ideas are useful, they are used and, as they are used, they shape practice discursively. Our ambition is for our book to be a model of recursivity, one that is capable of transforming the common sense of everyday practice. Reading this volume, we hope, will help future global leaders to be more effective, reach positive organizational performance, and contribute to creating organizations that function as genuine forces for good, by developing character strengths and virtues that resist the inevitable pathogens they will encounter.

By cultivating and developing virtuous attitudes, decisions, and actions while interacting with employees, suppliers, customers, partners, government authorities, NGOs, and local communities worldwide, global leaders may build *good businesses* (Csikszentmihalyi 2003), promote organizational virtuousness (Cameron et al. 2004; Wright and Goodstein 2007), and support peace and human development (Damon 2004; Fort and Schipani 2004; Kaku 1997; Maak 2009; Tashman and Marano 2010). They may also build positive networks of self-regulation, and influence governments and transnational authorities to focus on more sustainable development, improve legislation, and be better role models for organizational behaviour and more astute in the selection of future leadership contenders.

Trying to select those who are, or may become, potential virtuosi in virtue requires serious attention, especially in terms of detecting those potential candidates who excel in impression management but are less than wholly virtuous (Pearce et al. 2008). Impression management often counts a great deal: as Charan (2005) suggested, leaders are often selected through a less-than-rigorous process, even at the top of organizations.

> Past success, defined in terms of performance as seen in the enhancement of stock prices, is usually seen as the best predictor of future success. It may well be necessary, however, to enquire how the performativity being presented was actually constructed: Were costs slashed to produce a great bottom line? If so, how were they cut: Was there disinvestment in innovation, in sustainability, in the future? Or was there performance sustained through a carefully

planned and executed program of innovation? It makes a difference whether performance is achieved by disinvestment or investment.

Virtuosity nourishing leadership

Leadership development actions may also be carried out, not only to develop global leaders with positive qualities but also to signal the importance of virtuous behaviours across all parts of the organization. Developing virtuous behaviours such as courage, spirituality, and humility is not easy. It can be encouraged, however. Individuals may learn, for example, that adopting courageous and honest actions is valued, supported, and sanctioned at the highest levels of the organization, supporting the adoption of courageous acts. Global leaders who have been poor in spirituality or secular humanism may learn how employees may be mobilized by spiritual values and that it is important to respect such values and create conditions in which they can be nourished, especially in less secular societies. Imprudent global leaders may learn how perverse the consequences of thoughtless decisions can be.

Human strengths and virtues make individuals more willing to accept and to look for development opportunities (Osland et al. 2006). Individuals with high levels of curiosity, open-mindedness, love of learning, leadership, bravery, and vitality are more likely to accept and consider international assignments and responsibilities in international teams, and participate in international meetings and forums. If they are also rich in spirituality, they are more prone to accept international assignments in places where spirituality/religiosity is strongly valued and practised. Appreciative of beauty and excellence, they are inclined to accept missions in beautiful and exotic, although difficult, locations.

Individuals with higher bravery, persistence, and vitality are more likely to accept frequent short-term assignments and enjoy regular travelling. Individuals with higher curiosity, open-mindedness, and love of learning are more inclined to participate in international teams, action learning projects, and international meetings and forums. Individuals with higher citizenship are more likely to represent their organizations internationally in bodies such as the Global Compact, the Equator Principles or the Caux Round Table Principles. Humility, curiosity, open-mindedness, love of learning, hope, and social intelligence will impel individuals to accept coaching and mentoring before an international assignment, instead of adopting a presumptive 'know- it-all' attitude.

People with higher transcendence and humanity are more likely to adhere to initiatives such as *SeitenWechsel* ('PerspectiveChange'), where executives are assigned for a short period of time, usually two weeks, to social welfare projects involving less privileged members of society (e.g. homeless people, juvenile delinquents, HIV-patients, the terminally ill, immigrants seeking asylum). Through such initiatives, managers may learn how to perceive the world through the eyes of less-privileged people, and realize, standing in their shoes, what they must seem like: thus, they can develop competencies of care and dispositions that can make them better global leaders (Mendenhall et al. 2003). They may also develop gratitude and compassion (Gunther and Neal 2008).

Human strengths and virtues also enable individuals to learn from development experiences and opportunities. In exploring our argument, we consider the main components of the social learning process: (1) paying attention to the situation, (2) retaining the knowledge gained from the situation, (3) reproducing the behavioural skills observed and learned, and (4) having motivation to adopt the learned behaviour (Bandura 1997; Thomas 2006). First, individuals pay attention to and appreciate critical cultural differences. Second, they transfer knowledge gained from a specific cultural experience to broader principles that can be used in future interactions in other cultural settings. Third, individuals adopt the behaviours correspondent to the learned general principles (i.e. they convert principles into behaviours to adopt in further social contexts). Fourth, they repeat and reinforce behaviours, developing motivation for repeating (avoiding) such behaviours as they realize that the learned behaviours are effective (ineffective) and produce positive (negative) results.

Individuals with higher curiosity, open-mindedness, perspective, love of learning, and appreciation of beauty and excellence are more predisposed to pay attention to and to remember others' behaviours, attitudes, and values witnessed while participating in international assignments, short-term assignments, international teams, international meetings and forums, and international travelling. They pay more attention to what their coaches and mentors do and say. They are more predisposed to learn from contrasting views and values, thus forcing themselves to think globally (Gregersen et al. 1998). They are more motivated to translate observed behaviours into appropriate behaviours, thus satisfying their motivation for wisdom and for mastering new skills. They tend to adopt a more inquisitive attitude when participating in action learning activities and international training and development programmes, feeling an attraction for idiosyncratic behaviours of other people, and asking pertinent questions to improve their cross-cultural adaptability.

Social intelligence, love, kindness, humility, prudence, open-mindedness, and appreciation of beauty and excellence build opportunities for positive social interactions, increasing the individuals' cross-cultural adjustment (Caligiuri 2006) and providing them with longer exposure time and more opportunities to learn the cultural, social, and economic particularism of the global and cross-cultural landscape (i.e. models are repeatedly available to them, increasing opportunities for attention and retention).

Humility, bravery, vitality, and persistence motivate individuals to continue to learn even when facing difficulties (e.g. when working in distant cultures, or when participating in teams in which communication problems and conflicts emerge as a result of cultural diversity) and after making errors and experiencing failures. Such personal attributes also make the individuals more apt to cope effectively with the difficulties inherent in the culture shock experienced when living in distant cultures.

Prudence, open-mindedness, and appreciation of beauty and excellence allow individuals to avoid biased attributions when facing cultural idiosyncrasies. This way, they are more able to understand the behavioural and attitudinal complexity of their counterparts and identify the appropriate behaviours and ways of doing things of different places.

In short, human strengths and virtues make individuals more apt to develop their global mindset (Beechler and Javidan 2007) and cultural intelligence when facing development opportunities (Thomas 2006). They are more attentive and motivated to appreciate, understand, and learn the cultural idiosyncrasies of the context. They are motivated to translate the acquired knowledge and the observed behaviours into appropriate actions. They are able to face learning difficulties and cultural mistakes with vigour, perseverance, wisdom, and a desire to improve cross-cultural and global competencies.

Habituating virtuosity

Experiencing global leadership development opportunities also helps to develop character strengths. For example, an individual from a rich country who is working in a poor one may develop gratitude when realizing that, contrary to his/her previous perspective, his/her life is full of wonderful gifts. An individual working in an international team composed of successful expatriates of countries where humility is valued may learn to develop this force, observing the greatness of his/her humble partners.

A young global leader benefiting from mentoring by a prudent and self-disciplined professional may develop prudence and self-regulation. A brave though intemperate individual who takes advantage of all available development experiences may gain wisdom and prudence after experiencing the negative consequences of his/her behaviour. An extrovert, kind, and humorous individual who goes to work in a poor community in a developing country may develop gratitude and citizenship after realizing that his/her small efforts at community development do make a difference.

Virtues are developed through ongoing practices that, in the course of time, transform into habits. Looking for and accepting development experiences may be the starting point of an ongoing personal transformation (Fowers and Davidov 2006; Mendenhall et al. 2003), which, in turn, may foster the motivation for accepting and learning with development experiences, thus giving rise to ongoing virtuousness spirals.

Obviously, this is an ideal type—but virtuous leaders may lose virtuousness and become cynical observers of the global arena if they experience frustration at being unable to fight poor conditions and abusive and unethical practices in cultures in which their organizations operate. In some situations, moral bravery may jeopardize company performance, at least in the short run—and the emerging dilemma may force the adoption of moral compromises that are more compromising than moral.

Conclusion

We see global leaders' virtuousness as a social process driving organizations into positive spirals, rather than as leader traits not amenable to cultivation. The fact that global leaders are subject to intense scrutiny transforms them into role models for any aspirant to the same type of position. To the extent that they achieve virtuosity across the virtues, they can become cases for celebration.

Global leaders are role models both for current and future generations and, through intergenerational reciprocity (Hernandez 2008), they may promote future leaders' and organizations' virtuousness. We suggest that virtuosi virtuous global leaders can turn global companies into engines of economic and human progress. Such endeavour, while it may not be easy, especially for publically listed companies in short-term oriented economies, is important: the difference they make and the example they offer, even when flawed, offer remarkable opportunities for learning and improving the state of the world. We believe that

Table 7.1. Ten tests of the ethical compass

- **Test of the family perspective:** Can I be proud to tell my family members and friends that I adopted this decision/action?
- **The congruence test:** Is this consistent with my own personal principles?
- **The cost-benefit test:** Does a benefit for some cause harm to others?
- **The dignity test:** Are the dignity and humanity of others preserved?
- **The equal treatment test:** Are the rights of the disadvantaged given consideration?
- **The front-page test:** Would I be comfortable if this decision were on the front page?
- **The golden rule test:** Would I be willing to be treated in the same way?
- **The personal gain test:** Does personal gain cloud my judgement?
- **The procedural justice test:** Do the procedures stand up to scrutiny by those affected?
- **The sleep test:** Can I sleep with this decision I made?

Adapted from: Glynn and Jamerson (2006); Newton (2006)

this aim constitutes a realistic ambition (Rawls 1999), whose accomplishment is more plausible if global leaders express their virtues and submit the ethicality of their choices to the ten tests of Table 7.1.

Acting virtuously can be difficult and is no guarantee of good results. But, as successive waves of scandal suggest, the best way to unsustainable competitive advantage, to the degradation of the reputation of business in society, the ruination of profits, and the destruction of individual honour is to ignore the role of virtues. Those who ignore virtue do so at their own peril; stripped of virtue they might find themselves observed mired in the dirt of disdain and gossip, miserable muckraked creatures, where they could have been virtuous contenders, casting light, seen far and wide. Ethical virtuosity is not something just for puritans.

References

Adler, N. J. (2002) Global companies, global society: There is a better way, *Journal of Management Inquiry*, 11(3): 255–60.

—— (2008) Corporate global citizenship: Successful partnership with the world, in C. C. Manz, K. S. Cameron, K. P. Manz, and R. D. Marx (Eds.), *The virtuous organization: Insights from some of the world's leading management thinkers* (181–208), Singapore: World Scientific.

Ahmad, K. (2001) Corporate leadership and workplace motivation in Malaysia, *International Journal of Commerce and Management*, 11(1): 82–101.

Aitken, T. (1973) What it takes to work abroad. In T. Aitken (Ed.), *The multinational man: The role of the manager abroad*, New York: Halstead Press.

Alldredge, M. E. and Nilan, K. K. (2000) 3M's leadership competency model: An internally developed solution, *Human Resource Management*, 39(2/3): 133–45.

Allio, R. J. (2003) Interview: Noel M. Tichy explains why the 'virtuous teaching cycle' is integral to effective leadership, *Strategy & Leadership*, 31(5): 20–5.

Alon, I. and Higgins, J. M. (2005) Global leadership success through emotional and cultural intelligences, *Business Horizons*, 48(6): 501–12.

Alvey, J. E. (2005) Economics and religion: Globalization as the cause of secularization as viewed by Adam Smith, *International Journal of Social Economics*, 32(3): 249–67.

Ang, S., Van Dyne, L., Koh, C. K. S., Ng, K. Y., Templer, K. J., Tay, C. et al. (2007) The measurement of cultural intelligence: Effects on cultural judgment and decision-making, cultural adaptation, and task performance, *Management and Organization Review*, 3: 335–71.

Aristotle (1999) *The Nicomachean ethics* (translated by W. D. Ross), New York: Batoche Books.

Austin, E. J., Farrelly, D., Black, C., and Moore, H. (2007) Emotional intelligence, Machiavellianism and emotional manipulation: Does EI have a dark side? *Personality and Individual Differences*, 43: 179–89.

Autry, J. A. (1991) *Love and profit: The art of caring leadership*, New York: Avon Books.

Avolio, B., Howell, J., and Sosik, J. (1999) A funny things happened on the way to the bottom line: Humor as a moderator of leadership style effects, *Academy of Management Journal*, 42(2): 219–27.

Axtell, R. E. (1998) *Gestures: The do's and taboos of body language around the world*, New York: John Wiley.

Bandura, A. (1997) *Self-efficacy: The exercise of control*, New York: Freeman.

Barbe, B. and Kleiner, B. H. (2005) Can a good company achieve greatness? *Management Research News*, 28(2/3): 108–17.

Barbuto, J. E. and Wheeler, D. W. (2006) Scale development and construct clarification of servant leadership, *Group & Organization Management*, 31(3): 300–26.

Bartlett, C. A. and Ghoshal, S. (1992) What is a global manager? *Harvard Business Review*, September–October, 70: 124–32.

Bartlett, M. Y. and DeSteno, D. (2006) Gratitude and prosocial behavior: Helping when it costs you, *Psychological Science*, 17: 319–25.

Bass, B. M. (1999) Two decades of research and development in transformational leadership, *European Journal of Work and Organizational Psychology*, 8: 9–32.

Bastons, M. (2008) The role of virtues in the framing of decisions, *Journal of Business Ethics*, 78(3): 389–400.

Bates, S. (2007) The eight most frequent mistakes people make in front of an audience, *Business Strategy Series*, 8(4): 311–17.

Batten, J. (1999) Lead with love, *Executive Excellence*, 16(6): 14.

Beaver, W. (1995) Levi's is leaving China, *Business Horizons*, 38(2): 35–40.

Beck, M. (1982) The Tylenol scare, *Newsweek*, October 11: 32–9.

Beck, U. (1999) *World risk society*, Oxford: Polity Press.

Beechler, S. and Javidan, M. (2007) Leading with a global mindset, in M. Javidan, R. M. Steers, M. and A. Hitt (Eds.), *Advances in international management* (19: 131–69), Stamford, CT: JAI Press.

Beer, L. A. (2003) The gas pedal and the brake . . . Toward a global balance of diverging cultural determinants in managerial mindsets, *Thunderbird International Business Review*, 45(3): 255–273.

Bennis, W., Goleman, D., and O'Toole, J. (Eds.) (2008) *Transparency: Creating a culture of candor*, San Francisco: Jossey Bass.

Bierly III, P. E. Kessler, E. H., and Christensen, E. W. (2000) Organizational learning, knowledge and wisdom, *Journal of Organizational Change Management*, 13(6): 595–618.

Bingham, C., Black, J. S., and Felin, T. (2000) An interview with John Pepper: What it takes to be a global leader, *Human Resource Management*, 39(2/3): 287–92.

Bird, A. and Osland, J. S. (2004) Global competencies: An introduction, in H. W. Lane, M. L. Maznevski, M. E. Mendenhall, and J. McNett (Eds.), *The Blackwell Handbook of Global Management* (57–80), London: Blackwell.

Black, J. S. (2006) The mindset of global leaders: Inquisitiveness and duality, in W. H. Mobley and E. Weldon (Eds.), *Advances in global leadership* (181–200), Stamford, CT: JAI Press.

—— and Gregersen, H. B. (1999) The right way to manage expats, *Harvard Business Review*, 77: 52–63.

—— Morrison, A. J., and Gregersen, H. B. (1999) *Global explorers: The next generation of leaders*, New York: Routledge.

Boardman, C. M. and Kato, H. K. (2003) The Confucian roots of business Kyosei, *Journal of Business Ethics*, 48(4): 317–33.

Bollaert, H. and Petit, V. (2010) Beyond the dark side of executive psychology: Current research and new directions, *European Management Journal*, 28(5): 362–76.

Bono, G. and McCullough M. E. (2006) Positive responses to benefit and harm: Bringing forgiveness and gratitude into cognitive psychotherapy, *Journal of Cognitive Psychotherapy*, 20: 147–58.

—— —— and Root, L. M. (2008) Forgiveness, feeling connected to others, and well-being: Two longitudinal studies, *Personality and Social Psychology Bulletin*, 34: 182–95.

Box, T. and Byus, K. (2009) Southwest Airlines 2007, *Journal of the International Academy for Case Studies*, 15(1): 21–7.

Boyd, D. E., Spekpman, R. E., Kamauff, J. W., and Werhane, P. (2009) Corporate social responsibility in global supply chains: A procedural justice perspective, *Long Range Planning*, 40: 341–56.

Brady, C. (2010) An unlikely inspiration, *Financial Times/Business Education*, December 6: 14.

Bragues, G. (2006) Seek the good life, not money: The Aristotelian approach to business ethics, *Journal of Business Ethics*, 67: 341–57.

Branson, R. (1998) *Losing my virginity: How I've survived, had fun, and made a fortune doing business my way*, New York: Three Rivers Press.

Brenkert, G. (2009) Google, human rights, and moral compromise, *Journal of Business Ethics*, 85(4): 453–78.

Brett, J. M. (2001) *Negotiating globally*, San Francisco: Jossey Bass.

Briggs, D. (2008) Lead by example to reach global audiences, *Strategic Communication Management*, 12(2): 13–15.

Bright, D., Cameron, K., and Caza, A. (2006) The amplifying and buffering effects of virtuousness in downsized organizations, *Journal of Business Ethics*, 64: 249–69.

Bright, D. S. (2006) Forgiveness as an attribute of leadership, in E. D. Hess and K. S. Cameron (Eds.), *Leading with values* (172–93), Cambridge: Cambridge University Press.

—— Fry, R. E., and Cooperrider, D. L. (2008) Forgiveness from the perspectives of three response modes: Begrudgement, pragmatism, and transcendence, in C. C. Manz, K. S. Cameron, K. P. Manz, and R. D. Marx (Eds.), *The virtuous organization: Insights from some of the world's leading management thinkers* (67–95), Singapore: World Scientific.

Brockner, J., Ackerman, G., Greenberg, J., Gelfand, M. J., Francesco, A. M., Chen, Z. X., Leung, K., Bierbrauer, G., Gomez, G., Kirkman, B. L., and Shapiro, D. (2001) Culture and procedural justice: The influence of power distance on reactions to voice, *Journal of Experimental Social Psychology*, 37(4): 300–15.

Brown, R. M. (1998) *Spirituality and liberation: Overcoming the great fallacy*, Louisville: The Westminster Press.

Brownell, J. (2006) Meeting the competency needs of global leaders: A partnership approach, *Human Resource Management*, 45(3): 309–36.

Bruce, S. (2002) *God is dead: Secularization in the West*, Malden, MA: Blackwell.

Burns, P., Myers, A., and Kakabadse, A. (1995) Are national stereotypes discriminating? *European Management Journal*, 13(2): 212–17.

Burton, J. (1999) Samsung car company in receivership: Chaebol Swap with DAEWO fails, *Financial Times*, July 1: 32.

Cadbury, A. (1989) Ethical managers make their own rules, in K. R. Andrews (Ed.), *Ethics in practice: Managing the moral corporation* (70–6), Boston, MA: Harvard Business School Press.

—— (2010) *Chocolate wars*, New York: Harper.

Caldwell, C. and Dixon, R. (2010) Love, forgiveness, and trust: Critical values of the modern leader, *Journal of Business Ethics*, 93(1): 91–101.

Caligiuri, P. (2006) Developing global leaders, *Human Resource Management Review*, 16: 219–28.

—— and Tarique, I. (2009) Predicting effectiveness in global leadership activities *Journal of World Business* 44(3): 336–46.

—— Lazarova, M. and Tarique, I. (2005) Training, learning and development in multinational organizations, in H. Scullion and M. Linehan (Eds.), *International human resource management: A critical text* (71–90), New York: Palgrave MacMillan.

Cameron, K. S. (2010) Five keys to flourishing in trying times, *Leader to Leader*, 55: 45–51.

—— (2003) Organizational virtuousness and performance, in K. S. Cameron, J. E. Dutton, and R. E. Quinn (Eds.), *Positive organizational scholarship* (48–65), San Francisco: Berrett-Koehler.

—— and Caza, A. (2002) Organizational and leadership virtues and the role of forgiveness, *Journal of Leadership & Organizational Studies*, 9(1): 33–48.

—— —— (2004) Introduction: Contributions to the discipline of positive organizational scholarship, *American Behavioral Scientist*, 47(6): 731–9.

Cameron, K. S. and Spreitzer, G. M. (Eds.) (2012) *The Oxford Handbook of Positive Organizational Scholarship*, Oxford: Oxford University Press.

Cameron, K. S., Bright, D., and Caza, A. (2004) Exploring the relationships between organizational virtuousness and performance, *American Behavioral Scientist*, 47(6): 1–24.

Caminiti, S. (2005) The people company, *NYSE Magazine*, January/February, 12–16.

Carey, D., Patsalos-Fox, M., and Useem, M. (2009) Leadership lessons for hard times, *McKinsey Quarterly*, 4: 52–61.

Carpenter, M. A. and Sanders, W. G. (2004) The effects of top management team pay and firm internationalization on MNC performance, *Journal of Management*, 30(4): 509–28.

Castells, M. (2009) *Communication Power*, Cambridge: Polity.

Cavanagh, G. F. (2000) Executives' code of business conduct: Prospects for the Caux Principles, in O. F. Williams (Ed.), *Global codes of conduct: An idea whose time has come* (169–82), Notre Dame, IN: University of Notre Dame Press.

—— and Bandsuch, M. R. (2002) Virtue as a benchmark for spirituality in business, *Journal of Business Ethics,* 38(1/2): 109–17.

Charan, R. (2005) Ending the CEO succession crisis, *Harvard Business Review,* February, 83(2): 72–81.

Child, J. (2002) The international crisis of confidence in corporations, *Academy of Management Executive,* 16(3): 142–44.

Chun, R. (2005) Ethical character and virtue in organizations: An empirical assessment and strategic implications, *Journal of Business Ethics,* 57: 269–84.

Clark, M., Adjei, M., and Yancey, D. (2009) The impact of service fairness perceptions on relationship quality, *Services Marketing Quarterly,* 30(3): 287–302.

Clegg, S. R. (2008) 'Relationships of ownership, they whisper in the wings . . .', Review Article of Khurana, R. 2007 *From higher aims to hired hands: The social transformation of American business schools and the unfulfilled promise of management education,* Princeton: Princeton University Press, *Australian Review of Public Affairs,* March 2008, <http://www.australianreview.net/digest/2008/03/clegg.html>; retrieved December 27, 2011.

—— and Haugaard, M. (2009) *The Sage handbook of power,* London: Sage.

Cohen, S. L. (2010) Effective global leadership requires a global mindset, *Industrial and Commercial Training,* 42(1): 3–10.

Collier, P. and Dollar, D. (2002) *Globalization, growth, and poverty: Building an inclusive world economy,* New York: The World Bank.

Collins, D. (2009) Kozlowski's Tyco – 'I am the company', in A. Gini and A. M. Marcoux (Eds.), *Cases studies on business ethics* (115–25), Upper Saddle River, NJ: Pearson.

Collins, J. (2001) Level 5 leadership: The triumph of humility and fierce resolve, *Harvard Business Review,* January, 79(1): 67–76.

—— (2009) *How the mighty fall: And why some companies never give in,* New York: Arrow.

Conger, J. A. (1990) The dark side of leadership, *Organizational Dynamics,* Autumn, 19(2): 44–55.

—— (1999) Charismatic and transformational leadership in organizations: An insider's perspective on these developing streams of research, *Leadership Quarterly,* 10: 145–79.

Conlin, M. (1999) Religion in the workplace, *Business Week,* 3653: 150–8.

Conner, J. (2000) Developing the global leaders of tomorrow, *Human Resource Management,* 39(2/3): 147–57.

Cowherd, D. M. and Levine, D. I. (1992) Product quality and pay equity between lower-level employees and top management: An investigation of distributive justice theory, *Administrative Science Quarterly,* 37: 302–20.

Crossan, M., Vera, D., and Nanjad, L. (2008) Transcendent leadership: Strategic leadership in dynamic environments, *Leadership Quarterly,* 19: 569–81.

Csikszentmihalyi, M. (2003) *Good business: Leadership, flow and the making of meaning*, New York: Viking.

Cunha, M. P. and Cunha, R. C. (2004) Changing a cultural grammar? The pressure towards the adoption of 'Northern time' by Southern European managers, *Journal of Managerial Psychology*, 19(8): 795–808.

—— and Rego, A. (2010) Complexity, simplicity, simplexity, *European Management Journal*, 28(2): 85–94.

———— and D'Oliveira, T. (2006) Organizational spiritualities: An ideology-based typology, *Business and Society*, 45: 211–34.

Cunha, M. P., Guimarães-Costa, N., Rego, A., and Clegg, S. (2010) *Leading and following (un)ethically in* 'limen', *Journal of Business Ethics*, 97(2): 189–206.

Dalton, C. M. (2007) The science of customers: An interview with Youngsuk Chi, Vice Chairperson and Global Managing Director of Academic and Customer Relations, Elsevier, *Business Horizons*, 50: 193–8.

Damon, W. (2004) *The moral advantage*, San Francisco: Berrett-Koehler.

Danna, K. and Griffin, R. W. (1999) Health and well-being in the workplace: A review and synthesis of the literature, *Journal of Management*, 25(3): 357–84.

Dearlove, D. (2007) *Richard Branson Way: 10 secrets of the world greatest brand builder*, Chichester: Capstone.

DeCelles, K. A. and Pfarrer, M. D. (2004) Heroes or villains? Corruption and the charismatic leader, *Journal of Leadership and Organizational Studies*, 11(1): 67–77.

DeFrank, R. S., Konopaske, R., and Ivancevich, J. M. (2000) Executive travel stress: Perils of the road warrior, *Academy of Management Executive*, 14(2): 58–71.

Delbecq, A. L. (2008) The spiritual challenges of power, humility, and love as offsets to leadership hubris, in C. C. Manz, K. S. Cameron, K. P. Manz, and R. D. Marx (Eds.), *The virtuous organization: Insights from some of the world's leading management thinkers* (97–112), Singapore: World Scientific.

Den Hartog, D. N. (2004) Leading in a global context: Vision in complexity, in H. W. Lane, M. L. Maznevski, M. E. Mendenhall, and J. McNett (Eds.), *The Blackwell handbook of global management* (175–98), London: Blackwell.

—— and Verburg, R. M. (1997) Charisma and rhetoric: Communicative techniques of international business leaders, *Leadership Quarterly*, 8(4): 355–91.

Dennis, R. S. and Bocarnea, M. (2005) Development of the servant leadership assessment instrument, *Leadership and Organization Development Journal*, 26(7/8): 600–15.

DePree, M. (2004) *Leadership is an art*, New York: Doubleday.

Diamond, J. (1998) *Guns, germs and steel: A short history of everybody for the last 13,000 years*, London: Vintage.

Diener, E. and Seligman, M. E. P. (2004) Beyond money: Toward an economy of well-being, *Psychological Science in the Public Interest*, 5(1): 1–31.

Distefano, J. (1995) Tracing the vision and impact of Robert K. Greenleaf, in L. Spears (Ed.), *Reflections on leadership* (61–78), New York: Wiley.

Donal, P., Peasgood, T., and White, M. (2008) Do we really know what makes us happy? A review of the economic literature on the factors associated with subjective well-being, *Journal of Economic Psychology*, 29(1): 94–122.

Donaldson, T. (1989) *The ethics of international business*, Oxford: Oxford University Press.

—— and Dunfee, T. W. (1999) When ethics travel: The promise and peril of global business ethics, *California Management Review*, 41(4): 45–63.

Dorfman, P., Hanges, P. J., and Brodbeck, F. C. (2004) *Leadership and cultural variation: The identification of culturally endorsed leadership profiles, leadership, culture, and organizations: The GLOBE study of 62 societies*, Thousand Oaks, CA: Sage.

Dougherty, D. S. and Krone, K. J. (2002) Emotional intelligence as organizational communication, *Communication Yearbook*, 26(1): 202–29.

Driscoll, C. and McKee, M. (2007) Restoring a culture of ethical and spiritual values: A role for leader storytelling, *Journal of Business Ethics*, 73(2): 205–17.

Driver, M. (2005) From empty speech to full speech? Reconceptualizing spirituality in organizations based on a psychoanalytically-grounded understanding of the self, *Human Relations*, 58(9): 1091–110.

Dunlap, A. J. and Andelman, B. (1996) *Mean business: How I save bad companies and make good companies great*, New York: Fireside.

Earley, P. C. and Mosakowski, E. (2004) Cultural intelligence, *Harvard Business Review*, October, 82(10): 139–53.

—— Murnieks, C., and Mosakowski, E. (2007) Cultural intelligence and the global mindset, in M. Javidan, R. M. Steers, M. and A. Hitt (Eds.), *Advances in International Management* (19: 75–103), Stamford, CT: JAI Press.

Ecklund, E., Park, J., and Veliz, P. (2008) Secularization and religious change among elite scientists, *Social Forces*, 86(4): 1805–39.

Eden, R. (2010) BP oil spill: Tony Hayward's yacht sets sail again, Telegraph.co.uk, July 4 (<http://www.telegraph.co.uk/finance/newsbysector/energy/oilandgas/7870345/BP-oil-spill-Tony-Haywards-yacht-sets-sail-again.html>; retrieved December 27, 2011).

Edgecliffe-Johnson, A. (2010) 'I don't believe anger is an effective way of managing', *Financial Times*, November 29: 16.

Edmondson, A. (1999) Psychological safety and learning behavior in work teams, *Administrative Science Quarterly*, 44: 350–83.

Elaydi, R. and Harrison, C. (2010) Strategic motivations and choice in subsistence markets, *Journal of Business Research*, 63: 651–5.

Elias, N. (1969) *The Civilizing Process, Vol. I. The History of Manners*, Oxford: Blackwell.

Elkins, T. E. (1998) Participation in an international medical practice in West Africa, *Obstetrics & Gynecology*, 91(2): 302–4.

Emler, N. and Cook, T. (2001) Moral integrity in leadership: Why it matters and why it may be difficult to achieve, in B. W. Roberts and R. Hogan (Eds.), *Personality psychology in the workplace* (277–98), Washington, DC: American Psychological Association.

Enright, R.D. (2001) *Forgiveness is a choice: A step-by-step process for resolving anger and restoring hope*, Washington, DC: APA Life Tools.

Enron (2000) Annual Report of 2000. Enron (<http://picker.uchicago.edu/Enron/EnronAnnualReport2000.pdf>; retrieved December 28, 2011).

Entine, J. (2002) Body Shop's packaging starts to unravel, *Australian Financial Review*, December 18, accessed December 28, 2011 from <http://www.jonentine.com/reviews/Body_Shop_AFR.htm>

—— (2004) The strange-than-truth story of the Body Shop, in D. Wallis (2004) *Killed: Great journalism too hot to print*, New York: Nation Books.

Fairholm, G. W. (1993) *Organizational power politics: Tactics in organizational leadership*, Westport, CT: Praeger.

Farh, J. L., Dobbins, G. H., and Cheng, B. S. (1991) Cultural relativity in action: A comparison of self-ratings made by Chinese and US workers, *Personnel Psychology*, 44, 129–47.

Fassina, N. E., Jones, D. and Uggerslev, K. L. (2008) Meta-analytic tests of relationships between organizational justice and citizenship behavior: Testing agent-system and shared-variance models, *Journal of Organizational Behavior*, 29: 805–28.

Ferch, S. R. (2004) Servant-leadership, forgiveness, and social justice, in L. C. Spears and M. Lawrence (Eds.), *Practicing servant leadership: Succeeding through trust, bravery, and forgiveness* (225–39), San Francisco, CA: Jossey-Bass.

Ferraro, F., Pfeffer, J., and Sutton, R. I. (2005) Economic language and assumptions: How theories can become self-fulfilling, *Academy of Management Review*, 30: 8–24.

—————— (2009) How and why theories matter: A comment on Felin and Foss (2009), *Organization Science*, 20: 669–75.

Fey, C. F. and Shekshnia, S. (2011) The key commandments for doing business in Russia, *Organizational Dynamics*, 40: 57–66.

Financial Times (1999) Car crazy, *Financial Times*, July 1: 25.

Finkelstein, S. (1992) Power in top management teams: Dimensions, measurement, and validation, *Academy of Management Journal*, 35(3): 505–38.

Fischlmayr, I. and Kollinger, I. (2010) Work-life balance—a neglected issue among Austrian female expatriates, *The International Journal of Human Resource Management*, 21(4): 455–87.

Flannery, T. (1994) *The future eaters: An ecological history of the Australasian lands and people*, Sydney: Reed.

Flynn, G. (2008) The virtuous manager: A vision for leadership in business, *Journal of Business Ethics*, 78(3): 359–72.

Forster, N. (2000) Expatriates and the impact of cross-cultural training, *Human Resource Management Journal*, 10(3): 63–78.

Fort, T. L. and Junhai, L. (2002) Chinese business and the Internet: The infrastructure for trust, *Vanderbilt Journal of Transnational Law*, 35: 1545–99.

—— and Schipani, C. A. (2001) *The role of the corporation in fostering sustainable peace*, William Davidson Working Paper Number 422, November.

—— and Schipani, C. (2004) *The role of business in fostering peaceful societies*, Cambridge: Cambridge University Press.

—— Schipani, C. A. (2007) An action plan for the role of business in fostering peace, *American Business Law Journal*, 44(2): 359–77.

Fowers, B. J. and Davidov, B. J. (2006) The virtue of multiculturalism: Personal transformation, character, and openness to the other, *American Psychologist*, 61(6): 581–94.

Fraser, I. (2010) The great and the good aim to 'humanise globalization', *Financial Times*, June 21: 10.

Fredrickson, B. L. (2003) Positive emotions and upward spirals in organizational settings, in K. Cameron, J. Dutton, and R. Quinn (Eds.), *Positive organizational scholarship* (163–75), San Francisco: Berrett Koehler.

—— and Joiner, T. (2002) Positive emotions trigger upward spirals toward emotional well-being, *Psychological Science*, 13(2): 172–5.

Freiberg, K. and Freiberg, J. (2004) How gutsy leaders blow the doors off business-as-usual, *Leader to Leader*, 33: 32–7.

French, J. R. P., Jr. and Raven, B. H. (1959) The bases of social power, in D. Cartwright (Ed.), *Studies of social power* (150–67), Ann Arbor, MI: Institute for Social Research.

Friedman, M. (1970) The social responsibility of business is to increase its profits, *New York Times Magazine*, September 13, 32.

Friedman, T. L. (2002) India, Pakistan and G.E. *New York Times*, August 11 (<http://query.nytimes.com/gst/fullpage.html?res=940CEED9153AF932A2575-BC0A9649C8B63;> retrieved December 28, 2011)

—— (2005a) *The world is flat*, New York: Farrar, Strauss and Giroux.

—— (2005b) It's a flat world, after all, *New York Times*, April 3: 32–7.

Frost, P. J. (2003) *Toxic emotions at work*, Boston, MA: Harvard Business School Press.

Fry, L. W. (2003) Toward a theory of spiritual leadership, *Leadership Quarterly*, 14: 693–727.

—— (2008) Spiritual leadership: State-of -the-art and future directions for theory, research, and practice, in J. Biberman and L. Tishman (Eds.), *Spirituality in business: Theory, practice, and future directions* (106–24), New York: Palgrave.

—— and Matherly, L. L. (2007) Spiritual leadership and performance excellence, in S. G. Rogelberg (Ed.), *Encyclopedia of Industrial/Organizational Psychology*, Thousand Oaks, CA: Sage.

—— and Slocum Jr, J. W. (2008) Maximizing the triple bottom line through spiritual leadership, *Organizational Dynamics*, 37(1): 86–96.

—— Vitucci, S., and Cedillo, M. (2005) Spiritual leadership and army transformation: Theory, measurement, and establishing a baseline, *Leadership Quarterly*, 16: 835–62.

—— Hannah, S., Noel, M., and Walumbwa, F. (2011) Impact of spiritual leadership on unit performance, *Leadership Quarterly*, 22(2): 259–70.

Fujio, M. (2004) Silence during intercultural communication: A case study, *Corporate Communications*, 9(4): 331–9.

Fuller, S. (1997) The secularization of science and a new deal for science policy, *Futures*, 29(6): 483–503.

Gabel, M. (2004) Where to find 4 billion new customers: Expanding the world's marketplace, *The Futurist*, 38(4): 28–31.

Gannon, M. J. and Pillai, R. (2010) *Understanding global cultures: Metaphoric journeys through 29 nations, clusters of nations, continents and diversity* (4th ed.), Thousand Oaks: Sage.

Gaut, B. (1997) The structure of practical reason, in G. Cullity and B. Gaut (Eds.), *Ethics and practical reason* (161–88), Oxford: Oxford University Press.

Gavin, J. H. and Mason, R. O. (2004) The virtuous organization: The value of happiness in the workplace, *Organizational Dynamics*, 33(4): 379–92.

Ge, G. and Ding, D. (2008) A strategic analysis of surging Chinese manufacturers: The case of Galanz, *Asia Pacific Journal of Management*, 25(4): 667–83.

Gelfand, M. J., Erez, M., and Aycan, Z. (2007) Cross-cultural organizational behaviour, *Annual Review of Psychology*, 58: 479–514.

George, B. (2003) *Authentic leadership: Rediscovering the secrets to creating lasting value*, San Francisco, CA: Jossey Bass.

—— (2009) *Seven lessons for leading in crisis*, San Francisco: Jossey Bass.

—— Sims, P., McLean, A.N., and Mayer, D. (2007) Discovering your authentic leadership, *Harvard Business Review*, February, 85(2): 129–38.

Ghemawat, P. (2011) The cosmopolitan corporation, *Harvard Business Review*, 89(5): 92–9.

Ghoshal, S. (2005) Bad management theories are destroying good management practices, *Academy of Management Learning and Education*, 4(1): 75–91.

—— and Moran, P. (1996) Bad for practice: A critique of the transaction cost theory, *Academy of Management Review*, 21(1): 13–47.

—— —— (2005) Towards a good theory of management, in J. Birkinshaw and G. Piramal (Eds.), *Sumantra Ghoshal on management* (1–27), London: FT/Prentice-Hall.

—— Bartlett, C., and Moran, P. (1999) A new manifest for management, *Sloan Management Review*, Spring, 40(3): 9–20.

Glasman, M. (1996) Unnecessary suffering: managing market utopia, London: Verso.

Glynn, M. and Jamerson, H. (2006) Principled leadership: A framework for action, in E. D. Hess and K. S. Cameron (Eds.), *Leading values: Positivity, virtue, and high performance* (151–71), Cambridge: Cambridge University Press.

Goffee, R. and Jones, G. (2006) Getting personal on the topic of leadership: Authentic self-expression works for those at the top, *Human Resource Management International Digest*, 14(4): 32–4.

Goleman, D. (1998) What makes a leader? *Harvard Business Review*, November–December: 93–102.

—— Bennis, W., and O'Toole, J. (2008) *Transparency: How leaders create a culture of candor*, San Francisco: Jossey Bass.

Goodpaster, K. E. (2000) The Caux Round Table principles: Corporate moral reflection in a global business environment, in O. F. Williams (Ed.), *Global codes of conduct: An idea whose time has come* (183–95), Notre Dame, IN: University of Notre Dame Press.

Gorski, P. and Altinordu, A. (2008) After secularization? *Annual Review of Sociology,* 34: 55–85.

Gould, S. and Grein, A. (2009) Think glocally, act glocally: A culture-centric comment on Leung, Bhagat, Buchan, Erez and Gibson (2005), *Journal of International Business Studies,* 40(2): 237–54.

Gowri, A. (2007) On corporate virtue, *Journal of Business Ethics,* 70(4): 391–400.

Graham, C. (2005) The economics of happiness: Insights on globalization from a novel approach, *World Economics,* 6(3): 41–55.

—— (2006) The economics of happiness, in S. Durlauf and L. Blume (Eds.), *The new Palgrave dictionary of economics* (2nd ed.), London: Palgrave McMillan.

Grant, A. M., Christianson, M. K., and Price, R. H. (2007) Happiness, health, or relationships? Managerial practices and employee well-being tradeoffs, *Academy of Management Perspectives,* 21: 51–63.

Grant, K. (2008a) Who are the lepers in our organizations? A case for compassionate leadership, *Business Renaissance Quarterly,* 3(2): 75–91.

—— (2008b) Imperfect people leading imperfect people: Creating environments of forgiveness, *Interbeing,* 2(2): 11–17.

Grant-Vallone, E. J. and Ensher, E. A. (2001) An examination of work and personal life conflict, organizational support, and employee health among international expatriates, *International Journal of Intercultural Relations,* 25: 261–78.

Greenberg, J. (2001) Studying organizational justice cross-culturally: Fundamental challenges, *International Journal of Conflict Management,* 12(4): 365–75.

Greenleaf, R. K. (1998) *The power of servant leadership,* San Francisco, CA: Berrett-Koehler.

Greger, K. R and Peterson, J. S. (2000) Leadership profiles for the new millennium, *Cornell Hotel and Restaurant Administration Quarterly,* 41(1): 16–29.

Gregersen, H. B., Morrison, A. J., and Black, J. S. (1998) Developing leaders for the global frontier, *Sloan Management Review,* Fall, 40(1): 21–32.

Grieve, R. and Mahar, D. (2010) The emotional manipulation-psychopathy nexus: Relationships with emotional intelligence, alexithymia and ethical position, *Personality and Individual Differences,* 48(8): 945–50.

Griffith, D. A., Harvey, M. G., and Lusch, R. F. (2006) Social exchange in supply chain relationships: The resulting benefits of procedural and distributive justice, *Journal of Operations Management,* 24(2): 85–98.

Grint, K. (2010) The sacred in leadership: Separation, sacrifice and silence, *Organization Studies,* 31(1): 89–107.

Grol, P., Schoch, C. and CPA (1998) IKEA: Managing cultural diversity, in G. Oddou and M. Mendenhall (Eds.), *Cases in international organizational behavior* (88–112), Oxford: Blackwell.

Gunn, R.W. and Gullickson, B. R. (2006) Lucky Mud, *Strategic Finance,* 88(1): 8, 10.

Gunther, M. and Neal, J. (2008) *Fortune* Sr. Writer Marc Gunther on 'the role of virtuous in spiritual leadership', in C. C. Manz, K. S. Cameron, K. P. Manz, and

R. D. Marx (Eds), *The virtuous organization: Insights from some of the world's leading management thinkers* (259–78), Singapore: World Scientific.

Gupta, A. K. and Govindarajan, V. (2002) Cultivating a global mindset, *Academy of Management Executive*, 16(1): 116–26.

Gwynne, P. (2010) Google's experience raises doubts about high-tech business in China, *Research Technology Management*, 53(3): 2–3.

Hall, E. T. (1981) *Beyond culture*, New York: Doubleday.

Hamilton, E. A. (2006) An exploration of the relationship between loss of legitimacy and the sudden death of organizations, *Group & Organization Management*, 31(3): 327–58.

Hansen, M. T., Ibarra, H., and Peyer, U. (2010) The best-performing CEOs in the world, *Harvard Business Review*, January–February, 88: 104–13.

Hanson, K. and Rothlin, S. (2010) Taking your code to China, *Journal of International Business Ethics*, 3(1): 69–80.

Hart, S. L. (2005) *Capitalism at the crossroads*, New Jersey: Wharton School Publishing.

—— and Christensen, C. M. (2002) The great leap: Driving innovation from the base of the pyramid, *MIT Sloan Management Review*, 44(1): 51–6.

Harvey, M. G. (1995) The impact of dual-career families on international relocations, *Human Resource Management Review*, 5(3): 223–44.

—— and Novicevic, M. M. (2004) The development of political skill and political capital by global leaders through global assignments, *International Journal of Human Resource Management*, 15(7): 1173–88.

—— and Wiese, D. (1998) Global dual-career couple mentoring: A phase model approach, *HR. Human Resource Planning*, 21(2): 33–48.

Hayek, F. A. (1988) *The fatal conceit: The errors of socialism*, Chicago: University of Chicago Press.

Hayward, M. L. A. and Hambrick, D. D. (1997) Explaining the premiums paid for large acquisitions: Evidence of CEO hubris, *Administrative Science Quarterly*, 42: 103–27.

Helman, C. (2010) Slick performance (the optimism of Tony Hayward, chief executive at BP, about the future of the oil industry in the wake of the BP's Deepwater Horizon drilling rig disaster), *Forbes*, 185(10): 28–9.

Hendon, D. W. (2001) How to negotiate with Thai executives, *Asia Pacific Journal of Marketing and Logistics*, 13(3): 41–62.

Henry, K. (2009) Leading with your soul, *Strategic Finance*, 90(8): 44, 46–51.

Hernandez, M. (2008) Promoting stewardship behavior in organizations: A leadership model, *Journal of Business Ethics*, 80(1): 121–8.

Hill, A. and Stewart, I. (1999) Character education in business schools: Pedagogical strategies, *Teaching Business Ethics*, 3(2): 179–93.

Hill, D. (2008) Leaders and followers: How to build greater trust and commitment, *Ivey Business Journal Online*, 72(1) <www.siveybusinessjournal.com>.

Hitt, M.A., Javidan, M., and Steers, R.M. (2007) The global mindset: An introduction. In M. Javidan, R.M. Steers, M. and A. Hitt (Eds.), *Advances in international management*, (19: 1–10), Stamford, CT: JAI Press.

References

Hof, R. D., Rebello, K., and Burrows, P. (1996) Scott McNealy's rising sun, *Business Week*, January 22: 66–73.

Hoon, S. J. (1998) For love or money, *Far Eastern Economic Review*, 161(47): 14.

Hopkins, M. M. and Bilimoria, D. (2008) Social and emotional competencies predicting success for male and female executives, *Journal of Management Development*, 27(1): 13–35.

Hornibrook, S., Fearne, A., and Lazzarin, M. (2009) Exploring the association between fairness and organisational outcomes in supply chain relationships, *International Journal of Retail & Distribution Management*, 37(9): 790–803.

Howell, J. M. and Avolio, B. J. (1992) The ethics of charismatic leadership: submission or liberation? *Academy of Management Executive*, 6(2): 43–54.

Hruschka, D. J. and Henrich, J. (2006) Friendship, cliquishness, and the emergence of cooperation, *Journal of Theoretical Biology*, 239: 1–15.

Hughes, L. (2009) Leader levity: The effects of a leader's humor delivery on followers' positive emotions and creative performance, *Journal of Behavioral and Applied Management*, 10(3): 415–32.

Huppert, F. A. (2009) Psychological well-being: Evidence regarding causes and consequences, *Applied Psychology: Health and Well-Being*, 1(2): 137–64.

Hutzschenreuter, T., D'Aveni, R., and Voll, J. (2009) Temporal and geographical patterns of internationalization: An exploratory analysis, *Multinational Business Review*, 17(4): 45–75.

Imahori, T. T. and Cupach, W. R. (1994) A cross-cultural comparison of the interpretation and management of face: U.S. American and Japanese responses to embarrassing predicaments, *International Journal of Intercultural Relations*, 18(2): 193–219.

Imai, L. and Gelfand, M. (2010) The culturally intelligent negotiator: The impact of cultural intelligence (CQ) on negotiation sequences and outcomes, *Organizational Behavior and Human Decision Processes*, 112(2): 83–98.

Information Management Journal (2010) Google, China in Internet Scuffle, *Information Management Journal*, March/April, 44(2): 6.

Ingram, I. (2002) Producing the natural fiber naturally: Technological change and the US organic cotton industry, *Agriculture and Human Values*, 19(4): 325–36.

Ip, M. (2007) Consumer protection in China: An examination of the Toshiba notebook case from an Australian Perspective, *Asian Journal of Comparative Law*, 2(1): 1–25.

Irwin, T. H. (1997) Practical reason divided: Aquinas and his Critics, in G. Cullity and B. Gaut (Eds.), *Ethics and practical reason* (189–214), Oxford: Oxford University Press.

Jackson, S., Farndale, E., and Kakabadse, A. (2003) Executive development: Meeting the needs of top teams and boards, *Journal of Management Development*, 22(3): 185–265.

Jackson, T. (2002) *International HRM: A cross-cultural approach*, London: Sage.

Jassawalla, A. R., Asgary, N., and Sashittal, H. C. (2006) Managing expatriates: The role of mentors, *International Journal of Commerce and Management*, 16(2): 130–40.

Javidan, M., Steers, R. M., and Hitt, M. A. (2007) Putting it all together: So what is a global mindset and why is it important? In M. Javidan, R.M. Steers, M. and A. Hitt (Eds.), *Advances in international management* (19: 215–26), Stamford, CT: JAI Press.

—— Dorfman, P. W., Sully de Luque, M., and House, R. J. (2006) In the eye of the beholder: Cross cultural lessons in leadership from project GLOBE, *Academy of Management Perspectives*, 20: 67–90.

Jokinen, T. (2005) Global leadership competencies: A review and discussion, *Journal of European Industrial Training*, 29(2/3): 199–216.

Jordan, J. and Cartwright, S. (1998) Selecting expatriate managers: Key traits and competencies, *Leadership and Organization Development Journal*, 19(2): 89–96.

Kaku, R. (1997) The path of Kyosei, *Harvard Business Review*, July–August, 75(4): 55–63.

Kane, J. and Patapan, H. (2006) In search of prudence: The hidden problem of managerial reform, *Public Administration Review*, 66(5): 711–24.

Kanter, R. M. (2008) The corporate conduct continuum: From 'do not harm' to 'do lots of good', in C. C. Manz, K. S. Cameron, K. P. Manz, and R. D. Marx (Eds.), *The virtuous organization: Insights from some of the world's leading management thinkers* (279–86), Singapore: World Scientific.

—— (2010) Leadership in a globalizing world, in N. Nohria and R. Khurana (Eds.), *Handbook of leadership theory and practice* (569–609), Boston, MA: Harvard Business School Press.

Katz, J. (1996) Is this the perfect place to work? *Los Angeles Times Magazine*, June 9: 32.

Kay, J. (2011) *Obliquity*, London: Profile Books.

Kazmin, A. (2010) Microfinance backlash grows, *Financial Times*, December 8: 8.

Kedia, B. L. and Mukherji, A. (1999) Global managers: Developing a mindset for global competitiveness, *Journal of World Business*, 34(3): 230–51.

Kellerman, B. (2004) *Bad leadership*, Boston, MA: Harvard Business School Press.

Keough, D. (2008) *The ten commandments of business failure*, London: Penguin.

Ketchen Jr., D., Adams, G. L., and Shook, C. L. (2008) Understanding and managing CEO celebrity, *Business Horizons*, 51(6): 529–34.

Kets de Vries, M. F. R. (1998) Charisma in action: The transformational abilities of Virgin's Richard Branson and ABB's Percy Barnevik, *Organizational Dynamics*, 26(3): 7–21.

—— (2001) The anarchist within: Clinical reflections on Russian character and leadership style, *Human Relations*, 54(5): 585–627.

—— and Florent-Treacy, E. (2002) Creating high commitment organizations, *Organizational Dynamics*, 30(4): 295–309.

—— and Mead, C. (1992) The development of the global leader within the multinational corporation, in V. Pucik, N. M. Tichy, and C. K. Bartlett (Eds.), *Globalizing management: Creating and leading the competitive organization* (187–205), New York: John Wiley & Sons.

Khurana, R. (2007) *From higher aims to hired hands: The social transformation of American business schools and the unfulfilled promise of management education*, Princeton, NJ: Princeton University Press.

Kim, W. C. and Mauborgne, R. A. (1993) Procedural justice, attitudes, and subsidiary top management compliance with multinationals' corporate strategic decisions, *Academy of Management Journal*, 36(3): 502–26.

———— (1996) Procedural justice and managers' in-role and extra-role behavior: The case of the multinational, *Management Science*, 42(4): 499–515.

Kirkland, R. (2006) The real CEO pay problem, *Fortune*, July 10: 44–50.

Kolb, D. A. (1984) *Experiential learning: Experience as the source of learning and development*, Englewood Cliffs, NJ: Prentice-Hall.

Kollewe, J. (2010) Disgraced billionaire Lee Kun-Hee returns to lead Samsung, *The Guardian*, 25 March, 30 (<http://www.guardian.co.uk/business/2010/mar/24/samsung-billionaire-lee-kunhee>; retrieved December 27, 2011).

Koopman, P. L., Den Hartog, D. N., Konrad, E., and 44 co-authors (1999) National culture and leadership profiles in Europe: Some results from the GLOBE study, *European Journal of Work and Organizational Psychology*, 8(4): 503–20.

Kraar, L. (1997) Behind Samsung high-stakes push into cars the world is hardly waiting for another Korean auto. But this ambitious newcomer is betting $13 billion that Nissan can help it develop a crucial hedge: Quality, *Fortune*, May 12 (<http://money.cnn.com/magazines/fortune/fortune_archive/1997/05/12/226268/index.htm; retrieved December 27, 2011>).

Kraiger, K., Ford, J. K., and Salas, E. (1993) Application of cognitive, skill-based, and affective theories of learning outcomes to new methods of training evaluation, *Journal of Applied Psychology*, 78: 311–28.

Krishnan, V. R. (2003) Power and moral leadership: Role of self–other agreement, *Leadership & Organization Development Journal*, 24(5/6): 345–51.

Kroll, M. J., Toombs, L. A., and Wright, P. (2000) Napoleon's tragic march home from Moscow: Lessons in hubris, *The Academy of Management Executive*, 14(1): 117–28.

Krugman, P. and Wells, R. (2011) The Busts Keep Getting Bigger: Why? *New York Review of Books*, page 1, July 14, 2011, accessed at <http://www.nybooks.com/articles/archives/2011/jul/14/busts-keep-getting-bigger-why/?page=1> on December 27, 2011.

Kurtzberg, T. R. (1998) Creative thinking, cognitive aptitude, and integrative joint gain: A study of negotiator creativity, *Creativity Research Journal*, 11: 283–93.

Lane, H. W., Maznevski, M. L., and Mendenhall, M. E. (2004) Globalization: Hercules meets Buddha, in H. W. Lane, M. L. Maznevski, M. E. Mendenhall, and J. McNett, J. (Eds.), *The Blackwell handbook of global management* (3–25), London: Blackwell.

Law, K., Wong, C. S., and Wang, K. D. (2004) An empirical test of the model on managing the localization of human resources in the People's Republic of China, *International Journal of Human Resource Management*, 15(4/5): 635–48.

Lee, H. W. (2007) Factors that influence expatriate failure: An interview study, *International Journal of Management*, 24(3): 403–13.

——— and Liu, C. H. (2006) Determinants of the adjustment of expatriate managers to foreign countries: An empirical study, *International Journal of Management*, 23(2): 302–11.

Lee, W. and Lee, N. S. (2007) Understanding Samsung's diversification strategy: The case of Samsung Motors Inc, *Long Range Planning*, 40: 488–504.

Leigh, D. and Evans, R. (2010) The BAE files, *The Guardian*, December 21, <http://www.guardian.co.uk/baefiles/page/0,,2095864,00.html> accessed December 27, 2011.

Len, S. (1999) World business briefing: Asia; Samsung creditors deal, *The New York Times*, August 20, <http://www.nytimes.com/1999/08/20/business/world-business-briefing-asia-samsung-creditors-deal.html?ref=lee_kunhee;> retrieved December 27, 2011.

Leung, K. and Kwong, J. Y. Y. (2003) Human resource management practices in international joint ventures in mainland China: A justice analysis, *Human Resource Management Review*, 13: 85–105.

Levy, O., Beechler, S., Taylor, S. and Boyacigiller, N. (2007) What we talk about when we talk about 'Global Mindset', *Journal of International Business Studies*, 38: 231–58.

Levy, R. B. (2000) My experience as participant in the course on spirituality for executive leadership, *Journal of Management Inquiry*, 9(2): 129–31.

Lewis, T. and Turley, M. (1991) Strategic partnering in Eastern Europe, *The International Executive*, 32(4): 5–9.

Li, A. and Cropanzano, R. (2009) Do East Asians respond more/less strongly to organizational justice than North Americans? A meta-analysis, *Journal of Management Studies*, 46(5): 787–805.

Liden, R., Wayne, S., Zhao, H., and Henderson, D. (2008) Servant leadership: Development of a multidimensional measure and multi-level assessment, *Leadership Quarterly*, 19(2): 161–77.

Liker, J. K. and Hoseus, M. (2008) *Toyota culture*, New York: McGraw-Hill.

Lilius, J. M., Worline, M. C., Maitlis, S., Kanov, J., Dutton, J. E., and Frost, P. (2008) The contours and consequences of compassion at work, *Journal of Organizational Behavior*, 29: 193–218.

Lind, E. A., Tyler, T. R., and Huo, Y. J. (1997) Procedural context and culture: Variation in the antecedents of procedural justice judgments, *Journal of Personality and Social Psychology*, 73(4): 767–80.

Lips-Wiersma, M. S., Lund Dean, K. and Fornaciari, C. J. (2009) Theorizing the dark side of the workplace spirituality movement, *Journal of Management Inquiry*, 8(4): 288–300.

Liu, C., Tjosvold, D. and Wong, M. (2004) Effective Japanese leadership in China: Co-operative goals and applying abilities for mutual benefit, *International Journal of Human Resource Management*, 15(4/5): 730–49.

Lodge, G. C. (2002) The corporate key: Using big business to fight global poverty, *Foreign Affairs*, 81(4): 13–18.

London, T. (2009) Making better investments at the base of the pyramid, *Harvard Business Review*, 87(5): 106–13.

—— and Hart, S. (2004) Reinventing strategies for emerging markets: Beyond the transnational model, *Journal of International Business Studies*, 35(5): 350–70.

References

Longstaffe, C. (2005) Winston Churchill, a leader from history or an inspiration for the future? *Industrial and Commercial Training*, 37(2/3): 80–3.

Lucero, M., Kwang, A. T. T., and Pang, A. (2009) Crisis leadership: When should the CEO step up? *Corporate Communications*, 14(3): 234–48.

Luo, Y. (2007) An integrated anti-opportunism system in international exchange, *Journal of International Business Studies*, 38(6): 855–77.

—— (2008) Procedural fairness and interfirm cooperation in strategic alliances, *Strategic Management Journal*, 29(1): 27–46.

Luthans, F., Youssef, C. M., and Avolio, B. J. (2007) *Psychological capital: Developing the human competitive edge*. Oxford: Oxford University Press.

Lyall, S., Krauss, C., and Mouawad, J. (2010) In BP's record, a history of boldness and costly blunders, *New York Times*, July 12 <http://www.nytimes.com/2010/07/13/business/energy-environment/13bprisk.html>; retrieved December 27, 2011.

Lyubomirsky, S., King, L., and Diener, E. (2005) The benefits of frequent positive affect: Does happiness lead to success? *Psychological Bulletin*, 131(6): 803–55.

Maak, T. (2007) Responsible leadership, stakeholder engagement and the emergence of social capital, *Journal of Business Ethics*, 74(4): 329–43.

—— (2008) Undivided corporate responsibility: Towards a theory of corporate integrity, *Journal of Business Ethics*, 82(2): 353–68.

—— (2009) The cosmopolitical corporation, *Journal of Business Ethics*, 84(3): 361–72.

—— and Pless, N. M. (2006) Responsible leadership in a stakeholder society, *Journal of Business Ethics*, 66(1): 99–115.

—— and Pless, N. M. (2009) Business leaders as citizens of the world: Advancing humanism on a global scale, *Journal of Business Ethics*, 88(3): 537–50.

McCall, M. and Hollenbeck, G. (2002) *Developing global executives: The lessons of international experience*. Boston, MA: Harvard Business School Press.

McCuiston, V. E., Wooldridge, B. R., and Pierce, C. K. (2004) Leading the diverse workforce: Profit, prospects and progress, *Leadership & Organization Development Journal*, 25(1/2): 73–92.

McCullough, M. E., Emmons, R. A., and Tsang, J. (2002) The grateful disposition: A conceptual and empirical topography, *Journal of Personality and Social Psychology*, 82: 112–27.

—— Kilpatrick, S. D., Emmons, R. A., and Larson, D. B. (2001) Is gratitude a moral affect? *Psychological Bulletin*, 127: 249–66.

—— Kimeldorf, M. B., and Cohen, A. D. (2008) An adaptation for altruism? The social causes, social effects, and social evolution of gratitude, *Current Directions in Psychological Science*, 17: 281–4.

—— Root, L. M., Tabak, B., and Witvliet, C. (2009) Forgiveness, in S. J. Lopez (Ed.), *Handbook of positive psychology* 2nd edn: 427–35, New York: Oxford University Press.

—— Tsang, J., and Emmons, R. A. (2004) Gratitude in intermediate affective terrain: Links of grateful moods to individual differences and daily emotional experience, *Journal of Personality and Social Psychology*, 86: 295–306.

McManus, T. and Delaney, D. (2007) Dave Delaney's useful advice for your development as a manager, *Journal of Management Development*, 26(5): 468–74.

Machiavelli, N. (1992) *The Prince*, London: Penguin.

Madrick, J. (2011) *Age of Greed: The Triumph of Finance and the Decline of America, 1970 to the Present*, New York: Knopf.

Magnay, J. (2010) BP chief Tony Hayward avoids cutting corners in Round the Island yacht race, *The Telegraph* <http://www.telegraph.co.uk/sport/othersports/sailing/7841495/BP-chief-Tony-Hayward-avoids-cutting-corners-in-Round-the-Island-yacht-race.html> accessed December 27, 2011.

Mahy, B., Rycx, F., and Volral, M. (forthcoming) Wage dispersion and firm productivity in different working environments, *British Journal of Industrial Relations*. DOI: 10.1111/j.1467-8543.2009.00775.

Malloch, T. R. (2010) Spiritual capital and practical wisdom, *Journal of Management Development*, 29(7/8): 755–9.

Malone, M. S. (2007) *Bill and Dave: How Hewlett and Packard built the worlds' greatest company*, New York: Portfolio.

Mandela, N. (2010) *Conversations with myself*, London: Strauss, Farrar and Giroux.

Manz, C. C., Cameron, K. S., Manz, K. P., and Marx, R. D. (2008a) The virtuous organization: An introduction, in C. C. Manz, K. S. Cameron, K. P. Manz, and R. D. Marx (Eds.), *The virtuous organization: Insights from some of the world's leading management thinkers* (1–16), Singapore: World Scientific.

—— Cameron, K. S., Manz, K. P., and Marx, R. D. (Eds.) (2008b) *The virtuous organization: Insights from some of the world's leading management thinkers*, Singapore: World Scientific Publishing.

Manz, K. P., Marx, R. D., Manz, C. C., and Neal, J. A. (2008) The language of virtues: Toward an inclusive approach for integrating spirituality in management education, in C. C. Manz, K. S. Cameron, K. P. Manz, and R. D. Marx (Eds.), *The virtuous organization: Insights from some of the world's leading management thinkers* (117–39), Singapore: World Scientific.

Markovits, M. and Donop, K. (2007) Collaborate for growth: Deepening involvement through hope, *Organization Development Journal*, 25(4): P13–18.

Martin, G., Resick, C., Keating, M., and Dickson, M. (2009) Ethical leadership across cultures: A comparative analysis of German and US perspectives, *Business Ethics*, 18(2): 127–44.

Martin, J. (2002) *Organizational culture: Mapping the terrain*, Thousand Oaks, CA: Sage.

Martin, N. W. and Schinzinger, R. (1996) *Ethics in engineering*, New York: McGraw-Hill.

Martinez, S. and Dorfman, P. (1998) The Mexican entrepreneur: An ethnographic study of the Mexican *empresario*, *International Studies of Management and Organizations*, 28: 97–123.

Mason, R. and Roberts, L. (2010) BP oil spill: Tony Hayward pulls out of oil conference, Telegraph.co.uk, June 22 <http://www.telegraph.co.uk/finance/newsbysector/energy/oilandgas/7845790/BP-oil-spill-Tony-Hayward-pulls-out-of-oil-conference.html>; retrieved December 27, 2011.

Melé, D. (2009) Integrating personalism into virtue-based business ethics: The personalist and the common good principles, *Journal of Business Ethics*, 88(1): 227–44.

—— (2010) Practical wisdom in managerial decision making, *Journal of Management Development*, 29(7/8): 637–45.

Mendenhall, M. E. (2006) The elusive, yet critical challenge of developing global leaders, *European Management Journal*, 24(6): 422–9.

—— Jensen, R. J., Black, J. S., and Gregersen, H. B. (2003) Seeing the elephant: Human resource management challenges in the age of globalization, *Organizational Dynamics*, 32(3): 261–74.

—— and Osland, J. S. (2002) *An overview of the extant global leadership research*, Symposium presentation, Academy of International Business, Puerto Rico, June.

Mendonca, M. (2001) Preparing for ethical leadership in organizations, *Canadian Journal of Administrative Sciences*, 18(4): 266–76.

Merck and Co. (2005) *Corporate Responsibility 2006–2007 Report*, Merck and Co. <http://www.merck.com/corporate-responsibility/docs/cr2006-2007.pdf>; retrieved December 27, 2011.

Mezias, J. M. and Scandura, T. A. (2005) A needs-driven approach to expatriate adjustment and career development: A multiple mentoring perspective, *Journal of International Business Studies*, 36(5): 519–38.

Michaelson, C. (2008) Moral luck and business ethics, *Journal of Business Ethics*, 83(4): 773–87.

Miller, B. (2000) Spirituality for business leadership, *Journal of Management Inquiry*, 9(2): 132–3.

Millikin, J.P. and Fu, D. (2005) The global leadership of Carlos Ghosn at Nissan. *Thunderbird International Business Review*, 47(1): 121–37.

Mintzberg, H. (1971) Managerial work: Analysis from observation, *Management Science*, 18(2): B97–110.

—— (1983) *Power in and around organizations*, Englewood Cliffs, NJ: Prentice-Hall.

Mitchell, R. (1994) Managing by values, *Business Week*, August 1: 46–52.

Mokhiber, R. (1999) Crime wave! The top 100 corporate criminals of the 1990s, *Multinational Monitor*, 20(7/8): 9–29.

Moloney, L. and Pizzo, S. (2010) Parmalat's founder gets 18 years, *Wall Street Journal Europe*, December 10: 19.

Montville, J. V. and Davidson, W. D. (1981–1982) Foreign policy according to Freud, *Foreign Policy*, 45: 145–57.

Moore, G. (2005) Corporate character: Modern virtue ethics and the virtuous corporation, *Business Ethics Quarterly*, 15: 659–85.

—— and Beadle, R. (2006) In search of organizational virtue in business: Agents, goods, practices, institutions and environments, *Organization Studies*, 27: 369–89.

Moran, R T. and Riesenberger, J. R. (1994) *The global challenge: Building the new worldwide enterprise*, London: McGraw-Hill.

Morck, R. M., Shleifer, A., and Vishny, R. W. (1990) Do managerial objectives drive bad acquisitions? *Journal of Financial Economics*, 45(1): 31–48.

Morris, M. W. and Leung, K. (2000) Justice for all? Progress in research on cultural variation in the psychology of distributive and procedural justice, *Applied Psychology: An International Review*, 49(1): 100–32.

—— Leung, K., Ames, D., and Lickel, B. (1999) Views from inside and outside: Integrating emic and etic insights about culture and justice judgment, *Academy of Management Review*, 24(4): 781–96.

Morrison, A. J. (2001) Integrity and global leadership, *Journal of Business Ethics*, 31(1): 65–76.

—— (2006) Ethical standards and global leadership, in W. Mobley and E. Weldon (Eds.), *Advances in Global Leadership* (4: 165–79), Amsterdam: Elsevier.

—— (2000) Developing a global leadership model, *Human Resource Management*, 39(2/3): 117–31.

Mouawad, J. and Krauss, C. (2010) Another torrent BP works to stem: Its C.E.O. *New York Times*, June 3 (<http://www.nytimes.com/2010/06/04/us/04image.html>; retrieved December 27, 2011).

Muczyk, J. P. and Holt, D. T. (2008) Toward a cultural contingency model of leadership, *Journal of Leadership & Organizational Studies*, 14(4): 277–86.

Mulcahy, A. (2010a) Timeliness trumps perfection, *McKinsey Quarterly*, <http://mkqpreview1.qdweb.net/PDFDownload.aspx?ar=2541> accessed December 27, 2011.

—— (2010b) Xerox's former CEO on why succession shouldn't be a horse race, *Harvard Business Review*, 88(10): 47–51.

Mullins, L. H. (1990) CEOs lead by philanthropic example, *Management Review*, 79(12): 24–6.

Murphy-Berman, V., Berman, J. J., Singh, P., Pachauri, A., and Kumar, P. (1984) Factors affecting allocation to needy and meritorious recipients: A cross-cultural comparison, *Journal of Personality and Social Psychology*, 46: 1267–72.

Nagel, T. (1991) *Equality and partiality*. New York: Oxford University Press.

Nardon, L. and Steers, R. M. (2007) Learning cultures on the fly, in M. Javidan, R. M. Steers, M. and A. Hitt (Eds.), *Advances in international management* (19: 171–89), Stamford, CT: JAI Press.

Neff, J. (2010) Are marketers hiking ad spend at expense of product quality? *Advertising Age*, 81(29): 1–20.

Nevo, O., Nevo, B., and Yin, J. L. S. (2001) Singaporean humor: A cross-cultural, cross-gender comparison, *Journal of General Psychology*, 128(2): 143–56.

Newton, L. H. (2006) *Permission to steal: Revealing the roots of corporate scandal*, Malden, MA: Blackwell.

Ng, K., Van Dyne, L., and Ang, S. (2009) From experience to experiential learning: Cultural intelligence as a learning capability for global leader development, *Academy of Management Learning and Education*, 8(4): 511–26.

Nirenberg, J. (2001) Leadership: A practitioner's perspective on the literature, *Singapore Management Review*, 23(1): 1–34.

Nowak, M. and Sigmund, K. (1993) A strategy of win-stay, lose-shift that outperforms tit-for-tat in the Prisoner's Dilemma Game, *Nature*, 364: 56–8.

O'Hear, A. (1997) *Beyond evolution: Human nature and the limits of evolutionary explanation*, Oxford: Clarendon Press.

O'Rourke IV, J. S., Harris, B., and Ogilvy, A. (2007) Google in China: Government censorship and corporate reputation, *Journal of Business Strategy*, 28(3): 12–22.

Oddou, G., Mendenhall, M. E., and Ritchie, J. B. (2000) Leveraging travel as a tool for global leadership development, *Human Resource Management*, 39(2/3): 159–72.

Okoroafo, S. C. (1992) International countertrade at the crossroads, *Management Decision*, 30(5): 47–9.

Ordeix-Rigo, E. and Duarte, J. (2009) From public diplomacy to corporate diplomacy: Increasing corporation's legitimacy and influence, *The American Behavioral Scientist*, 53(4): 549–64.

Orfalea, P., Helfert, L., Lowe, A. and Zatkowsky, D. (2008) *The entrepreneurial investor: The art, science, and business of value investing*, Singapore: John Wiley & Sons.

Organ, D. W. and Paine, J. B. (2000) A new kind of performance for industrial and organizational psychology: Recent contributions to the study of organizational citizenship behavior, *International Review of Industrial and Organizational Psychology*, 14: 338–68.

Osland, J. S., Bird, A., Mendenhall, M., and Osland, A. (2006) Developing global leadership capabilities and global mindset: A review, in K. Stahl and I. Bjorkman (Eds.), *Handbook of research in international human resource management* (197–222), Cheltenham: Edward Elgar.

Otazo, K. L. (1999) Global leadership: The inside story, in W. H. Mobley, M. J. Gessner, and V. Arnold (Eds.), *Advances in global leadership* (1: 317–35), Stamford, CT: JAI Press.

Ozer, M. (2002) The role of flexibility on online business, *Business Horizons*, January–February, 45(1): 61–9.

Paine, L. S. (2010) The China Rules, *Harvard Business Review*, June, 88(6): 103–8.

Park, N. and Peterson, C. (2003) Virtues and organizations, in K. S. Cameron, J. E. Dutton, and R. E. Quinn (Eds.), *Positive organizational scholarship: Foundations of a new discipline* (33–47), San Francisco: Berrett-Koehler.

Pearce, C. L., Waldman, D. A., and Csikszentmihalyi, M. (2008) Virtuous leadership: A theoretical model and a research agenda, in C. C. Manz, K. S. Cameron, K. P. Manz, and R. D. Marx (Eds.), *The virtuous organization: Insights from some of the world's leading management thinkers* (211–30), Singapore: World Scientific.

People's Daily (2000) *Toshiba faces media fire in China, People's Daily*, May 30 <http://english.peopledaily.com.cn/english/200005/30/eng20000530_41874.html>; retrieved December 27, 2011.

Peters, D. H. and Philips, T. (2004) Mectizan Donation Program: Evaluation of a public–private partnership, *Tropical Medicine and International Health*, 9(4): A4–15.

Peterson, C. and Seligman, M. E. P. (2001) *VIA Inventory of Strengths* (VIA-IS).

—––—— (2003) Character strengths before and after September 11, *Psychological Science*, 14(4): 381–4.

—––—— (2004) *Character strengths and virtues: A handbook and classification*, Washington: American Psychological Association.

Pfeffer, J. (1992a) Understanding power in organizations, *California Management Review*, 34(2): 29–50.

—— (1992b) *Managing with power: Politics and influence in organizations*, Boston MA: Harvard Business School Press.

—— (2007) *What were they thinking?* Boston, MA: Harvard Business School Press.

—— (2010a) Building sustainable organizations: The human factor, *Academy of Management Perspectives*, 24(1): 34–45.

—— (2010b) *Power*, New York: Harper Collins.

—— and Langton, N. (1993) The effect of wage dispersion on satisfaction, productivity, and working collaboratively: Evidence from college and university faculty, *Administrative Science Quarterly*, 38: 382–407.

—— and Sutton, R. I. (2006) *Hard facts, dangerous half-truths and total nonsense: Profiting from evidence-based management*, Boston, MA: Harvard Business School Press.

Podolny, J. M., Khurana, R., and Besharov, M. L. (2010) Revisiting the meaning of leadership, in N. Nohria and R. Khurana (Eds.), *Handbook of leadership theory and practice* (65–105), Boston, MA: Harvard Business School Press.

Polak, E. and McCullough, M. E. (2006) Is gratitude an alternative to materialism? *Journal of Happiness Studies*, 7: 343–60.

Porter, M. E. and Kramer, M. R. (2002) The competitive advantage of corporate philanthropy, *Harvard Business Review*, 80(12): 56–68.

—––—— (2006) Strategy and society: The link between competitive advantage and corporate social responsibility, *Harvard Business Review*, 84(12): 78–92.

—––—— (2011) Creating shared value, *Harvard Business Review*, 89(1/2): 62–77.

Powley, E. H. and Cameron, K. S. (2008) Organizational healing: Lived virtuousness amidst organizational crisis, in C. C. Manz, K. S. Cameron, K. P. Manz, and R. D. Marx (Eds.), *The virtuous organization: Insights from some of the world's leading management thinkers* (21–44), Singapore: World Scientific.

—— and Taylor, S. N. (2006) *Values and leadership in organizational crisis*, in E. D. Hess and K. S. Cameron (Eds.), *Leading values: Positivity, virtue, and high performance* (194–212), Cambridge: Cambridge University Press.

Prahalad, C. K. (2005) *The fortune at the base of the pyramid: Eradicating poverty through profits*, Philadelphia, PA: Wharton School Publishing.

Pu, H. and Que, Y. (2004) Why have some transnational corporations failed in China? *China & World Economy*, 12(5): 67–79.

Purkayastha, D. and Fernando, R. (2007) *The Body Shop: Social Responsibility or Sustained Greenwashing* (<http://www.oikos-international.org/fileadmin/oikos-international/international/Case_competition/Inspection_copy_ICFAI2007.pdf>; accessed December 27, 2011)

References

Ragins, B. R. and Cotton, J. L. (1999) Mentor functions and outcomes: A comparison of men and women in formal and informal mentoring relationships, *Journal of Applied Psychology*, 84(4): 529–50.

Rarick, C. and Feldman, L. (2008) Patagonia: Climbing to new highs with a smaller carbon footprint, *Journal of the International Academy for Case Studies*, 17(4): 121–4.

Raven, B. H. (2001) Power/interaction and interpersonal influence: Experimental investigations and case studies, in A. Y. lee-Chai and J. A. Bargh (Eds.), *The use and abuse of power: Multiple perspectives on the causes of corruption* (217–40), Philadelphia, PA: Psychology Press.

Rawls, J. (1999) *The law of peoples*, Cambridge, MA: Harvard University Press.

Reave, L. (2005) Spiritual values and practices related to leadership effectiveness, *Leadership Quarterly*, 16(5): 655–87.

Redding, G. (1993) *The Spirit of Chinese Capitalism*, New York: de Gruyter.

Rego, A. and Cunha, M. P. (2008a) Cross-cultural teams, in S. R. Clegg and J. Bailey (Eds.), *International encyclopaedia of organization studies* (1530–3), Thousand Oaks, CA: Sage.

—— (2008b) Organisational citizenship behaviours and effectiveness: An empirical study in two small insurance companies, *Service Industries Journal*, 28(4): 541–54.

—— Clegg, S., and Cunha, M. P. (2011) The positive power of character strengths and virtues for global leaders, in K. S. Cameron and G. M. Spreitzer (Eds.), *Handbook of positive organizational scholarship* (366–81), Oxford: Oxford University Press.

—— Machado, F., Leal, S. and Cunha, M.P. (2009) Are hopeful employees more creative? An empirical study, *Creativity Research Journal*, 21(2/3): 223–31.

—— Sousa, F., Marques, S., and Cunha, M. P. C. (2012) Authentic leadership promoting employees' psychological capital and creativity, *Journal of Business Research* 65: 429–37.

Rhee, S. Y., Dutton, J. E., and Bagozzi, R. P. (2008) Making sense of organizational actions with virtues frames and its links to organizational attachment, in C. C. Manz, K. S. Cameron, K. P. Manz, and R. D. Marx (Eds.), *The virtuous organization: Insights from some of the world's leading management thinkers* (45–65), Singapore: World Scientific.

Riggio, R. E. and Reichard, R. J. (2008) The emotional and social intelligences of effective leadership: An emotional and social skill approach, *Journal of Managerial Psychology*, 23(2): 169–85.

Robertson, R. (1995) Glocalization: Time-space and Homogeneity-heterogeneity, in M. Featherstone et al. (Eds.), *Global modernities* (25–44), London: Sage.

Rockoff, J. D. (2010) Pfizer CEO Kindler resigns, *Wall Street Journal* (Europe) December 7: 18.

—— and Kamp, J. (2010) J&J's latest recall: Hip-repair implants, *Wall Street Journal* (Eastern Edition), August 27: B1.

Roll, R. (1986) The hubris hypothesis of corporate takeovers, *Journal of Business*, 59(2): 197–216.

Rosenbloom, A. H. (Ed.) (2002) *Due diligence for global deal making*, Princeton, NJ: Bloomberg Press.

Roth, G. (1975) Socio-historical model and development theory: Charismatic community, charisma of reason and the counterculture, *American Sociological Review*, 40(2): 148–57.

Russell, R. and Aquino-Russell, C. (2010) Expatriate managers: Powerful or powerless? *The International Business & Economics Research Journal*, 9(2): 101–8.

San, G. and Jane, W. (2008) Wage dispersion and team performance: Evidence from the small size professional baseball league in Taiwan, *Applied Economics Letters*, 15(11): 883–6.

Sanders III, J. E., Hopkins, W. E., and Geroy, G. D. (2003) From transactional to transcendental: Toward and integrated theory of leadership, *Journal of Leadership and Organizational Studies*, 9(4): 21–31.

Sang-Hun, C. (2009) Korean leader pardons Samsung's ex-chairman, *The New York Times*, December 30, B3, (<http://www.nytimes.com/2009/12/30/business/global/30samsung.html?ref=lee_kunhee>; retrieved December 27, 2011).

Schell, M. S. and Solomon, C. M. (1997) *Capitalizing on the global workforce*, New York: McGraw-Hill.

Schriesheim, C. and Neider, L. (Eds.) (2006) *Power and influence in organizations: New empirical and theoretical perspectives*, Hartford, CT: Information Age Publishing.

Schroeder, A. (2009) *The snowball: Warren Buffett and the business of life*, New York: Bantam Books.

Schudt, K. (2000) Taming the corporate monster: An Aristotelian approach to corporate virtue, *Business Ethics Quarterly*, 10: 711–23.

Schuster, C. P. and Copeland, M. J. (1999) Executive insights: Global business exchanges–similarities and differences around the world, *Journal of International Marketing*, 7(2): 63–80.

Schwass, J. and Lief, C. (2008) About family, business and philanthropy, *Perspectives for Managers*, 165: 1–4.

Sehgal, V., Dehoff, K., and Panneer, G. (2010) The importance of frugal engineering, *Strategy + Business*, Summer, 59: 20–5.

Seligman, M. E. P. and Csikszentmihalyi, M. (2000) Positive psychology: An introduction, *American Psychologist*, 55(1): 5–14.

Selmer, J. (2003) Staff localization and organizational characteristics: Western business operations in China, *Asia Pacific Business Review*, 10(1): 43–57.

—— (2004) Expatriates' hesitation and the localization of Western business operations in China, *International Journal of Human Resource Management*, 15 (6): 1094–107.

Seth, A., Song, K. P., and Petit, R. (2000) Synergy, managerialism or hubris? An empirical examination of motives for foreign acquisitions of US firms, *Journal of International Business Studies*, 31(3): 387–405.

Shelton, C. D. and Darling, J. R. (2003) From theory to practice: Using new science concepts to create learning organizations, *The Learning Organization*, 10(6): 353–60.

References

Shrivastava, P., Mitroff, I. I., Miller, D., and Miglani, A. (1988) Understanding industrial crises, *Journal of Management Studies*, 25: 285–303.

Simanis, E. and Hart, S. (2009) Innovation from the inside out, *MIT Sloan Management Review*, 50(4): 77–86.

Simpson, K. F. Jr. (1994) Organizational power politics: Tactics in organizational leadership, *Personnel Psychology*, 47(2): 436–9.

Singer, P. (2002) *One world*, New Haven, CT: Yale University Press.

Sliter, J. (2007) The price of corporate crime: The risks to business, *Journal of Financial Crime*, 14(1): 12–16.

Sluyterman, K. (2010) Royal Dutch Shell: Company strategies for dealing with environmental issues, *Business History Review*, 84(2): 203–27.

Small, M. W. (2004) Wisdom and now managerial wisdom: Do they have a place in management development programs? *Journal of Management Development*, 23(7/8): 751–64.

Smith, C. (Ed.) (2003) *The secular revolution: Power, interests and conflict in the secularization of American public life*, Berkeley, CA: University of California Press.

Solomon, R.C. (1999) *A better way to think about business*, New York: Oxford University Press.

Sonne, P., Bryan-Low, C., and Adams, R. (2001) Tabloid to close amid scandal, *The Wall Street Journal*. July 8th <http://online.wsj.com/article/SB1000142405 2702303365804576431833214832352.html>; retrieved December 27, 2011.

Spreitzer, G. M., McCall, Jr., M. W., and Mahoney, J. D. (1997) The early identification of international executives, *Journal of Applied Psychology*, 82: 6–29.

—— and Sonenshein, S. (2004) Toward the construct definition of positive deviance, *American Behavioral Scientist*, 77(6): 828–47.

Stenebo, J. (2010) *The truth about Ikea: The secret behind the world's fifth richest man and the success of the Swedish flatpack giant*, London: Gibson Square.

Stengel, R. (2008) Mandela: His 8 lessons of leadership, *Time*, July (<http://www.time.com/time/world/article/0,8599,1821467,00.html>; retrieved December 27, 2011)

Sternberg, R. J. (1997) Managerial intelligence: Why IQ isn't enough, *Journal of Management*, 23: 475–93.

Stone, R. J. (2002) *Human resource management*, Melbourne: John Wiley.

Striker, J., Dimberg, L., and Liese, B. H. (2000) Stress and business travel: Individual, managerial, and corporate concerns, *National Productivity Review*, 20(1): 3–9.

Stroh, L. K. and Caligiuri, P. M. (1998) Increasing global competitiveness through effective people management, *Journal of World Business*, 33: 1–16.

Sueda, K. and Wiseman, R. L. (1992) Embarrassment remediation in Japan and the United States, *International Journal of Intercultural Relations*, 16(2): 159–73.

Sugawara, H. (2010) Japanese business and poverty reduction, *Society and Business Review*, 5(2): 198–216.

Suutari, V. (2002) Global leader development: An emerging research agenda, *Career Development International*, 7(4): 218–33.

Swartz, J. (2010) Timberland's CEO on standing up to 65,000 angry activists, *Harvard Business Review*, 88(9): 39–43.

Takeuchi, H., Osono, E., and Shimizu, N. (2008) The contradictions that drive Toyota's success, *Harvard Business Review*, 86(6): 96–104.

Tashman, P. and Marano, V. (2010) Dynamic capabilities and base of the pyramid business strategies, *Journal of Business Ethics*, 89: 495–514.

Tata, J., Fu, P. P., and Wu, R. (2003) An examination of procedural justice principles in China and the U.S., *Asia Pacific Journal of Management*, 20: 205–16.

Tavis, L. E. (2000) The globalization phenomenon and multinational corporate developmental responsibility, in O. F. Williams (Ed.), *Global codes of conduct: An idea whose time has come* (13–36), Notre Dame, IN: University of Notre Dame Press.

Terrion, J. L. and Ashforth, B. E. (2002) From 'I' to 'we': The role of putdown humor and identity in the development of a temporary group, *Human Relations*, 55(1): 55–88.

Thayer, L. (1988) Leadership/communication: A critical review and a modest model, in G. M. Goldhaber and G. A. Barnett (eds.), *Handbook of organizational communication* (231–63), Norwood, New Jersey: Ablex.

The Economist (2010a) BP and golden parachutes: The wages of failure, *The Economist*, July 29 (<http://www.economist.com/node/16693567?story_id=16693567>; retrieved December 27, 2011).

—— (2010b) Under water, December 11: 63.

—— (2011a) The end of the World as we know it, *The Economist*, July 7 <http://www.economist.com/blogs/newsbook/2011/07/newspapers-0>; retrieved December 27, 2011.

—— (2011b) Street of shame: A full judicial inquiry is needed immediately to clean up British journalism, *The Economist*, July 7th <http://www.economist.com/node/18928406> retrieved December 27, 2011.

Thomas, D. C. (2006) Domain and development of cultural intelligence: The importance of mindfulness, *Group & Organization Management*, 31(1): 78–99.

—— and Ravlin, E. C. (1995) Responses of workers to cultural adaptation by a foreign manager, *Journal of Applied Psychology*, 80(1): 133–46.

Thompson, A. D., Grahek, M., Phillips, R. E., and Fay, C. L. (2008) The search for worthy leadership, *Consulting Psychology Journal: Practice and Research*, 60(4): 366–82.

Tichy, N. M. and Devanna, M. A. (1986) *The transformational leader*, New York: John Wiley & Sons.

Townsend, P. and Cairns, L. (2003) Developing the global manager using a capability framework, *Management Learning*, 34(3): 313–27.

Treasurer, B. (2009) Courageous leadership: Modeling the way, *Leader to Leader*, 52: 13–17.

Tredget, D. A. (2010) Practical wisdom and the Rule of Benedict, *Journal of Management Development*, 29(7/8): 716–23.

Trompenaars, F. and Hampden-Turner, C. (1997) *Riding the waves of culture* (2nd ed.), London: Brealey.

—————— (2004) *Managing people across cultures*, Chichester: Capstone.

Tsang, J., McCullough, M. E., and Fincham, F. D. (2006) The longitudinal association between forgiveness and relationship closeness and commitment, *Journal of Social and Clinical Psychology*, 25: 448–72.

Useem, M. (2003) Leading your boss, *The Economic Times*, November 13 <http://leadership.wharton.upenn.edu/l_change/up_lead/ET_Nov_13_03.shtml>; retrieved October 8, 2010.

Van Knippenberg, D. and Hogg, M. A. (Eds.) (2006) *Leadership and power: Identity processes in groups and organizations*, Thousand Oaks, CA: Sage.

Vandenberghe, C. (1999) Transactional vs. transformational leadership: Suggestions for future research, *European Journal of Work and Organizational Psychology*, 8: 26–32.

Vecchio, R., Justin, J., and Pearce, C. (2009) The influence of leader humor on relationships between leader behavior and follower outcomes, *Journal of Managerial Issues*, 21(2): 171–94.

Vera, D. and Rodriguez-Lopez, A. (2004) Strategic virtues: Humility as a source of competitive advantage, *Organizational Dynamics*, 33(4): 393–406.

Viswesvaran, C. and Ones, D. S. (2002) Examining the construct of organizational justice: A meta-analytic evaluation of relations with work attitudes and behaviors, *Journal of Business Ethics*, 38(3): 193–203.

Waddock, S. and Smith, N. (2000) Relationships: The real challenge of corporate global citizenship, *Business and Society Review*, 105(1): 47–62.

Weber, M. (1978) *Economy and society*, Berkeley, CA: University of California Press.

—— (2001) *The protestant ethic and the spirit of capitalism*, London: Routledge.

Weddings, Parties, Anything (1993) 'Monday's Experts', from the album *King Tide*, Melbourne: Roo Art.

Weiss, S. E. and Stripp, W. (1998) Negotiating with foreign business persons, in S. Niemeier, C. P. Campbell, and R. Dirven (Eds.), *The cultural context in business communications* (51–118), Amsterdam: John Benjamins.

Whalen, J. and MacDonald, A. (2011) Amid turmoil, newspaper bids readers final farewell, *The Wall Street Journal*, July 11 <http://online.wsj.com/article/SB10001424052702303812104576437142421401166.html>; retrieved December 27, 2011.

Whetstone, J. T. (2003) The language of managerial excellence: Virtues as understood and applied, *Journal of Business Ethics*, 44(4): 343–57.

Whyte, W. H. (1956) *The organization man*, New York: Doubleday.

Wilkinson, T. L. and Omidi, M. (2010) Greed is for wimps: Today's gilded youth are shunning high salaries in favor of charity, *Wall Street Journal*, December 13: R.7.

Williams, R. J. and Barrett, J. D. (2000) Corporate philanthropy, criminal activity, and firm reputation: Is there a link? *Journal of Business Ethics*, 26(4): 341–50.

Wong, A. (2009) The essays of Warren Buffett: Lessons for investors and managers, *Journal of Accountancy*, 208(3): 70.

Wong, C. and Law, K. S. (2002) The effects of leader and follower emotional intelligence on performance and attitude: An exploratory study, *Leadership Quarterly*, 13: 243–74.

Wright, P. C., Szeto, W. F., and Lee, S. K. (2003) Ethical perceptions in China: The reality of business ethics in an international context, *Management Decision*, 41 (1/2): 180–9.

Wright, T. A. and Cropanzano, R. (2004) The role of psychological well-being in job performance: A fresh look at an age-old quest, *Organizational Dynamics*, 33(4): 338–51.

—— and Goodstein, J. (2007) Character is not 'dead' in management research: A review of individual character and organizational-level virtue, *Journal of Management*, 33(6): 928–58.

Yifeng, N. C. and Tjosvold, D. (2008) Goal interdependence and leader-member relationship for cross-cultural leadership in foreign ventures in China, *Leadership & Organization Development Journal*, 29(2): 144–66.

Yoosuf, S. (2005) What factors influence the development of a leader? *The Business Review, Cambridge*, 4(2): 149–52.

Yukl, G. (2009) *Leadership in organizations* (7th ed.), Englewood Cliffs, NJ: Prentice Hall.

Yunus, M. (2006) Nobel Lecture, Oslo, December 10 (accessed December 27, 2011, at <http://nobelprize.org/nobel_prizes/peace/laureates/2006/yunus-lecture-en.html>)

—— Moingeon, B. and Lehmann-Ortega, L. (2010) Building social business models: Lessons from the Grameen experience, *Long Range Planning*, 43: 308–25.

Index

213

Index